Handbook of International Trade

Handbook of International Trade

Evelyn Stewart

MURPHY & MOORE
www.murphy-moorepublishing.com

Handbook of International Trade
Evelyn Stewart
ISBN: 978-1-63987-285-5 (Hardback)

MURPHY & MOORE
Published by Murphy & Moore Publishing,
1 Rockefeller Plaza,
New York City, NY 10020, USA

Cataloging-in-Publication Data

Handbook of international trade / Evelyn Stewart.
p. cm.
Includes bibliographical references and index.
ISBN 978-1-63987-285-5
1. International trade. 2. Commerce. 3. International economic relations.
I. Stewart, Evelyn.
HF1379 .H36 2022
382--dc23

For more information regarding Murphy & Moore Publishing and its products, please visit the publisher's website www.murphy-moorepublishing.com

Table of Contents

Preface

The exchange of goods, capital and services across international borders is termed as international or global trade. It is a complex process that occurs between a minimum of two countries. A wide variety of factors such as government, currency, trade policies, economy, judiciary, laws and market regulations have a considerable influence on international trade. Products sold by a country are termed as its exports. International trade opens up horizons for consumers and nations with exposure to unknown markets and products. Some of the common commodities of international trade are oil, food, clothes jewelry, spare parts and currencies. Various theories and models are utilized for the analysis of international trade. A few of them are the Heckscher-Ohlin model, specific factors model, Ricardian model and Adam Smith's model. The topics included in this book on international trade are of utmost significance and bound to provide incredible insights to readers. Some of the diverse topics covered herein address the varied branches that fall under this category. Those with an interest in the international trade field would find this book helpful.

To facilitate a deeper understanding of the contents of this book a short introduction of every chapter is written below:

Chapter 1- International trade is the exchange of capital goods and services across international borders and different nations of the world. It gives the consumers the opportunity to be exposed to certain goods and services that may not be available in their own countries. Export trade, import trade and entrepot trade are significant aspects of international trade. This chapter deals with international trade and its types in an elaborate manner.

Chapter 2- There are policies and laws that govern the way international trade is conducted and directly affect the flow of goods and services between countries. These include but are not limited to import tariffs, import quotas, voluntary export restraints, export taxes, export subsidies, etc. International trade policy, free trade policy, international trade law and international trade regulation fall under its domain. This chapter examines the different policies and laws related to international trade in detail.

Chapter 3- International Trade theory analyses the patterns of international trade, its origins and implications. Various models and theories have been established which aim to promote certain techniques and procedures as the basis on which international trade can be conducted. Brander-Spencer model, balanced trade, gravity model of trade, Linder hypothesis, new trade theory, etc. are some models and theories which are discussed in-depth to provide a better understanding of the subject matter.

Chapter 4- Heckscher-Ohlin Theorem, Factor Price Equalization Theorem, Stopler-Samuelson Theorem and Rybczynski Theorem are the theorems covered in this chapter. These theorems are based on various factors like the theory of comparative advantage, endowment changes and changes in product prices. This chapter has been carefully written to provide an easy understanding of these concepts and theories.

Chapter 5- An exchange rate is the value of a nation's currency in terms of another nation or economic zone. It can also be defined as the rate at which one currency will be exchanged for another. A few of its aspects are forward exchange rate, foreign exchange spot, forward exchange swap, cross rates, interest rate arbitrage, triangular arbitrage, etc. All the aspects related to exchange rate theories have been carefully analyzed in this chapter.

Chapter 6- International trade barriers are government-induced restrictions on international trade, which decrease overall economic deficiency. They can be broadly classified into tariff and non-tariff barriers. The custom levies or taxes on imported goods are called tariff barriers. The barriers outside the purview of tariff barriers like import licenses, export licenses, import quotas, subsidies, etc. are known as Non-tariff. This chapter discusses the subject of trade barriers and their effects on International trade.

Finally, I would like to thank the entire team involved in the inception of this book for their valuable time and contribution. This book would not have been possible without their efforts. I would also like to thank my friends and family for their constant support.

Evelyn Stewart

1

Basics of International Trade

International trade is the exchange of capital goods and services across international borders and different nations of the world. It gives the consumers the opportunity to be exposed to certain goods and services that may not be available in their own countries. Export trade, import trade and entrepot trade are significant aspects of international trade. This chapter deals with international trade and its types in an elaborate manner.

Trade

Trade is a basic economic concept involving the buying and selling of goods and services, with compensation paid by a buyer to a seller, or the exchange of goods or services between parties. Trade can take place within an economy between producers and consumers. International trade allows countries to expand markets for both goods and services that otherwise may not have been available to it. It is the reason why an American consumer can pick between a Japanese, German, or American car. As a result of international trade, the market contains greater competition and therefore, more competitive prices, which brings a cheaper product home to the consumer. In financial markets, trading refers to the buying and selling of securities, such as the purchase of stock on the floor of the New York Stock Exchange (NYSE).

How Trade Works

Trade broadly refers to transactions ranging in complexity from the exchange of baseball cards between collectors to multinational policies setting protocols for imports and exports between countries. Regardless of the complexity of the transaction, trading is facilitated through three primary types of exchanges.

Trading globally between nations allows consumers and countries to be exposed to goods and services not available in their own countries. Almost every kind of product can be found on the international market: food, clothes, spare parts, oil, jewelry, wine, stocks, currencies, and water. Services are also traded: tourism, banking, consulting, and transportation. A product that is sold to the global market is an export, and a product that is bought from the global market is an import. Imports and exports are accounted for in a country's current account in the balance of payments.

International trade not only results in increased efficiency but also allows countries to participate in a global economy, encouraging the opportunity of foreign direct investment (FDI), which is the amount of money that individuals invest into foreign companies and other assets. In theory, economies can, therefore, grow more efficiently and can more easily become competitive economic participants. For the receiving government, FDI is a means by which foreign currency and expertise can enter the country. These raise employment levels, and, theoretically, lead to a growth in the gross domestic product. For the investor, FDI offers company expansion and growth, which means higher revenues.

A trade deficit is a situation where a country spends more on aggregate imports from abroad than it earns from its aggregate exports. A trade deficit represents an outflow of domestic currency to foreign markets. This may also be referred to as a negative balance of trade (BOT).

Comparative Advantage: Increased Efficiency of Trading Globally

Global trade, in theory, allows wealthy countries to use their resources–whether labor, technology, or capital– more efficiently. Because countries are endowed with different assets and natural resources (land, labor, capital, and technology), some countries may produce the same good more efficiently and therefore sell it more cheaply than other countries. If a country cannot efficiently produce an item, it can obtain the item by trading with another country that can. This is known as specialization in international trade.

Let's take a simple example. Country A and Country B both produce cotton sweaters and wine. Country A produces ten sweaters and ten bottles of wine a year while Country B also produces ten sweaters and ten bottles of wine a year. Both can produce a total of 20 units without trading. Country A, however, takes two hours to produce the ten sweaters and one hour to produce the ten bottles of wine (total of three hours). Country B, on the other hand, takes one hour to produce ten sweaters and one hour to produce ten bottles of wine (a total of two hours).

But these two countries realize by examining the situation that they could produce more, in total, with the same amount of resources (hours) by focusing on those products with which they have a comparative advantage. Country A then begins to produce only wine, and Country B produces only cotton sweaters. Country A, by specializing in wine, can produce 30 bottles of wine with its 3 hours of resources at the same rate of production per hour of resource used (10 bottles per hour) before specialization. Country B, by specializing in sweaters, can produce 20 sweaters with its 2 hours of resources at the same rate of production per hour (10 sweaters per hour) before specialization. Total output of both countries is now the same as before in terms of sweaters–20–but they are making 10 bottles of wine more than if they did not specialize. This is the gain from specialization that can result from trading. Country A can send 15 bottles of wine to Country B for 10 sweaters and then each country is better off–10 sweaters and 15 bottles of wine each compared with 10 sweaters and 10 bottles of wine before trading.

Note that, in the example above, Country B could produce wine more efficiently than Country A (less time) and sweaters as efficiently. This is called an absolute advantage in wine production and at an equal cost in terms of sweaters. Country B may have these advantages because of a higher level of technology. However, as the example shows Country B can still benefit from specialization and trading with Country A.

A contemporary example: China's comparative advantage with the United States is in the form of cheap labor. Chinese workers produce simple consumer goods at a much lower opportunity cost. The United States' comparative advantage is in specialized, capital-intensive labor. American workers produce sophisticated goods or investment opportunities at lower opportunity costs. Specializing and trading along these lines benefit each.

The theory of comparative advantage helps to explain why protectionism is typically unsuccessful. Adherents to this analytical approach believe that countries engaged in international trade will have already worked toward finding partners with comparative advantages. If a country removes itself from an international trade agreement, if a government imposes tariffs, and so on, it may produce a local benefit in the form of new jobs and industry. However, this is not a long-term solution to a trade problem. Eventually, that country will be at a disadvantage relative to its neighbors: countries that were already better able to produce these items at a lower opportunity cost.

Criticisms of Comparative Advantage

Why doesn't the world have open trading between countries? When there is free trade, why do some countries remain poor at the expense of others? Perhaps comparative advantage does not work as suggested. There are many reasons this could be the case, but the most influential is something that economists call rent-seeking. Rent-seeking occurs when one group organizes and lobbies the government to protect its interests.

Say, for example, the producers of American shoes understand and agree with the free-trade argument–but they also know that cheaper foreign shoes would negatively impact their narrow interests. Even if laborers would be most productive by switching from making shoes to making computers, nobody in the shoe industry wants to lose his or her job or see profits decrease in the short run.

This desire leads the shoemakers to lobby for, say, special tax breaks for their products and/or extra duties (or even outright bans) on foreign footwear. Appeals to save American jobs and preserve a time-honored American craft abound–even though, in the long run, American laborers would be made relatively less productive and American consumers relatively poorer by such protectionist tactics.

Free Trade vs. Protectionism

As with other theories, there are opposing views. International trade has two contrasting views regarding the level of control placed on trade: free trade and protectionism. Free trade is the simpler of the two theories: a laissez-faire approach, with no restrictions on trade. The main idea is that supply and demand factors, operating on a global scale, will ensure that production happens efficiently. Therefore, nothing needs to be done to protect or promote trade and growth because market forces will do so automatically.

In contrast, protectionism holds that regulation of international trade is important to ensure that markets function properly. Advocates of this theory believe that market inefficiencies may hamper the benefits of international trade, and they aim to guide the market accordingly. Protectionism exists in many different forms, but the most common are tariffs, subsidies, and quotas. These strategies attempt to correct any inefficiency in the international market.

Currency as a Medium of Exchange Facilitating Trade

Money, which also functions as a unit of account and a store of value, is the most common medium of exchange, providing a variety of methods for fund transfers between buyers and sellers, including cash, ACH transfers, credit cards, and wired funds. Money's attribute as a store of value also assures that funds received by sellers as payment for goods or services can be used to make purchases of equivalent value in the future.

Barter Transactions

Cashless trades involving the exchange of goods or services between parties are referred to as barter transactions. While barter is often associated with primitive or undeveloped societies, these transactions are also used by large corporations and individuals as a means of gaining goods in exchange for excess, underutilized or unwanted assets. For example, in the 1970s, PepsiCo Inc. set up a barter agreement with the Russian government to trade cola syrup for Stolichnaya vodka. In 1990, the deal was expanded to $3 billion dollars and included 10 Russian-built ships, which PepsiCo leased or sold in the years following the agreement.

International Trade

International trade is the sale and purchase of goods and services across international borders. International trade is governed by a vast set of rules, codified in treaties and trade agreements. To clarify, the rules we are referring to are those governing the actions of states and governments with regard to international trade.

Now that we have a basic definition of international trade, perhaps we should begin to answer the question of "why do states trade?" The answer, again, is rather simple. We buy goods and services from other countries because we cannot domestically produce all the goods and services that each individual consumer wants and needs. The reason for this is that each country has different factors of production. Factors of production are the resources used to build an economy and produce goods and services; they are land, labor, and capital. Each country is endowed with different combinations of these factors, and therefore each country is capable of producing different combinations of goods and services. When domestic production is greater than domestic demand for a good, excess production is traded on the international market. The act of selling domestically produced goods to international consumers is known as exportation.

The previous example involved only two countries and one product. However, the international trading system in which we operate is comprised of dozens of countries and the thousands—if not more—of products they individually produce. Moreover, it is often the case that several countries are similarly suited to produce the same types of goods and services, and this places them in direct competition with each other.

Arguments in Favor of International Trade

Economic Arguments in Favor of International Trade

The example, in which Sweden and Lebanon became trading partners, is based on the theory of absolute advantage. According to this theory, country X has an absolute advantage in the production of a good when country X is able to produce more of that specific good than country Y. Most countries have an absolute advantage in the production of certain goods. Given that each country is better than others at producing certain goods, they specialize and trade their excess production.

As you might have intuited, the world is more complicated than the scenario we presented above between Sweden and Lebanon. Often, countries have very similar factors of production, and therefore are able to produce similar amounts of the same goods. To rationalize trade in such a scenario, a more complete and complex theory is needed. This theory is called the theory of comparative advantage. A comparative advantage exists whenever a country has "a greater margin of superiority or a smaller margin of inferiority" 1 in the production of a good. It is possible for a country not to have an absolute advantage in the production of a good, but it may still have a comparative advantage if it is relatively better suited for the production of a certain good than another country might be.

Let us use the following scenario to understand the theory of comparative advantage. In this scenario, there are two countries: Techno and Agro. Techno is an industrialized country, and Agro is still developing and has not yet reached the same level of industrialization as Techno. Notwithstanding, both countries produce televisions and lamps, and both countries have 1,000 workers.

To produce one television per hour, Techno uses 10 workers, and Agro uses 100; and to produce one lamp per hour, Techno uses 2 workers, whereas Agro uses 4. Let us assume that half of each country's workers produce televisions, and the other half produces lamps. If we do the math, we will find that Techno can produce 50 televisions and 250 lamps per hour. Conversely, Agro can produce 5 televisions and 125 lamps per hour. In this example, Techno has an absolute advantage in the production of both goods.

Let us now think about how lamp production would change if each country decided to produce more televisions. Assume Techno wants to produce 51 televisions instead of 50, and that Agro wants to produce 6 televisions instead of 5. Given that instead of producing lamps, some workers will produce televisions, the output of lamps for Techno decreases to 245, and the output of lamps for Agro decreases to 100 lamps. It costs Techno 5 lamps to produce 1 television, whereas it costs Agro 25 lamps to produce 1 television.

Now let us think about what would happen if each country decided to produce one more lamp instead of one more television. Again, because some workers that were producing televisions will now be producing lamps, the television output must decrease in some amount. A simple calculation will show us that increasing lamp output to 251 will decrease Techno's television output to 49.8 televisions, whereas increasing lamp output to 126 would decrease Agro's television output to 4.96. It costs Techno .2 televisions to produce one lamp, whereas it costs Agro .04 televisions to produce one lamp.

If we compare the costs of producing 1 additional television and 1 additional lamp for each country, we will discover the following: it is relatively cheaper for Techno to produce televisions, and relatively cheaper for Agro to produce lamps. Therefore, Techno has a comparative advantage in the production of televisions and Agro has a comparative advantage in the production of lamps. If Techno and Agro specialize in the production of the good they have a comparative advantage in, they will be left with more televisions and lamps than they can consume domestically. If they trade, they will be able to consume more of both goods than if they each attempted to produce televisions and lamps independently.

The theory of comparative advantage tells a compelling story of why international trade is beneficial. However, there are many more arguments in favor of increased trade amongst countries. For instance, trade between countries tends to expand the markets that domestic producers can access, allowing them to produce at a scale that will keep their costs down. Additionally, trade may lead to the spread of new technologies, which can be particularly valuable in developing economies.

The economic rationales in favor of international trade are strong, but they are not a complete representation of the pro-trade argument. Nonetheless, understanding them is a key element to fully grasping the underpinnings of many rules and goals of the current international trade system.

Non-Economic Arguments in Favor of International Trade

In addition to the economic arguments articulated above, there are many non-economic rationales supporting international trade. Some scholars argue that international trade, and more specifically free trade—defined as trade without barriers—promotes peace. The idea behind this argument is that countries that actively trade with each other are less likely to engage in a war or conflict against one another. As evidence of this, scholars point to history, and note that only on rare occasions has this theory been contradicted in modern times.

Some have argued that trade promotes democracy and peace, forming a 'virtuous cycle.' They suggest that trade and economic integration tend to promote the introduction of democratic ideas to society. This is ostensibly because increased trade also leads to an increase in the inflow of books, and other forms of "political and social content." Moreover, scholars contend that "[f]oreign investment and services trade create opportunities for foreign travel and study, allowing citizens to experience first-hand the civil liberties and more representative political institutions of other nations." Additionally, they introduce three main ways in which trade and globalization reinforce the "trend toward democracy." First, as explained above, it is rather unlikely that democracies that trade with each other will fight one another. Second, trade promotes economic integration, which means that economies are more linked and thus that countries have more to lose from fighting each other. Third, trade allows countries to depend on production and exchange to acquire wealth instead of depending on war and conquest.

Characteristics of International Trade

International trade is characterised by the following features:

- Territorial specialization: International trade takes place basically due to geographical specialisation. Every country specialises in the production of goods and services in which it has a specific advantage. For example, India has specific advantage in the production of jute and tea. Therefore, India exports these commodities to U.K. India imports steel from U.K. which U.K. can produce at a lower cost than India.
- International competition: Producers from many countries complete with another to sell their products. Therefore, there is intense competition in international trade. Here the quality, design, packing, price, advertisement, etc., all play a significant role in deciding the winner in the market.
- Separation of sellers from buyers: In international trade sellers and buyers belong to different countries. They may have no chance of ever meeting one another. Therefore, they have to depend upon middlemen for transactions.
- Long chain of middlemen: The procedure of international trade is very long

and complex. It is very difficult for buyers and sellers to perform all the formalities themselves. They require the services of expert middlemen such as, indent houses, forwarding agents, clearing agents, foreign exchange banks, etc.

- Mutually acceptable currency: The currencies of importing and exporting countries generally are different. Therefore, it is necessary to find out a mutually acceptable currency. Generally, dollar and pound sterling are selected. These currencies are known as hard currencies because they are acceptable all over the world.
- International rules and regulations: Businessmen engaged in international trade require knowledge of international laws and trade restrictions.
- Government control: The government of every country exercises control over imports and exports for national interest.
- Several documents: A large number of documents are required in international trade.

Features, Advantages and Disadvantages of International Trade

Salient Features of International Trade

The following are the distinguishing features of international trade:

Immobility of Factors

The degree of immobility of factors like labour and capital is generally greater between countries than within a country. Immigration laws, citizenship, qualifications, etc. often restrict the international mobility of labour.

International capital flows are prohibited or severely limited by different governments. Consequently, the economic significance of such mobility of factors tends to equality within but not between countries. For instance, wages may be equal in Mumbai and Pune but not in Bombay and London.

It thus follows that domestic trade consists largely of exchange of goods between producers who enjoy similar standards of life, whereas international trade consists of exchange of goods between producers enjoying widely differing standards. Evidently, the principles which determine the course and nature of internal and international trade are bound to be different in some respects at least. In this context, it may be pointed out that the price of a commodity in the country where it is produced tends to equal its cost of production.

The reason is that if in an industry the price is higher than its cost, resources will flow into it from other industries, output will increase and the price will fall until it is equal to the cost of production. Conversely, resources will flow out of the industry, output will decline, the price will go up and ultimately equal the cost of production.

But, as among different countries, resources are comparatively immobile; hence, there is no automatic influence equalising price and costs. Therefore, there may be permanent difference between the cost of production of a commodity.

In one country and the price obtained in a different country for it. For instance, the price of tea in India must, in the long run, be equal to its cost of production in India. But in the U.K., the price of Indian tea may be permanently higher than its cost of production in India. In this way, international trade differs from home trade.

Heterogeneous Markets

In the international economy, world markets lack homogeneity on account of differences in climate, language, preferences, habit, customs, weights and measures, etc. The behaviour of international buyers in each case would, therefore, be different.

Different National Groups

International trade takes place between differently cohered groups. The socio-economic environment differs greatly among different nations.

Different Political Units

International trade is a phenomenon which occurs amongst different political units.

Different National Policies and Government Intervention

Economic and political policies differ from one country to another. Policies pertaining to trade, commerce, export and import, taxation, etc., also differ widely among countries though they are more or less uniform within the country. Tariff policy, import quota system, subsidies and other controls adopted by governments interfere with the course of normal trade between one country and another.

Different Currencies

Another notable feature of international trade is that it involves the use of different types of currencies. So, each country has its own policy in regard to exchange rates and foreign exchange.

Differences between Internal Trade and International Trade

Characteristically, there are marked differences between internal and international trade as stated below:

Specific Terms

Exports and Imports: Internal trade is the exchange of domestic output within the political boundaries of a nation, while international trade is the trade between two or more nations. Thus, unlike internal trade, the terms "export" and "import" are used in foreign trade. To export means to sell goods to a foreign country. To import goods means to buy goods from a foreign country.

Heterogeneous Group

An obvious difference between home trade and foreign trade is that trade within a country is trade among the same group of people, whereas trade between countries takes place between differently cohered groups. The socio-economic environment differs greatly between nations, while it is more or less uniform within a country. Frederick List, therefore, put that: "Domestic trade is among us, international trade is between us and them."

Political Differences

International trade occurs between different political units, while domestic trade occurs within the same political unit. The government in each country is keen about the welfare of its own nationals against that of the people of other countries. Hence, in international trade policy, each government tries to see its own interest at the cost of the other country.

Different Rules

National rules, laws and policies relating to trade, commerce, industry, taxation, etc. are more or less uniform within a country, but differ widely between countries. Tariff policy, import quota system, subsidies and other controls adopted by a government interfere with the course of normal trade between it and other countries. Thus, state interference causes different problems in international trade while the value of theory, in its pure form, which is laissez faire, cannot be applied in toto to the international trade theory.

Different Currencies

Perhaps the principal difference between domestic and international trade is that the latter involves the use of different types of currencies and each country follows different foreign exchange policies. That is why there is the problem of exchange rates and foreign exchange. Thus, one has to study not only the factors which determine the value of each country's monetary unit, but also the divergent practices and types of exchange resorted to.

Heterogeneous World Markets

In a way, home trade has a homogeneous market. In foreign trade, however, the world markets lack homogeneity on account of differences in climate, language, preferences, habits, customs, weights and measures etc.

The behaviour of international buyers in each case would, therefore, be different. For instance, Indians have right-hand drive cars, while Americans have left-hand driven cars. Hence, the markets for automobiles are effectively separated. Thus, one peculiarity of international trade is that it involves heterogeneous national markets.

Factor Immobility

Another major difference between internal and international trade is the degree of immobility of factors of production like labour and capital which is generally greater between countries than within the country. Immigration laws, citizenship qualifications, etc., often restrict international mobility of labour. International capital flows are prohibited or severely limited by different governments.

Advantages of International Trade

The following are the major gains claimed to be emerging from international trade:

- Optimum Allocation: International specialisation and geographical division of labour leads to the optimum allocation of world's resources, making it possible to make the most efficient use of them.
- Gains of Specialisation: Each trading country gains when the total output increases as a result of division of labour and specialisation. These gains are in the form of more aggregate production, larger number of varieties and greater diversity of qualities of goods that become available for consumption in each country as a result of international trade.
- Enhanced Wealth: Increase in the exchangeable value of possessions, means of enjoyment and wealth of each trading country.
- Larger Output: Enlargement of world's aggregate output.
- Welfare Contour: Increase in the world's prosperity and economic welfare of each trading nation.

- Cultural Values: Cultural exchange and ties among different countries develop when they enter into mutual trading.
- Better International Politics: International trade relations help in harmonising international political relations.
- Dealing with Scarcity: A country can easily solve its problem of scarcity of raw materials or food through imports.
- Advantageous Competition: Competition from foreign goods in the domestic market tends to induce home producers to become more efficient to improve and maintain the quality of their products.
- Larger Size of Market: Because of foreign trade, when a country's size of market expands, domestic producers can operate on a larger scale of production which results in further economies of scale and thus can promote development. Synchronised application of investment to many industries simultaneously become possible. This helps industrialisation of the country along with balanced growth.

Disadvantages of International Trade

When a country places undue reliance on foreign trade, there is a likelihood of the following disadvantages:

- Exhaustion of Resources: When a country has larger and continuous exports, her essential raw materials and minerals may get exhausted, unless new resources are tapped or developed (e.g., the near-exhausting oil resources of the oil-producing countries).
- Blow to Infant Industry: Foreign competition may adversely affect new and developing infant industries at home.
- Dumping: Dumping tactics resorted to by advanced countries may harm the development of poor countries.
- Diversification of Savings: A high propensity to import may cause reduction in the domestic savings of a country. This may adversely affect her rate of capital formation and the process of growth.
- Declining Domestic Employment: Under foreign trade, when a country tends to specialize in a few products, job opportunities available to people are curtailed.
- Over Interdependence: Foreign trade discourages self-sufficiency and self-reliance in an economy. When countries tend to be interdependent, their economic independence is jeopardised. For instance, for these reasons, there is no free trade in the world. Each country puts some restrictions on its foreign trade under its commercial and political policies.

Export Trade

Exports are the goods and services produced in one country and purchased by residents of another country. It doesn't matter what the good or service is. It doesn't matter how it is sent. It can be shipped, sent by email, or carried in personal luggage on a plane. If it is produced domestically and sold to someone in a foreign country, it is an export.

Exports are one component of international trade. The other component is imports. They are the goods and services bought by a country's residents that are produced in a foreign country. Combined, they make up a country's trade balance. When the country exports more than it imports, it has a trade surplus. When it imports more than it exports, it has a trade deficit.

As an example, the United States imported $1.68 trillion in goods between January and August 2018. During that same period, it exported $1.12 trillion in goods. This created a deficit of $565.6 billion.

What Countries Export

Businesses export goods and services where they have a competitive advantage. That means they are better than any other companies at providing that product. They also export things that reflect the country's comparative advantage. Countries have comparative advantages in the commodities they have a natural ability to produce. For example, Kenya, Jamaica, and Colombia have the right climate to grow coffee. That gives their industries an edge in exporting coffee.

India's population is its comparative advantage. Its workers speak English, which gives them an edge as affordable call center workers. China has a similar advantage in manufacturing due to its lower standard of living. Its workers can live on lower wages than people in developed countries.

How Exports Affect the Economy

Most countries want to increase their exports. Their companies want to sell more. If they've sold all they can to their own country's population, then they want to sell overseas as well. The more they export, the greater their competitive advantage. They gain expertise in producing the goods and services. They also gain knowledge about how to sell to foreign markets.

Governments encourage exports. Exports increase jobs, bring in higher wages, and raise the standard of living for residents. As such, people become happier and more likely to support their national leaders.

Exports also increase the foreign exchange reserves held in the nation's central bank. Foreigners pay for exports either in their own currency or the U.S. dollar. A country with large reserves can use it to manage their own currency's value. They have enough foreign currency to flood the market with their own currency. That lowers the cost of their exports in other countries.

Countries also use currency reserves to manage liquidity. That means they can better control inflation, which is too much money chasing too few goods. To control inflation, they use the foreign currency to purchase their own currency. That decreases the money supply, making the local currency worth more.

Three Ways Countries Boost Exports

There are three ways countries try to increase exports. First, they use trade protectionism to give their industries an advantage. This usually consists of tariffs that raise the prices of imports. They also provide subsidies on their own industries to lower prices. But once they start doing this, other countries retaliate with the same measures. These trade wars lower international commerce for everyone. For example, the Smoot-Hawley tariff lowered trade by 65% and worsened the Great Depression.

Countries also increase exports by negotiating trade agreements. They boost exports by reducing trade protectionism. The World Trade Organization tried to negotiate a multilateral agreement among its 149 members. The so-called Doha agreement almost succeeded. But the European Union and the United States refused to eliminate their farm subsidies.

As a result, most countries relied on bilateral agreements or regional trade agreements for years. But in 2015, the Obama administration negotiated the Trans-Pacific Partnership. In 2017, the Trump administration dropped out.12 But the other countries completed the agreement without the United States.

The third way countries boost exports is to lower the value of their currencies. This makes their export prices comparatively lower in the receiving country. Central banks do this by lowering interest rates. A government can also print more currency or buy up foreign currency to make its value higher. Countries that try to compete by devaluing their currencies are accused of being in currency wars.

Import Trade

Import trade refers to the purchase of goods from a foreign country. The procedure for import trade differs from country to country depending upon the import policy, statutory requirements and customs policies of different countries. In almost all countries of the world import trade is controlled by the government. The objectives of these controls are proper use of foreign exchange restrictions, protection of indigenous industries etc. The imports of goods have to follow a procedure. This procedure involves a number of steps. The steps taken in import procedure are discussed as follows:

Trade Enquiry

The first stage in an import transaction, like any other transaction of purchase and sale relates to making trade enquiries. An enquiry is a written request from the intending buyer or his agent for information regarding the price and the terms on which the exporter will be able to supply goods.

The importer should mention in the enquiry all the details such as the goods required, their description, catalogue number or grade, size, weight and the quantity required. Similarly, the time and method of delivery, method of packing, terms and conditions in regard to payment should also be indicated.

In reply to this enquiry, the importer will receive a quotation from the exporter. The quotation contains the details as to the goods available, their quality etc., the price at which the goods will be supplied and the terms and conditions of the sale.

Procurement of Import Licence and Quota

Under a general licence goods can be imported from any country, whereas a specific or individual licence authorises to import only from specific countries. Every importer must first find out whether he can import the goods he wants or not, and how much of a certain class of goods he can import during the period covered by the relevant Red Book. For the purpose of issuing licence, the importers are divided into three categories:

- Established importer,
- Actual users,
- Registered exporters, i.e., those import under any of the export promotion schemes.

In order to obtain an import licence, the intending importer has to make an application in the prescribed form to the licensing authority. If the person imported goods of the class in which he is interested now during the basic period prescribed for such class, he is treated as an established importer.

An established importer can make an application to secure a Quota Certificate. The certificate specifies the quantity and value of goods which the importer can import. For this, he furnishes details of the goods imported in any one year in basic period prescribed for the goods together with documentary evidence for the same, including a certificate from a chartered accountant in the prescribed form certifying the c.i.f. value of the goods imported in the selected year.

The c.i.f. value includes the invoice price of the goods and the freight and insurance paid for the goods in transit. The quota certificate entitles the established importer to import upto the value indicated therein (called Quota) which is calculated on the basis of past imports. If the importer is an actual user, that is, he wants to import goods for his own use in industrial manufacturing process he has to obtain licence through the prescribed sponsoring authority.

The sponsoring authority certifies his requirements and recommends the grant of licence. In case of small industries having a capital of less than Rs. 5 lakhs, they have to apply for licences through the Director of Industries of the state where the industry is located or some other authority expressly prescribed by the Government.

Registered exporter importing against exports made under a scheme of export promotion and others have to obtain licence from the Chief Controller of Exports and Imports. The Government issues from time to time a list of commodities and products which can be imported by obtaining a general permission only. This is called as O.G.L. or Open General Licence list.

Obtaining Foreign Exchange

After obtaining the licence (or quota, in case of an established importer), the importer has to make arrangement for obtaining necessary foreign exchange since the importer has to make payment for the imports in the currency of the exporting country.

The foreign exchange reserves in many countries are controlled by the Government and are released through its central bank. In India, the Exchange Control Department of the Reserve Bank of India deals with the foreign exchange. For this the importer has to submit an application in the prescribed form along-with the import licence to any exchange bank as per the provisions of Exchange Control Act.

The exchange bank endorses and forwards the applications to the Exchange Control Department of the Reserve Bank of India. The Reserve Bank of India sanctions the release of foreign exchange after scrutinizing the application on the basis of exchange policy of the Government of India in force at the time of application.

The importer gets the necessary foreign exchange from the exchange bank concerned. It is to be noted that whereas import licence is issued for a particular period, exchange is released only for a specific transaction. With liberalisation of economy, most of the restrictions have been removed as rupee has become convertible on current account.

Placing the Indent or Order

After the initial formalities are over and the importer has obtained the licence quota and the necessary amount of foreign exchange, the next step in the import of goods is that of placing the order. This order is known as Indent. An indent is an order placed by an importer with an exporter for the supply of certain goods.

It contains the instructions from the importer as to the quantity and quality of goods required, method of forwarding them, nature of packing, mode of settling payment and the price etc. An indent is usually prepared in duplicate or triplicate. The indent may be of several types like open indent, closed indent and Confirmatory indent.

In open indent, all the necessary particulars of goods, price, etc. are not mentioned in the indent, the exporter has the discretion to complete the formalities, at his own end. On the other hand, if full particulars of goods, the price, the brand, packing, shipping, insurance etc. are mentioned clearly, it is called a closed indent. A confirmatory indent is one where an order is placed subject to the confirmation by the importer's agent.

Despatching a Letter of Credit

Generally, foreign traders are not acquainted to each other and so the exporter before shipping the goods wants to be sure about the creditworthiness of the importer. The exporter wants to be sure that there is no risk of non-payment. Usually, for this purpose he asks the importers to send a letter of credit to him.

A letter of credit, popularly known as 'L/C or 'L.C is an undertaking by its issuer (usually importer's bank) that the bills of exchange drawn by the foreign dealer, on the importer will be honoured on presentation upto a specified amount.

Obtaining Necessary Documents

After despatching a letter of credit, the importer has not to do much. On receipt of the letter of credit, the exporter arranges for the shipment of goods and sends Advice Note to the importer immediately after the shipment of goods. An Advice Note is a document sent to a purchaser of goods to inform him that goods have been despatched. It may also indicate the probable date on which the ship is expected to reach the port of destination.

The exporter then draws a bill of exchange on the importer for the invoice value of goods. The shipping documents such as the bill of lading, invoice, insurance policy, certificate of origin, consumer invoice etc., are also attached to the bill of exchange. Such bill of exchange with all these attached documents is called Documentary Bill. Documentary bill of exchange is forwarded to the importer through a foreign exchange bank which has a branch or an agent in the importer's country for collecting the payment of the bill. There are two types of documentary bills:

- D/P, D.P. (or Documents against payment) bills.
- D/A, D.A. (or Document against acceptance) bills.

Customs Formalities and Clearing of Goods

After receiving the documents of title of the goods, the importer's only concern is to take delivery of the goods, when the ship arrives at the port and to bring them to his own place of business. The importer has to comply with many formalities for taking delivery of goods. Unless the following mentioned formalities are complied with, the goods lie in the custody of the Custom House.

To Obtain Endorsement for Delivery or Delivery Order

When the ship carrying the goods arrives at the port, the importer, first of all, has to obtain the endorsement on the back of the bill of lading by the shipping company. Sometimes the shipping company, instead of endorsing the bill in his favour, issues a delivery order to him. This endorsement of delivery order will entitle the importer to take the delivery of the goods.

The shipping company makes this endorsement or issues the delivery order only after the payment of freight. If the exporter has not paid the freight, i.e., when the bill, of lading is marked freight forward, the importer has to pay the freight in order to get green signal for the delivery of goods.

To Pay Dock Dues and Obtain Port Trust Dues Receipts

The importer has to submit two copies of a form known as 'Application to import' duly filled in to the 'Lading and Shipping Dues Office'. This office levies a charge on all imported goods for services rendered by the dock authorities in connection with lading of goods. After paying the necessary charges, the importer receive back one copy of the application to import as a receipt 'Port Trust Dues Receipt'.

Bill of Entry

The importer will then fill in form called Bill of Entry. This is a form supplied by the custom office and is to be filled in triplicate. The bill of entry contains the particulars regarding the name and address of the importer, the name of the ship, packages number, marks, quantity, value, description of goods, the name of the country wherefrom goods have been imported and custom duty payable.

The bill of entry forms are of three types and are printed in three colours-Black, Blue and Violet. A black form is used for non-dutiable or free goods, the blue form is used for goods to be sold within the country and the violet form is used for re-exportable goods, i.e., goods meant for re-export. The importer has to submit three forms of bill of entry along-with Port Trust Dues Receipt to the customs office.

Bill of Sight

If the importer is not is a position to supply the detailed particulars of goods because of insufficiency of information supplied to him by the exporter, he has to prepare a statement called a bill of sight. The bill of sight contains only the information possessed by the importer along-with a remark that he is not in a position to give complete information about the goods. The bill of sight enables him to open the package and examine the goods in the presence of custom officer so as to complete the bill of entry.

To Pay Customs or Import Duty

There are three types of imported goods:

- Non dutiable or free goods.
- Goods which are to be sold within the country or which are for home consumption.
- Re-exportable goods i.e. goods meant for re-export. If the goods are duty free, no import duty is to be paid at the custom office.

Custom authorities will permit the delivery of such goods after usual examination of the goods. But if the goods are liable for duty, the importer has to pay custom or import duty which may be based on weight or measurement of goods, called Specific Duty or on the value of imported goods Ad-valorem Ditty.

There are three types of import duties. On some goods quite low duties are levied and they are called revenue duties. On some others, quite high duties are charged to give protection to home industries against foreign competition. While goods imported from certain nations are given preferential treatment for the levy of import duties and in their case full protective duties are not charged.

Bonded and Duty Paid Warehouses

The port trust and custom authorities maintain two types of warehouses-Bonded and Duty paid. These warehouses are situated near the dock and are very useful to importers who do not have godown of their own to store the imported goods or who, for business reasons, do not wish to carry them to their own godowns.

The goods on which the duty has already been paid by the importer can be kept in the duty paid warehouses for which a receipt called 'warehouse receipt' is issued to him. This receipt is a document of title and is transferable. The bonded warehouses are meant for goods on which duty has been paid by the importer. If the importer cannot pay the duty, he may keep the goods in Bonded warehouses for which he is issued a receipt, called 'Dock Warrant'. Dock Warrant, also like warehouses receipt, is a document of title and is transferable. The bonded warehouses are used by the importer when:

- He has no godown of his own.
- He cannot pay the duty immediately.
- He wants to re-export the goods and thereby does not want to pay the duty.
- He wants to pay the duty in installments.

A nominal rent is charged for the use of these warehouses. One special advantage of these warehouses is that the importer can sell the goods and transfer the title of goods merely by endorsing warehouse receipt or dock-warrant. This will save the importer from the trouble and expenses of carrying the goods from the warehouses to his godown.

Appointment of Clearing Agents

By now we understand that the importer has to fulfill many legal formalities before he can take delivery of goods. The importer may take the delivery of the goods himself at the port. But it involves much of time, expenses and difficulty. Thus, to save himself from the botheration of complying with all the complicated formalities, the importer may appoint clearing agents for taking the delivery of the goods for him. Clearing agents are the specialised persons engaged in the work of performing various formalities required for taking the delivery of goods on behalf of others. They charge some remuneration on performing these valuable services.

Making the Payment

The mode and time of making payment is determined according to the terms and conditions as agreed to earlier between the importer and the exporter. In case of a D/P bill the documents of title are released to the importer only on the payment of the bill in full. If the bill is a D/A bill, the documents of title of the goods are released to the importer on his acceptance of the bill. The bill is retained by the banker till the date of maturity. Usually, 30 to 90 days are allowed to the importer for making the payment of such bills.

Closing the Transactions

The last step in the import trade procedure is closing the transaction. If the goods are to the satisfaction of the importer, the transaction is closed. But if he is not satisfied with the quality of goods or if there is any shortage, he will write to the exporter and settle the matter. In case the goods have been damaged in transit, he will claim compensation from the insurance company. The insurance company will pay him the compensation under an advice to the exporter.

Entrepôt Trade

The term entrepôt, also called a transshipment port and historically referred to as a port city, is a trading post, port, city, or warehouse where merchandise may be imported, stored, or traded before re-export, with no additional processing taking place and with no customs duties imposed.

These port cities originated as a result of the growth of long-distance trade during the era of wind-powered shipping. In the modern age, customs areas of countries have rendered entrepôts obsolete. However, the term is still used to refer to duty-free ports where a large volume of re-exporting takes place.

The use of entrepôts dates back to the days of long-distance, wind-powered sea routes. These seaports enabled traders to utilize part of a route to sell their goods without having to bear the risks and costs associated with long-distance travel over an entire route.

The use of trade entrepôts has become largely obsolete as transportation options and safety have improved, and as the establishment of customs areas in seaports and airports have negated the financial benefits of entrepôts. Goods in customs areas are stored for re-export and because they do not technically enter the country in which they are located, no customs duties are charged.

Historically, entrepôts were usually ports located at strategic points along the sea trade routes. Entrepôts flourished especially during the height of colonialism when ships would travel long distances to bear goods, such as commodities and spices, from the colonies in the Americas and Asia back to Europe. Many of these commercial cities were spawned as a result of the burgeoning, long-distance sea trading. In the past, entrepôts removed the need for ships to travel the whole distance of the shipping route, making this their main benefit. Ships would sell their goods into the entrepôt and the entrepôt would, in turn, sell them to another ship traveling a further leg of the route.

For example, at the height of the spice trade in Europe, the long trade routes necessary for the delivery of spices to Europe made the market price of the goods much more expensive than the original buying price. If a trader did not want to travel the entire route, they may use entrepôts on the way to sell their goods.

However, entrepôt trade has continued in some regions. Indirect trade through an entrepôt may provide savings in transportation costs and is a way to take advantage of specialized agents processing and distribution. In particular, Hong Kong and Singapore have remained centers of entrepôt trade through the twentieth century and beyond. Entrepôt trade still accounts for about a third of Singapore's exports. Hong Kong's position, geographically and as a free port, made it an entrepôt for trade with China, especially in the first part of the twentieth century. In this arrangement, traders in Hong Kong imported goods from China and then distributed them to a final destination.

However, in 1951 a United Nations trade embargo on China and North Korea reduced that role. Now, with the re-integration of China into the world economy and the country adopting a more open foreign policy in the past few decades, Hong Kong has resumed the role of intermediating trade between China and the rest of the world.

The term can also be used to refer to a financial entrepôt, which a financial center where most activity is foreign traders is dealing with each other, so that money flows through the center, but not much is retained in the local market.

References

- Education, what-are-the-characteristics-of-international-trade-21484: preservearticles.com, Retrieved 24, May 2020
- International-trade-features-advantages-and-disadvantages-of-international-trade-26009: yourarticlelibrary.com, Retrieved 16, April 2020
- Entrepot: investopedia.com, Retrieved 14, March 2020
- Exports-definition-examples-effect-on-economy-3305838: thebalance.com, Retrieved 11, March 2020
- Export-management, procedure-and-steps-involved-in-import-of-goods-42106: yourarticlelibrary.com, Retrieved 16, February 2020

2

International Trade: Policies and Law

There are policies and laws that govern the way international trade is conducted and directly affect the flow of goods and services between countries. These include but are not limited to import tariffs, import quotas, voluntary export restraints, export taxes, export subsidies, etc. International trade policy, free trade policy, international trade law and international trade regulation fall under its domain. This chapter examines the different policies and laws related to international trade in detail.

International Trade Policy

Regulation of international trade supposes purposeful influence of the state on trade relations with other countries. The main goals of foreign trade policy are:

- The volume change of exports and imports.
- Changes in the structure of foreign trade.
- providing the country with the necessary resources.
- The change in the ratio of export and import prices.

There are three main approaches to the regulation of international trade:

- A system of unilateral measures, in which the instruments of state control used by the government unilaterally and not coordinated with the trading partner.
- The undertaking of bilateral agreements, in which trade policy measures agreed between trading partners.
- The undertaking of multilateral agreements. Trade policy is coordinated and regulated by the participating countries.

The state can use each of approaches in any combination. The basic line of government control of international trade is the application of two different types of foreign trade policy in combination: liberalization (free trade policy) and protectionism.

Under the free trade policy is understood the minimum of state interference in foreign trade, which developed on the basis of free market forces of supply and demand, and under the protectionism - the state policy, which provides the protecting of the domestic market from foreign competition through the use of tariff and non-tariff trade policy instruments.

These two types of trade policy characterize the measure of state intervention into international trade. If under the conditions of liberalization policy, a basic regulator of foreign trade is a market, then the protectionism practically excludes the operation of free market forces. It is assumed that economic potential and competitiveness at the world market of separate countries is different. Therefore a free action of market forces can be unprofitable for the less developed countries. Unlimited competition from more powerful states can result to economic stagnation and the formation of inefficient economic structure in less-developed countries.

The protectionism policy contributes to the development of certain industries in the country and often is a necessary condition for industrialization of agrarian countries and unemployment reduction. However, the removal of foreign competition reduces the interest of domestic producers in the implementation of scientific and technological progress, improving the efficiency of production. There are such forms of protectionism:

- Selective protectionism, directed against some countries or some commodities.
- Industrial protectionism, which protects certain industries.
- Collective protectionism Countries, which belong to economic integration organizations, conduct this form to countries, which do not belong to a union.
- Hidden protectionism, which is carried out by methods of domestic economic policy.

Every country has economic, social and political arguments, protecting interests of protectionism. The main arguments for restrictions on foreign trade are:

- Necessity of defense providing.
- Increase of domestic employment.
- Diversification for the sake of stability.
- Protection of infant industries.
- Protection from dumping.
- Cheap foreign labor force.

So, the art of trading policy is to find the point of balance between two trends: free trade and protectionism. Each policy has its own advantages and disadvantages, depending on the circumstances, time and place of its applying. The instruments of state regulation of international trade include the following:

- Tariff methods that regulate mostly the imports and protect domestic producers from foreign competition. They make foreign goods less competitive.

- Non-tariff methods, regulating both imports and exports (they help to bring more domestic products on the world market, making them more competitive).

To indicate the nature of trade policy, the following two indicators are used:

- The average level of customs tariff. It is calculated as the average rate of import duties, according to the value of imported goods, to which the rate is applied. This indicator is defined only for the goods whose imports are imposed by duties.

- The average level of nontariff barriers. It is calculated as the value share of the imports or exports, which are subject to the restrictions.

Mode of implemented restrictions for each of the indicators is considered as open one if its level is less than 10%, the moderate one if less than 10-15%, the limited one if over 25% and the restrictive one if 40-100%.

Free Trade Policy

A free trade agreement is a pact between two or more nations to reduce barriers to imports and exports among them. Under a free trade policy, goods and services can be bought and sold across international borders with little or no government tariffs, quotas, subsidies, or prohibitions to inhibit their exchange. The concept of free trade is the opposite of trade protectionism or economic isolationism.

How a Free Trade Agreement Works

In the modern world, free trade policy is often implemented by means of a formal and mutual agreement of the nations involved. However, a free-trade policy may simply be the absence of any trade restrictions. A government doesn't need to take specific action to promote free trade. This hands-off stance is referred to as "laissez-faire trade" or trade liberalization.

Governments with free-trade policies or agreements in place do not necessarily abandon all control of imports and exports or eliminate all protectionist policies. In modern international trade, few free trade agreements (FTAs) result in completely free trade.

For example, a nation might allow free trade with another nation, with exceptions that forbid the import of specific drugs not approved by its regulators, or animals that have not been vaccinated, or processed foods that do not meet its standards. Or, it might have policies in place that exempt specific products from tariff-free status in order to protect home producers from foreign competition in their industries.

The Economics of Free Trade

In principle, free trade on the international level is no different from trade between neighbors, towns, or states. However, it allows businesses in each country to focus on producing and selling the goods that best use their resources while other businesses import goods that are scarce or unavailable domestically. That mix of local production and foreign trade allows economies to experience faster growth while better meeting the needs of its consumers.

This view was first popularized in 1817 by economist David Ricardo in his book, On the Principles of Political Economy and Taxation. He argued that free trade expands the diversity and lowers the prices of goods available in a nation while better exploiting its homegrown resources, knowledge, and specialized skills.

Public Opinion on Free Trade

Few issues divide economists and the general public as much as free trade. Research suggests that faculty economists at American universities are seven times more likely to support free-trade policies than the general public. In fact, the American economist Milton Friedman said: "The economics profession has been almost unanimous on the subject of the desirability of free trade."

Free-trade policies have not been as popular with the general public. The key issues include unfair competition from countries where lower labor costs allow price-cutting and a loss of good-paying jobs to manufacturers abroad. The call on the public to Buy American may get louder or quieter with the political winds, but it never goes silent.

The View from Financial Markets

Not surprisingly, the financial markets see the other side of the coin. Free trade is an opportunity to open another part of the world to domestic producers. Moreover, free trade is now an integral part of the financial system and the investing world. American investors now have access to most foreign financial markets and to a wider range of securities, currencies, and other financial products.

However, completely free trade in the financial markets is unlikely in our times. There are many supranational regulatory organizations for world financial markets, including the Basel Committee on Banking Supervision, the International Organization of Securities Commission (IOSCO), and the Committee on Capital Movements and Invisible Transactions.

Real-World Examples of Free Trade Agreements

The European Union is a notable example of free trade today. The member nations form an essentially borderless single entity for the purposes of trade, and the adoption of the euro by most of those nations smooths the way further. It should be noted that this system is regulated by a bureaucracy based in Brussels that must manage the many trade-related issues that come up between representatives of member nations.

U.S. Free Trade Agreements

The United States currently has a number of free trade agreements in place. These include multi-nation agreements such as the North American Free Trade Agreement (NAFTA), which covers the U.S., Canada, and Mexico, and the Central American Free Trade Agreement (CAFTA), which includes most of the nations of Central America. There are also separate trade agreements with nations from Australia to Peru.

Collectively, these agreements mean that about half of all goods entering the U.S. come in free of tariffs, according to government figures. The average import tariff on industrial goods is 2%.

All these agreements collectively still do not add up to free trade in its most laissez-faire form. American special interest groups have successfully lobbied to impose trade restrictions on hundreds of imports including steel, sugar, automobiles, milk, tuna, beef, and denim.

International Trade Law

International trade law is the set of laws and agreements that govern commerce between countries. International trade laws create the rules that countries and businesses must follow in order to do business across borders.

The General Agreement on Tariffs and Trade (GATT)

The General Agreement on Tariffs and Trade (GATT) is a multilateral agreement regulating international trade. The General Agreement on Tariffs and Trade (GATT) is a multilateral agreement regulating international trade. According to its preamble, its purpose is the "substantial reduction of tariffs and other trade barriers and the elimination of preferences, on a reciprocal and mutually advantageous basis." GATT was negotiated during the UN Conference on Trade and Employment and was the outcome of the failure of negotiating governments to create the International Trade Organization (ITO). GATT was signed in 1947 and lasted until 1993, when it was replaced by the

World Trade Organization (WTO) in 1995. The original GATT text (GATT 1947) is still in effect under the WTO framework, subject to the modifications of GATT 1994. GATT held a total of eight rounds, during which countries exchanged tariff concessions and reduced tariffs.

In 1993, the GATT was updated (GATT 1994) to include new obligations upon its signatories. One of the most significant changes was the creation of the WTO. The 75 existing GATT members and the European Communities became the founding members of the WTO on January 1, 1995. The other 52 GATT members rejoined the WTO in the following two years, the last being Congo in 1997. Since the founding of the WTO, 21 new non-GATT members have joined and 29 are currently negotiating membership. There are a total of 157 member countries in the WTO, with Russia and Vanuatu being new members as of 2012.

Of the original GATT members, Syria and SFR Yugoslavia (SFRY) have not rejoined the WTO. Because FR Yugoslavia (later renamed Serbia and Montenegro) is not recognized as a direct SFRY successor state, its application is considered a new (non-GATT) one. The General Council of WTO, on 4 May 2010, agreed to establish a working party to examine the request of Syria for WTO membership. The contracting parties who founded the WTO ended official agreement of the "GATT 1947" terms on 31 December 1995. Serbia and Montenegro are in the decision stage of the negotiations and are expected to become the newest members of the WTO in 2012 or in the near future.

The European Union

The European Union (EU) is an economic and political union made up of 27 member states that are located primarily in Europe. The European Union (EU) is an economic and political union or confederation of 27 member states that are located in Europe, including: Austria, Belgium, Bulgaria, Cyprus, the Czech Republic, Denmark, Estonia, Finland, France, Germany, Greece, Hungary, Ireland, Italy, Latvia, Lithuania, Luxembourg, Malta, the Netherlands, Poland, Portugal, Romania, Slovakia, Slovenia, Spain, Sweden, and the United Kingdom.

The EU operates through a system of supranational independent institutions and intergovernmental decisions negotiated by the member states. Important institutions of the EU include the European Commission, the Council of the European Union, the European Council, the Court of Justice of the European Union, and the European Central Bank. The European Parliament is elected every five years by EU citizens. The EU has developed a single market through a standardized system of laws that apply in all member states. Within the Schengen Area (which includes EU and non-EU states) passport controls have been abolished. EU policies aim to ensure the free movement of people, goods, services, and capital, enact legislation in justice and home affairs, and maintain common policies on trade, agriculture, fisheries, and regional development. A monetary union, the eurozone, was established in 1999, and as of January 2012, is composed of 17 member states. Through the Common Foreign and Security Policy the EU has developed a limited role in external relations and defense. Permanent diplomatic missions have been established around the world. The EU is represented at the United Nations, the WTO, the G8 and the G-20.

The Euro

The creation of a single European currency became an official objective of the European Economic Community in 1969. However, it was only with the advent of the Maastricht Treaty in 1993 that member states were legally bound to start the monetary union. In 1999 the euro was duly launched by eleven of the then fifteen member states of the EU. It remained an accounting currency until 1 January 2002, when euro notes and coins were issued and national currencies began to phase out in the Eurozone, which by then consisted of twelve member states. The Eurozone (constituted by the EU member states that have adopted the euro) has since grown to seventeen countries, the most recent being Estonia, which joined on 1 January 2011. All other EU member states, except Denmark and the United Kingdom, are legally bound to join the euro when the convergence criteria are met, however only a few countries have set target dates for accession. Sweden has circumvented the requirement to join the euro by not meeting the membership criteria.

The euro is designed to help build a single market by easing travel of citizens and goods, eliminating exchange rate problems, providing price transparency, creating a single financial market, stabilizing prices, maintaining low interest rates, and providing a currency used internationally and protected against shocks by the large amount of internal trade within the Eurozone. It is also intended as a political symbol of integration. The euro and the monetary policies of those who have adopted it in agreement with the EU are under the control of the European Central Bank (ECB). The ECB is the central bank for the Eurozone, and thus controls monetary policy in that area with an agenda to maintain price stability. It is at the center of the European System of Central Banks, which comprises all EU national central banks and is controlled by its General Council, consisting of the President of the ECB, who is appointed by the European Council, the Vice-President of the ECB, and the governors of the national central banks of all 27 EU member states. The monetary union has been shaken by the European sovereign-debt crisis since 2009.

The North American Free Trade Agreement (NAFTA)

NAFTA is an agreement signed by Canada, Mexico, and the United States, creating a trilateral trade bloc in North America. The North American Free Trade Agreement (NAFTA) is an agreement signed by the governments of Canada, Mexico, and the United States, creating a trilateral trade block in North America. The agreement came into force on January 1, 1994. It superseded the Canada – United States Free Trade Agreement between the U.S. and Canada.

In terms of combined GDP of its members, the trade bloc is the largest in the world as of 2010. NAFTA has two supplements: the North American Agreement on Environmental Cooperation (NAAEC) and the North American Agreement on Labor Cooperation (NAALC). The goal of NAFTA was to eliminate barriers to trade and investment among the U.S., Canada, and Mexico.

The implementation of NAFTA on January 1, 1994 brought the immediate elimination of tariffs on more than one-half of Mexico's exports to the U.S. and more than one-third of U.S. exports to Mexico. Within 10 years of the implementation of the agreement, all U.S.–Mexico tariffs would be eliminated except for some U.S. agricultural exports to Mexico that were to be phased out within 15 years. Most U.S.–Canada trade was already duty free. NAFTA also seeks to eliminate non-tariff trade barriers and to protect the intellectual property right of the products.

The agreement opened the door for open trade, ending tariffs on various goods and services, and implementing equality between Canada, America, and Mexico. NAFTA has allowed agricultural goods such as eggs, corn, and meats to be tariff-free. This allowed corporations to trade freely and import and export various goods on a North American scale.

The Asia-Pacific Economic Cooperation

APEC is a forum for 21 Pacific Rim countries that seeks to promote free trade and economic cooperation throughout the Asia-Pacific region. The Asia-Pacific Economic Cooperation (APEC) is a forum for 21 Pacific Rim countries (formally Member Economies) that seeks to promote free trade and economic cooperation throughout the Asia-Pacific region. Established in 1989 in response to the growing interdependence of Asia-Pacific economies and the advent of regional economic blocs (such as the European Union) in other parts of the world, APEC works to raise living standards and education levels through sustainable economic growth and to foster a sense of community and an appreciation of shared interests among Asia-Pacific countries.

Member countries are: Australia, Brunei, Canada, Chile, China, Hong Kong (Hong Kong, China), Indonesia, Japan, South Korea, Mexico, Malaysia, New Zealand, Papua New Guinea, Peru, Philippines, Russia, Singapore, Taiwan (Chinese Taipei), Thailand, United States, and Vietnam.

During the meeting in 1994 in Bogor, Indonesia, APEC leaders adopted the Bogor Goals that aim for free and open trade and investment in the Asia-Pacific by 2010, for industrialized economies and by 2020, for developing economies. In 1995, APEC established a business advisory body named the APEC Business Advisory Council

(ABAC), composed of three business executives from each member economy. To meet the Bogor Goals, APEC carries out work in three main areas:

- Trade and investment liberalization.
- Business facilitation.
- Economic and technical cooperation.

APEC is considering the prospects and options for a Free Trade Area of the Asia-Pacific (FTAAP), which would include all APEC member economies. Since 2006, the APEC Business Advisory Council, promoting the theory that a free trade area has the best chance of converging the member nations and ensuring stable economic growth under free trade, has lobbied for the creation of a high-level task force to study and develop a plan for a free trade area. The proposal for a FTAAP arose due to the lack of progress in the Doha round of World Trade Organization negotiations, and as a way to overcome the "spaghetti bowl" effect created by overlapping and conflicting elements of the umpteen free trade agreements. There are approximately 60 free trade agreements, with an additional 117 in the process of negotiation in Southeast Asia and the Asia-Pacific region.

The World Bank

The World Bank is an international financial institution that provides loans to developing countries for various programs. The World Bank is an international financial institution that provides loans to developing countries for capital programs. The World Bank's official goal is the reduction of poverty. According to the World Bank's Articles of Agreement (as amended effective February 16, 1989), all of its decisions must be guided by a commitment to promote foreign investment, international trade, and facilitate capital investment.

The World Bank differs from the World Bank Group, in that the World Bank comprises only two institutions: the International Bank for Reconstruction and Development (IBRD) and the International Development Association (IDA), whereas the former incorporates these two in addition to three more: International Finance Corporation (IFC), Multilateral Investment Guarantee Agency (MIGA), and International Centre for Settlement of Investment Disputes (ICSID). The current President of the Bank, Jim Yong Kim, is responsible for chairing the meetings of the boards of directors and for overall management of the bank. Traditionally, the bank president has always been a U.S. citizen nominated by the United States, the largest shareholder in the bank. The nominee is subject to confirmation by the board of executive directors, to serve for a five-year, renewable term.

The International Bank for Reconstruction and Development (IBRD) has 188 member countries, while the International Development Association (IDA) has 172 members.

Each member state of IBRD should be also a member of the International Monetary Fund (IMF), and only members of IBRD are allowed to join other institutions within the Bank (such as IDA).

For the poorest developing countries in the world, the bank's assistance plans are based on poverty reduction strategies; by combining a cross-section of local groups with an extensive analysis of the country's financial and economic situation, the World Bank develops a strategy pertaining uniquely to the country in question. The government then identifies the country's priorities and targets for the reduction of poverty, and the World Bank aligns its aid efforts correspondingly. Forty-five countries pledged $25.1 billion in "aid for the world's poorest countries," aid that goes to the World Bank International Development Association (IDA) which distributes the loans to 80 poorer countries.

The International Monetary Fund (IMF)

The IMF seeks to promote international economic cooperation, international trade, employment, and exchange rate stability. The International Monetary Fund (IMF) is an international organization that was created on July 22, 1944 at the Bretton Woods Conference and came into existence on December 27, 1945 when 29 countries signed the IMF Articles of Agreement. It originally had 45 members. The IMF's stated goal was to stabilize exchange rates and assist the reconstruction of the world's international payment system post-World War II. Countries contribute money to a pool through a quota system from which countries with payment imbalances can borrow funds on a temporary basis. Through this activity and others, such as surveillance of its members' economies and policies, the IMF works to improve the economies of its member countries. The IMF describes itself as "an organization of 188 countries, working to foster global monetary cooperation, secure financial stability, facilitate international trade, promote high employment and sustainable economic growth, and reduce poverty."

The organization's stated objectives are to promote international economic cooperation, international trade, employment, and exchange rate stability, including by making financial resources available to member countries to meet balance of payments needs. Member countries of the IMF have access to information on the economic policies of all member countries, the opportunity to influence other members' economic policies, technical assistance in banking, fiscal affairs, and exchange matters, financial support in times of payment difficulties, and increased opportunities for trade and investment. Voting power in the IMF is based on a quota system. Each member has a number of "basic votes" (each member's number of basic votes equals 5.502% of the total votes), plus one additional vote for each Special Drawing Right (SDR) of 100,000 of a member country's quota. The Special Drawing Right is the unit of account of the IMF and represents a claim to currency. It is based on a basket of key international currencies. The basic votes generate a slight bias in favor of small countries, but the additional votes determined by SDR outweigh this bias.

The IMF works to foster global growth and economic stability. It provides policy advice and financing to members in economic difficulties and also works with developing nations to help them achieve macroeconomic stability and reduce poverty. The rationale for this is that private international capital markets function imperfectly, and many countries have limited access to financial markets. Such market imperfections, together with balance of payments financing, provide the justification for official financing, without which many countries could only correct large external payment imbalances through measures with adverse effects on both national and international economic prosperity. The IMF can provide other sources of financing to countries in need that would not be available in the absence of an economic stabilization program supported by the fund.

The IMF is mandated to oversee the international monetary and financial system and monitor the economic and financial policies of its 188 member countries. This activity is known as "surveillance" and facilitates international cooperation. Since the demise of the Bretton Woods system of fixed exchange rates in the early 1970s, surveillance has evolved largely by way of changes in procedures rather than through the adoption of new obligations. The responsibilities of the fund changed from those of guardian to those of overseer of members' policies. The fund typically analyzes the appropriateness of each member country's economic and financial policies for achieving orderly economic growth, and assesses the consequences of these policies for other countries and for the global economy.

IMF conditionality is a set of policies or "conditions" that the IMF requires in exchange for financial resources. The IMF does not require collateral from countries for loans but rather requires the government seeking assistance to correct its macroeconomic imbalances in the form of policy reform. If the conditions are not met, the funds are withheld. Conditionality is the most controversial aspect of IMF policies. These loan conditions ensure that the borrowing country will be able to repay the fund and that the country won't attempt to solve their balance of payment problems in a way that would negatively impact the international economy. The incentive problem of moral hazard, which is the actions of economic agents maximizing their own utility to the detriment of others when they do not bear the full consequences of their actions, is mitigated through conditions rather than providing collateral; countries in need of IMF loans do not generally possess internationally valuable collateral anyway. Conditionality also reassures the IMF that the funds lent to them will be used for the purposes defined by the Articles of Agreement and provides safeguards that country will be able to rectify its macroeconomic and structural imbalances. In the judgment of the fund, the adoption by the member of certain corrective measures or policies will allow it to repay the fund, thereby ensuring that the same resources will be available to support other members.

Common Markets

A common market is the first stage towards a single market and may be limited initially to a free trade area. A common market is a first stage towards a single market and may be limited initially to a free trade area with relatively free movement of capital and of services, but not so advanced in reduction of the rest of the trade barriers.

The European Economic Community (EEC) (also known as the Common Market in the English-speaking world and sometimes referred to as the European Community even before it was renamed as such in 1993) was an international organization created by the 1957 Treaty of Rome. Its aim was to bring about economic integration, including a common market, among its six founding members: Belgium, France, Germany, Italy, Luxembourg, and the Netherlands.

It gained a common set of institutions along with the European Coal and Steel Community (ECSC) and the European Atomic Energy Community (EURATOM) as one of the European Communities under the 1965 Merger Treaty (Treaty of Brussels).

Upon the entry into force of the Maastricht Treaty in 1993, the EEC was renamed the European Community (EC) to reflect that it covered a wider range of policy. This was also when the three European Communities, including the EC, were collectively made to constitute the first of the three pillars of the European Union (EU), which the treaty also founded. The EC existed in this form until it was abolished by the 2009 Treaty of Lisbon, which merged the EU's former pillars and provided that the EU would "replace and succeed the European Community." The main aim of the EEC, as stated in its preamble, was to "preserve peace and liberty and to lay the foundations of an ever closer union among the peoples of Europe." Calling for balanced economic growth, this was to be accomplished through:

- The establishment of a customs union with a common external tariff.
- Common policies for agriculture, transport, and trade.
- Enlargement of the EEC to the rest of Europe.

For the customs union, the treaty provided for a 10% reduction in custom duties and up to 20% of global import quotas. Progress on the customs union proceeded much faster than the 12 years planned. However, France faced some setbacks due to its war with Algeria.

The six states that founded the EEC and the other two communities were known as the "inner six" (the "outer seven" were those countries who formed the European Free Trade Association). The six were France, West Germany, Italy, and the three Benelux countries: Belgium, the Netherlands, and Luxembourg. The first enlargement was in 1973, with the accession of Denmark, Ireland, and the United Kingdom. Greece, Spain, and Portugal joined in the 1980s. Following the creation of the EU in 1993, it has enlarged to include an additional 15 countries by 2007.

There were three political institutions that held the executive and legislative power of the EEC, plus one judicial institution and a fifth body created in 1975. These institutions (except for the auditors) were created in 1957 by the EEC but from 1967 on, they applied to all three communities. The council represents governments, the Parliament represents citizens, and the commission represents the European interest.

The Export-Import Bank of the United States

The Export-Import Bank of the United States (Ex-Im Bank) is the official export credit agency of the United States federal government. The Export-Import Bank of the United States (Ex-Im Bank) is the official export credit agency of the United States federal government. It was established in 1934 by an executive order and made an independent agency in the Executive branch by Congress in 1945. Its purpose is to finance and insure foreign purchases of United States goods for customers unable or unwilling to accept credit risk.

The mission of the Ex-Im Bank is to create and sustain U.S. jobs by financing sales of U.S. exports to international buyers. Ex-Im Bank is the principal government agency responsible for aiding the export of American goods and services through a variety of loan, guarantee, and insurance programs. Generally, its programs are available to any American export firm regardless of size. The Bank is chartered as a government corporation by the Congress of the United States; it was last chartered for a five year term in 2006. Its Charter spells out the Bank's authorities and limitations. Among them is the principle that Ex-Im Bank does not compete with private sector lenders, but rather provides financing for transactions that would otherwise not take place because commercial lenders are either unable or unwilling to accept the political or commercial risks inherent in the deal. Ex-Im Bank provides the following services:

- The Export-Import Bank of the United States focuses much of its energy and resources on providing support to small American businesses for export of American-made products.
- Export Credit Insurance provides insurance policies to U.S. companies and banks to mitigate risks of non-collection from foreign buyers and borrowers.
- The Working Capital Guarantee program provides loan guarantees to banks willing to lend to exporting companies.

- Two types of loans: Direct loans to foreign buyers of American exports and intermediary loans to responsible parties, such as foreign government lending agencies that re-lend to foreign buyers of capital goods and related services (for example, a maintenance contract for a jet passenger plane).

International Trade Regulation

Traditionally, trade was regulated through bilateral treaties between two nations. After World War II, as free trade emerged as the dominant doctrine, multilateral treaties like the GATT and World Trade Organization (WTO) became the principal regime for regulating global trade.

The WTO, created in 1995 as the successor to the General Agreement on Tariffs and Trade (GATT), is an international organization charged with overseeing and adjudicating international trade. The WTO deals with the rules of trade between nations at a near-global level; is responsible for negotiating and implementing new trade agreements; and is in charge of policing member countries' adherence to all the WTO agreements, signed by the majority of the world's trading nations and ratified in their parliaments. Additionally, it is the WTO's duty to review the national trade policies and to ensure the coherence and transparency of trade policies through surveillance in global economic policy making.

Headquartered in Geneva, Switzerland, the WTO has more than 150 members, which represent more than 95% of total world trade. It is governed by a ministerial conference, which meets every 2 years; a general council, which implements the conference's policy decisions and is responsible for day-to-day administration; and a director-general, who is appointed by the ministerial conference. Five basic principles guide the WTO's role in overseeing the global trading system:

- Nondiscrimination: This principle inspired two major policies—the most favored nation (MFN) rule and the national treatment policy—embedded in the main WTO rules on goods, services, and intellectual property. The MFN rule requires that a WTO member must apply the same conditions on all trade with other WTO members, that is, a WTO member has to grant the most favorable conditions under which it allows trade in a certain product type to all other WTO members. The national treatment policy, adopted to address nontariff barriers to trade (e.g., technical standards, security standards) dictates that imported and locally produced goods should be treated equally (at least after the foreign goods have entered the market).
- Reciprocity: This principle reflects both a desire to limit the scope of free riding that that may arise because of the MFN rule and a desire to obtain better access to foreign markets.

- Binding and enforceable commitments: The tariff commitments made by WTO members in a multilateral trade negotiation and on accession are enumerated in a list of concessions. A country can change its commitments but only after negotiating with its trading partners, which could mean compensating them for loss of trade. If satisfaction is not obtained, the complaining country may invoke the WTO dispute settlement procedures.
- Transparency: WTO members are required to publish their trade regulations, to maintain institutions charged with review of administrative decisions affecting trade, to respond to requests for information by other members, and to notify changes in trade policies to the WTO.
- Safety valves: Under specific circumstances, governments can (within limits) restrict trade to attain noneconomic objectives, to ensure "fair competition," and under special economic circumstances.

The WTO operates on a "one country, one vote" system, but actual votes have never been taken. Ostensibly, decisions are made by consensus, with relative market size as the primary source of bargaining power. In reality, most WTO decisions are made through a process of informal negotiations between small groups of countries, often referred to as the "green room" negotiations (after the color of the WTO director-general's office in Geneva) or "miniministerials" when they occur in other countries. These processes have been regularly criticized by many of the WTO's developing-country members who are often excluded from these negotiations.

The WTO oversees about 60 different agreements that have the status of international legal texts. Member countries must sign and ratify all WTO agreements on accession. Some of the most important agreements concern agriculture, services, and intellectual-property rights.

Regional arrangements such as Mercosur in South America; the North American Free Trade Agreement (NAFTA) between the United States, Canada, and Mexico; ASEAN in Southeast Asia; and the European Union (EU) between 27 independent states constitute a second dimension of the international trade regulatory framework.

The EU is an economic and political union of 27 member states. Committed to regional integration, the EU was established by the Treaty of Maastricht on November 1, 1993, upon the foundations of the preexisting European Economic Community. With almost 500 million citizens, the EU combined generates an estimated 30% share of the nominal gross world-product.

The EU has developed a single market through a standardized system of laws that apply in all member states, ensuring the freedom of movement of people, goods, services, and capital. It maintains common policies on trade, agriculture, fisheries, and regional development. A common currency, the euro, has been adopted by 16 member states known as the Eurozone. The EU has developed a limited role in foreign policy, having representation at the WTO, G8 summits, and at the UN. It enacts legislation in justice and home affairs, including the abolition of passport controls between many member states. Twenty-one EU countries are also members of NATO, those member states outside NATO being Austria, Cyprus, Finland, Ireland, Malta, and Sweden.

Mercosur is a regional trade agreement among Argentina, Brazil, Paraguay, and Uruguay, founded in 1991 by the Treaty of Asunción, which was later amended and updated by the 1994 Treaty of Ouro Preto. Its purpose is to promote free trade and the fluid movement of goods, people, and currency.

Bolivia, Chile, Colombia, Ecuador, and Peru currently have associate-member status. Venezuela signed a membership agreement on June 17, 2006, but before becoming a full member, its entry has to be ratified by the Paraguayan and the Brazilian parliaments.

The NAFTA is an agreement signed by the governments of the United States, Canada, and Mexico, creating a trilateral trade bloc in North America. The agreement came into force on January 1, 1994. It superseded the Canada–United States Free Trade Agreement. In terms of combined purchasing power, parity GDP of its members, as of 2007 the trade block, is the largest in the world and second largest by nominal GDP comparison. NAFTA has two supplements: the North American Agreement on Environmental Cooperation (NAAEC) and the North American Agreement on Labor Cooperation (NAALC).

The Association of Southeast Asian Nations, commonly abbreviated ASEAN, is a geopolitical and economic organization of 10 countries located in Southeast Asia, which was formed on August 8, 1967, by Indonesia, Malaysia, the Philippines, Singapore, and Thailand. Since then, membership has expanded to include Brunei, Burma (Myanmar), Cambodia, Laos, and Vietnam. Its aims include the acceleration of economic growth, social progress, cultural development among its members, and the protection of the peace and stability of the region.

3

Theories of International Trade

International Trade theory analyses the patterns of international trade, its origins and implications. Various models and theories have been established which aim to promote certain techniques and procedures as the basis on which international trade can be conducted. Brander-Spencer model, balanced trade, gravity model of trade, Linder hypothesis, new trade theory, etc. are some models and theories which are discussed in-depth to provide a better understanding of the subject matter.

Brander–Spencer Model

The Brander–Spencer model is an economic model in international trade originally developed by James Brander and Barbara Spencer in the early 1980s. The model illustrates a situation where, under certain assumptions, a government can subsidize domestic firms to help them in their competition against foreign producers and in doing so enhances national welfare. This conclusion stands in contrast to results from most international trade models, in which government non-interference is socially optimal.

The basic model is a variation on the Stackelberg–Cournot "leader and follower" duopoly game. Alternatively, the model can be portrayed in game theoretic terms as initially a game with multiple Nash equilibria, with government having the capability of affecting the payoffs to switch to a game with just one equilibrium. Although it is possible for the national government to increase a country's welfare in the model through export subsidies, the policy is of beggar thy neighbor type. This also means that if all governments simultaneously attempt to follow the policy prescription of the model, all countries would wind up worse off.

The model was part of the "New Trade Theory" that was developed in the late 1970s and early 1980s, which incorporated then recent developments from literature on industrial organization into theories of international trade. In particular, like in many other New Trade Theory models, economies of scale (in this case, in the form of fixed entry costs) play an important role in the Brander–Spencer model.

Entry Game Version

A simplified version of the model was popularized by Paul Krugman in the 1990s in his book *Peddling Prosperity*. In this set up there are two firms, one foreign and one domestic which are considering entering a new export market in a third country (or possibly the whole world). The demand in the export market is such that if only one firm enters, it will make a profit, but if they both enter each will make a loss, perhaps because of initial set up, infrastructure, product development, marketing or other fixed costs of entry. The matrix below presents a stylized example of the game that the two firms are engaged in.

The game with no government subsidy to the domestic firm is shown in Figure 1 on the left. If both firms enter, they each suffer a loss of 10 million dollars and if they both stay out of the market neither firm makes a profit or a loss. If only one firm enters however, that firm will realize a profit of 50 million dollars while the other firm will make nothing. The two Nash equilibria of this game (marked in purple) are the situations in which only one firm enters – but which firm, domestic or foreign, is indeterminate. In such a situation if the foreign firm has a slight initial advantage over the domestic firm (perhaps because it began product development earlier) the domestic firm will stay out and the foreign firm will enter.

Enter	−10, −10	50, 0
Stay Out	0, 50	0, 0

Fig. 1*: Entry game with multiple equilibria*

	Enter	Stay Out
Enter	10, −10	70, 0
Stay Out	0, 50	0, 0

Fig. 2*: Entry game with subsidy, single equilibrium*

The available choices of the domestic firms are given on the left, while those of the foreign firm are on top. The first number in each cell denotes the payoff to the domestic firm while the second number is the payoff to the foreign firm.

The game changes however if the government credibly promises to subsidize the domestic firm if it enters the market, as illustrated in Figure 2. Suppose the government promises a subsidy of twenty million, regardless of whether the foreign firm also enters or not. In that case, if the foreign firm enters the domestic firm will lose ten million from entry costs but will be more than compensated by the government subsidy, ending up with a net payoff of ten million. If the foreign firm does not enter of course, it is still profitable for the domestic firm to enter. As a result, regardless of the action of the foreign firm, the domestic firm's incentive is to enter the market. Anticipating this, the foreign firm will stay out of the market itself, since otherwise it would incur a loss.

From the point of view of the domestic country, the subsidy is welfare improving. The 20 million subsidy is a transfer from the government to the firm hence it has no effect on national welfare (ignoring costs of taxation; as long as these are not too large the basic insight of the model goes through). Additionally the domestic firm gains 50 million which would have otherwise gone to the foreign firm.

Stackelberg–cournot Version

The original Brander and Spencer paper presented the game in the framework of a Cournot competition model.

Letting x denote the output of the domestic firm and y denote the output of the foreign firm, the inverse demand function (price as a function of total quantity) is given by $p(x+y)$. Hence the profit function for the domestic firm is $\pi^h = xp(x+y) - c(x) + sx$ where $xp(x+y)$ is total revenue, $c(x)$ is total cost of producing x units, and s is per unit subsidy provided by the government. The profit function for the foreign firm is similar except that it does not include a subsidy, $\pi^f = yp(x+y) - c(y)$.

Each firm chooses the quantity to supply in order to maximize profits, taking the other's choice as given. The (first order) conditions for profit maximization are $xp_x + p - c_q + s = 0$ for the domestic firm and $yp_y + p - c_y = 0$ for the foreign firm, where subscripted variables denote partial derivatives. Solving these for y implicitly defines a best response function for each firm; $y = R1(x;s)$ and $y = R2(x)$. These are illustrated in the figure below, with the domestic firm's output on the x axis and foreign firm's output on the y axis.

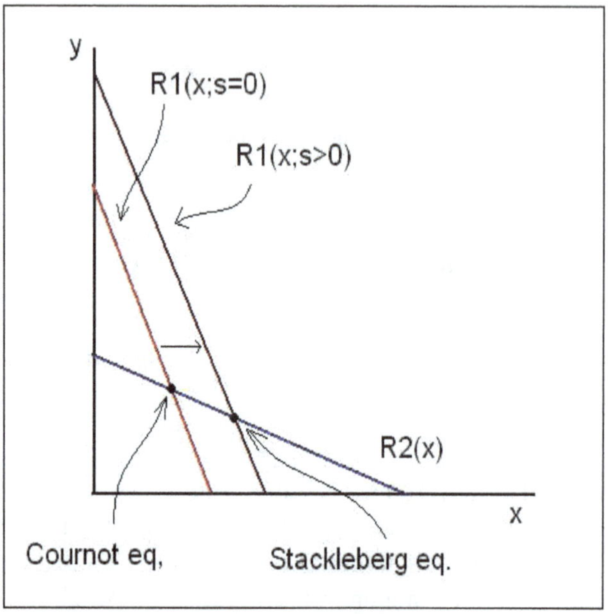

With no government subsidy (s=o) the resulting equilibrium will be the standard Cournot outcome, as shown in the graph by the intersection of the best response functions. A subsidy however has the effect of shifting the domestic firm's best response function to the right. Because its output is subsidized, the domestic firm increases production. This in turn means that the foreign firm's best response is to cut output, although not proportionally (hence, the market price falls). In the new equilibrium domestic firm produces more and foreign firm produces less.

In the model, domestic social welfare can be defined as the home firm's profit net of the subsidy (the model can be extended so that social welfare includes the firm's monopoly profit as well as the wages paid to the firm's workers; the results are qualitatively the same). It can be shown that the profit function evaluated at equilibrium quantity levels is concave in s and eventually negatively sloped. As a result, there is an "optimal subsidy" which maximizes the domestic firm's profits and hence domestic social welfare. As it turns out, if the government sets the subsidy exactly at the optimal level, the resulting equilibrium is the same as that of the "leader and follower" Stackelberg model. In that case one of the firms (in this case the domestic firm) has the ability to choose its output first. This creates the ability to credibly commit to a particular action, resulting in "first mover advantage". In the Brender–Spencer model, the government's subsidy creates this credible commitment even when the private firm does not have that ability.

Extensions

Domestic Consumption of Export Good

In standard models of international trade a fall in the price of a country's export good – a deterioration in its terms of trade – generally decreases the home country's welfare. In the Brander–Spencer model however the opposite is true. This is because in this model the markets are not perfectly competitive and the revenue from the expanded quantity sold compensates the firm for the revenue lost from the lower export price. If the good produced by the firm is also consumed domestically however the result is a bit more complicated. In the case where the firm is able to separate the home and export market (charge different prices in each with no possibility of third party arbitrage) then the level of the optimal subsidies will depend on whether marginal costs of production are constant, increasing or decreasing. The optimal subsidy level is either the same, higher or lower, respectively, compared to the level with no domestic consumption. This underscores the need on the part of the government for very precise information on industry structure and firm's cost functions.

In the more general case where the firm cannot price discriminate between domestic and foreign consumers the effects of a subsidy are less clear since both an expansion of exports and deterioration of terms of trade are present. However, Brender and Spencer show that starting out from the position of no subsidy, introducing a small subsidy can improve a country's welfare.

Extended Government Game

The basic model can be extended to incorporate a supra-game played by the governments of the respective countries. In this case, each government chooses the level of subsidy it will provide to its firm, taking the other government's action as given, and anticipating the reaction of the firms (in terms of quantity produced) to the subsidy. Brander and Spencer show that in the resulting Nash equilibrium the governments choose a level of subsidy that is too high and hence they do not manage to maximize social welfare. In fact, if the good produced is not consumed domestically, then the optimal level of subsidy is negative – an export tax.This is because the total quantity produced in the Cournot and the Stackelberg equilibrium is higher than the profit maximizing collusive monopoly level of output. Since both the home and foreign firm are producing for a third market, an export tax could reduce the total quantity produced down to the monopoly level, thus increasing both firms' profits. In that way the governments can effect a collusive outcome between their firms, at the expanse of the third country which imports the good.

Policy Applications and Applied Work

General Difficulties

As pointed out by Paul Krugman, the Brander–Spencer model, due to the sensitivity of the results to its assumptions, does not establish a generally applicable policy prescription in favor of government subsidies. Rather, it provides an example for when such intervention may be justifiable and points to some conditions which may favor it.

Paul Krugman popularized the model, but was also critical of it being misapplied to industries which did not meet the model's criteria.

A general difficulty with the application of the model, like many game theoretic models, is that it does not easily lend itself to econometric testing and parameter estimation. As a result, the two avenues of empirical research that have been pursued in subsequent literature have been estimates of a "conjectural variation" parameter for particular industries, and calibration of the models using behavioral parameters from other studies. The former approach assumes that firms have a "conjecture" as to how the other firms will react to their own choice of output and base their decision on this belief. However, the approach is problematic, both from an analytical (it is not internally consistent) and an empirical point of view (there's no guarantee that the parameter, even if it makes conceptual sense, remains stable when a new policy – the government's subsidy – is introduced[note 4]). Calibrations of models of industry structure on the other hand have generally found that most industry are neither Cournot (in which case the Brander–Spencer policy prescription would be an export subsidy) nor Bertrand (in which case the optimal policy is an export tax). As a result, it is hard to say in which industries exactly the Brander–Spencer policy prescription may apply.

Agriculture

Marie Thursby has used an extended version of the model to examine international trade in wheat, 60% of which is produced by the United States and Canada. Thursby includes marketing boards, possibility of a monopsony, and a variety of government policies in the analysis. She finds that while there are significant economies of scale in the industry, the barriers to entry are not high and regardless of the extent of market power that US firms have in the industry, the optimal policy is actually an export tax, rather than a subsidy.

Aircraft

In his book which presented the model to the general public, Paul Krugman used the example of the aircraft industry, with the two players being Airbus and Boeing. In fact, Krugman and Baldwin examined the industry for wide bodied aircraft in the context of the model in a 1988 paper. The authors calibrate an extended version of the model in order to examine the effect of a subsidy to Airbus by European governments, and its presence in a market which can only support two firms at most, worldwide. They find that the subsidy had an unambiguously negative effect on welfare of the United States and a positive effect on rest of the world, which benefits from lower prices. The result for Europe hinges on price elasticity of demand; for relatively inelastic demand the net effect of subsidy is positive with most of the benefits accruing to European consumers, but for elastic demand, social welfare in Europe goes down. Importantly, unlike in the baseline Brander and Spencer model, Krugman and Baldwin find that the changes to consumer surplus resulting from the subsidy and entry, dominate the effect of changes in firm profits in social welfare calculations.

Gernot Klepper, in an analysis similar to Krugman and Baldwin, has also used the Brander Spencer and other models to analyze the effects of entry into the transport aircraft industry. He included the effects of learning during the production process which depends on the scale of production. His calibrated model suggested that per unit production costs can fall by as much as 20% if total production is doubled. In that case, the entry of another firm (in this case, Airbus) into the market would decrease per firm output and reduce the learning and scale effects. In his analysis, the entry of Airbus would cause an increase in consumer surplus, but this would be smaller than the resulting loss in producer surplus.

Criticism

In general, like with many of the New Trade Theory models, the results of the Brander Spencer model and the policy prescriptions it generates are very sensitive to the underlying assumptions on the nature of the industry in question, the information available to the national government, its ability to credibly commit to an action and the likely response of foreign governments. Some of these criticisms were already noted by Brander and Spencer in their paper, where they advised caution.

Further work on the model has shown that a slight difference in assumptions can produce completely different results. For example, Eaton and Grossmann showed that if the firms compete in prices rather in quantities (Bertrand competition rather than Cournot) then the optimal policy is an export tax rather a subsidy – a policy rarely used in practice, politically unpopular and contrary to protectionist sentiment which generally touted New Trade Theory models as an argument for their favored policies.

Influence

The 1985 paper "Export Subsidies and International Market Share Rivalry", which presented the original version of the model, was the most cited paper in the *Journal of International Economics* since the inception of the journal in 1971 (as of 2000).

Balanced Trade

Balanced trade is an alternative economic model to free trade. Under balanced trade nations are required to provide a fairly even reciprocal trade pattern; they cannot run large trade deficits.

The concept of Balanced Trade arises from an essay by Michael McKeever Sr. of the McKeever Institute of Economic Policy Analysis. According to the essay, "BT is a simple concept which says that a country should import only as much as it exports so that trade and money flows are balanced. A country can balance its trade either on a trading partner basis in which total money flows between two countries are equalized or it can balance the overall trade and money flows so that a trade deficit with one country is balanced by a trade surplus with another country."

Implementation

Balanced trade was first popularized by Warren Buffett in a November 2003 Fortune Magazine article. Therein he proposed a system of "Import Certificates" (ICs) – exporters would receive $1 of ICs for each $1 of goods they exported, and importers would be required to present $1 of ICs for every $1 of goods they import. This would limit the value of imports to at most the value of exports (and presumably exactly the value of imports, assuming no leakage), and create a market of exporters to sell ICs to importers, effectively subsidizing exporters and taxing importers – compare cap and trade.

A year before Warren Buffett's article, a nascent form of Balanced Trade was hinted at by William Hawkins, who advocated direct limitation of imports: "the Bush Administration should be taking direct measures to reduce the trade deficit -- which means limiting imports, both to defend the dollar's integrity and America's economic strength."

In the United States, the idea was first introduced legislatively in the Balanced Trade Restoration Act of 2006. The proposed legislation was sponsored by Senators Byron Dorgan (ND) and Russell Feingold (WI), two Democrats in the United States senate. Since then there has been no action on the bill.

A more extensive argument for balanced trade, and a program to achieve balanced trade is presented by Raymond Richman, Howard Richman and Jesse Richman. In their 2008 book Trading Away Our Future, they argued "A minimum standard for ensuring that trade does benefit all is that trade should be relatively in balance." The Richmans published another book in 2014, Balanced Trade: Ending the Unbearable Costs of America's Trade Deficits, in which they propose a "scaled tariff...be applied to all imported goods from trade surplus countries that have had a sizable trade surplus with the United States over the most recent four economic quarters. The tariff rate would be designed to take in a portion (e.g. 50%) of the bilateral trade deficit (goods plus services) as revenue."

Another advocate of Balanced Trade has been Kenneth Davis Jr., former Assistant Secretary of Commerce and former Vice President and Chief Financial Officer for IBM Inc. In 2014 Mr. Davis and Will Wilkin formed Balanced Trade Associates to advocate for a Balanced Trade policy in the United States. They drafted model legislation, the Balanced Trade Restoration Act of 2014, that would use an electronic form of Import Certificates to taper down imports 10% each year for 3 years, then, beginning in the 4th year, limit imports each year to the same value as the previous year's exports.

The goal of Balanced Trade is also advanced by Mike Stumo the CEO of the Coalition for a Prosperous America (CPA). CPA has initiated a petition requesting that "Congress adopt balanced trade as the primary national trade goal by adding the following language to future trade-related bills: 'The principal national objective for trade in goods, services and agriculture is to achieve an overall balance of payments over a reasonable period of time, eliminate persistent trade deficits and reverse the accumulation of foreign debt.'"

Gravity Model of Trade

The gravity model of international trade in international economics, similar to other gravity models in social science, predicts bilateral trade flows based on the economic sizes (often using GDP measurements) and distance between two units. The model was first used by Jan Tinbergen in 1962. The basic model for trade between two countries (*i* and *j*) takes the form of,

$$F_{ij} = G\frac{M_i^{\beta_1} M_j^{\beta_2}}{D_{ij}^{\beta_3}}$$

Where F is the trade flow, M is the economic mass of each country, D is the distance and G is a constant. The model has been used by economists to analyse the determinants of bilateral trade flows such as common borders, common languages, common legal systems, common currencies, common colonial legacies, and it has been used to test the effectiveness of trade agreements and organizations such as the North American Free Trade Agreement (NAFTA) and the World Trade Organization (WTO) (Head and Mayer 2014). The model has also been used in international relations to evaluate the impact of treaties and alliances on trade (Head and Mayer).

The model has also been applied to other bilateral flow data (also 'dyadic' data) such as migration, traffic, remittances and foreign direct investment.

Theoretical Justifications and Research

The model has been an empirical success in that it accurately predicts trade flows between countries for many goods and services, but for a long time some scholars believed that there was no theoretical justification for the gravity equation. However, a gravity relationship can arise in almost any trade model that includes trade costs that increase with distance.

The gravity model estimates the pattern of international trade. While the model's basic form consists of factors that have more to do with geography and spatiality, the gravity model has been used to test hypotheses rooted in purer economic theories of trade as well. One such theory predicts that trade will be based on relative factor abundances. One of the common relative factor abundance models is the Heckscher–Ohlin model. This theory would predict that trade patterns would be based on relative factor abundance. Those countries with a relative abundance of one factor would be expected to produce goods that require a relatively large amount of that factor in their production. While a generally accepted theory of trade, many economists in the Chicago School believed that the Heckscher–Ohlin model alone was sufficient to describe all trade, while Bertil Ohlin himself argued that in fact the world is more complicated. Investigations into real world trading patterns have produced a number of results that do not match the expectations of comparative advantage theories. Notably, a study by Wassily Leontief found that the United States, the most capital endowed country in the world, actually exports more in labor-intensive industries. Comparative advantage in factor endowments would suggest the opposite would occur. Other theories of trade and explanations for this relationship were proposed in order to explain the discrepancy between Leontief's empirical findings and economic theory. The problem has become known as the Leontief paradox.

An alternative theory, first proposed by Staffan Linder, predicts that patterns of trade will be determined by the aggregated preferences for goods within countries. Those countries with similar preferences would be expected to develop similar industries. With continued similar demand, these countries would continue to trade back and forth in differentiated but similar goods since both demand and produce similar products. For instance, both Germany and the United States are industrialized countries with a high preference for automobiles. Both countries have automobile industries, and both trade cars. The empirical validity of the Linder hypothesis is somewhat unclear. Several studies have found a significant impact of the Linder effect, but others have had weaker results. Studies that do not support Linder have only counted countries that actually trade; they do not input zero values for the dyads where trade could happen but does not. This has been cited as a possible explanation for their findings. Also, Linder never presented a formal model for his theory, so different studies have tested his hypothesis in different ways.

Elhanan Helpman and Paul Krugman asserted that the theory behind comparative advantage does not predict the relationships in the gravity model. Using the gravity model, countries with similar levels of income have been shown to trade more. Helpman and Krugman see this as evidence that these countries are trading in differentiated goods because of their similarities. This casts some doubt about the impact Heckscher–Ohlin has on the real world. Jeffrey Frankel sees the Helpman–Krugman setup here as distinct from Linder's proposal. However, he does say Helpman–Krugman is different from the usual interpretation of Linder, but, since Linder made no clear model, the association between the two should not be completely discounted. Alan Deardorff adds the possibility, that, while not immediately apparent, the basic gravity model can be derived from Heckscher–Ohlin as well as the Linder and Helpman–Krugman hypotheses. Deardorff concludes that, considering how many models can be tied to the gravity model equation, it is not useful for evaluating the empirical validity of theories.

Bridging economic theory with empirical tests, James Anderson and Jeffrey Bergstrand develop econometric models, grounded in the theories of differentiated goods, which measure the gains from trade liberalizations and the magnitude of the border barriers on trade (see McCallum Border puzzle).

Adding to the problem of bridging economic theory with empirical results, some economists have pointed to the possibility of intra-industry trade not as the result of differentiated goods, but because of "reciprocal dumping." In these models, the countries involved are said to have imperfect competition and segmented markets in homogeneous goods, which leads to intra-industry trade as firms in imperfect competition seek to expand their markets to other countries and trade goods that are not differentiated yet for which they do not have a comparative advantage, since there is no specialization. This model of trade is consistent with the gravity model as it would predict that trade depends on country size.

The reciprocal dumping model has held up to some empirical testing, suggesting that the specialization and differentiated goods models for the gravity equation might not fully explain the gravity equation. Feenstra, Markusen, and Rose (2001) provided evidence for reciprocal dumping by assessing the *home market effect* in separate gravity equations for differentiated and homogeneous goods. The home market effect showed a relationship in the gravity estimation for differentiated goods, but showed the inverse relationship for homogeneous goods. The authors show that this result matches the theoretical predictions of reciprocal dumping playing a role in homogeneous markets.

Past research using the gravity model has also sought to evaluate the impact of various variables in addition to the basic gravity equation. Among these, price level and exchange rate variables have been shown to have a relationship in the gravity model that accounts for a significant amount of the variance not explained by the basic gravity equation. According to empirical results on price level, the effect of price level varies according to the relationship being examined. For instance, if exports are being examined, a relatively high price level on the part of the importer would be expected to increase trade with that country. A non-linear system of equations are used by Anderson and van Wincoop (2003) to account for the endogenous change in these price terms from trade liberalization. A more simple method is to use a first order log-linearization of this system of equations (Baier and Bergstrand (2009)), or exporter-country-year and importer-country-year dummy variables. For counterfactual analysis, however, one would still need to account for the change in world prices.

Econometric Estimation of Gravity Equations

Since the gravity model for trade does not hold exactly, in econometric applications it is customary to specify,

$$F_{ij} = G\frac{M_i^{\beta_1} M_j^{\beta_2}}{D_{ij}^{\beta_3}}\eta_{ij}$$

where F_{ij} represents volume of trade from country i to country j, M_i and M_j M_j typically represent the GDPs for countries i and j, D_{ij} denotes the distance between the two countries, and η represents an error term with expectation equal to 1.

The traditional approach to estimating this equation consists in taking logs of both sides, leading to a log-log model of the form (note: constant G becomes part of β_0):

$$\ln(F_{ij}) = \beta_0 + \beta_1 \ln(M_i) + \beta_2 \ln(M_j) - \beta_3 \ln(D_{ij}) + \varepsilon_{ij}.$$

However, this approach has two major problems. First, it obviously cannot be used when there are observations for which F_{ij} is equal to zero. Second, it has been argued by Santos Silva and Tenreyro (2006) that estimating the log-linearized equation by least squares (OLS) can lead to significant biases. As an alternative, these authors have suggested that the model should be estimated in its multiplicative form, i.e.,

$$F_{ij} = \exp[\beta_0 + \beta_1 \ln(M_i) + \beta_2 \ln(M_j) - \beta_3 \ln(D_{ij})]\eta_{ij},$$

using a Poisson pseudo-maximum likelihood (PPML) estimator usually used for count data (see the original paper for details). One of the authors' more surprising findings was that, when controlling for sharing a common language, having past colonial ties does not increase trade. This is despite the fact that simpler methods, such as taking simple averages of trade shares of countries with and without former colonial ties suggest that countries with former colonial ties continue to trade more. Santos Silva and Tenreyro (2006) did not explain where their result came from and even failed to realize their results were highly anomalous. Martin and Pham (2008) argued that using PPML on gravity severely biases estimates when zero trade flows are frequent. However, their results were challenged by Santos Silva and Tenreyro (2011), who argued that the simulation results of Martin and Pham (2008) are based on misspecified models and showed that the PPML estimator performs well even when the proportions of zeros is very large.

In applied work, the model is often extended by including variables to account for language relationships, tariffs, contiguity, access to sea, colonial history, and exchange rate regimes. Yet the estimation of structural gravity, based on Anderson and van Wincoop (2003), requires the inclusion of importer and exporter fixed effects, thus limiting the gravity analysis to bilateral trade costs (Baldwin and Taglioni 2007).

Linder Hypothesis

The Linder hypothesis is an economics conjecture about international trade patterns: The more similar the demand structures of countries, the more they will trade with one another. Further, international trade will still occur between two countries having identical preferences and factor endowments (relying on specialization to create a comparative advantage in the production of differentiated goods between the two nations).

Development of the Theory

The hypothesis was proposed by economist Staffan Burenstam Linder in 1961 as a possible resolution to the Leontief paradox, which questioned the empirical validity of the Heckscher-Ohlin theory (H-O). H-O predicts that patterns of international trade will be determined by the relative factor-endowments of different nations. Those with relatively high levels of capital in relation to labor would be expected to produce capital-intensive goods while those with an abundance of labor relative to (immobile) capital would be expected to produce labor-intensive goods. H-O and other theories of factor-endowment based trade had dominated the field of international economics until Leontief performed a study empirically rejecting H-O. In fact, Leontief found that the United States (then the most capital abundant nation) exported primarily labor-intensive goods. Linder proposed an alternative theory of trade that was consistent with Leontief's findings. The Linder hypothesis presents a demand based theory of trade in contrast to the usual supply based theories involving factor endowments. Linder hypothesized that nations with similar demands would develop similar industries. These nations would then trade with each other in similar, but differentiated goods.

Empirical Tests

Examinations of the Linder hypothesis have observed a "Linder effect" consistent with the hypothesis. Econometric tests of the hypothesis usually proxy the demand structure in a country from its per capita income: it is convenient to assume that the closer are the income levels per consumer the closer are the consumer preferences. (That is, the proportionate demand for each good becomes more similar, for example following Engel's law on food and non-food spending.)Econometric test of the hypothesis has been difficult because countries with similar levels of per capita income are generally located close to each other geographically and distance is a very important factor in explaining the intensity of trade between two countries. Generally a Linder effect has been found to be more significant for trade in manufactures than for non-manufactures, and within manufactures the effect is more significant for trade in capital goods than in consumer goods and more significant for differentialted products than for standardized products.

Marginal Intra-Industry Trade

Marginal Intra-Industry Trade, a concept originating in international economics, refers to the degree to which the change in a country's exports over a certain period of time are essentially of the same products as its change in imports over the same period. The concept is therefore closely related to that of intra-industry trade, that being the export and import of the same items, but concerns changes in exports and imports between two points in time as opposed to their values at a given point in time. The concept is thought to be useful for ascertaining the amount of adjustment costs associated with changing trade flows or the degree to which changes in trade might be responsible for changes in the distribution of income. Several formulas have been proposed to quantify this concept but the most widely used is that of Shelburne (1993).

$$MIIT=1-(|\Delta X-\Delta M|/(|\Delta X|+|\Delta M|))$$

where ΔX represents the change in exports between two points in time and ΔM represents the change in imports over the same period of time. The absolute values are needed because these changes in trade flows can sometimes be negative. Thus when exports and imports of a good change by the same amount the index would be one while if exports increase while imports do not (or vice versa) then the index would be zero. Generally adjustment costs or distribution effects are thought to be small if the MIIT index is high. The choice of the time period to use in making this calculation is somewhat arbitrary but can nevertheless significantly affect the results. The index is usually calculated as a sum of the different changes in imports and exports in the different sub-sectors (i). Thus more formally the index is:

$$MIIT=1-\sum_i(|\Delta X_i-\Delta M_i|)/(|\Delta X_i|+|\Delta M|_i)$$

Brülhart (1994) has further analyzed the properties of this index and popularized its use.

New Trade Theory

New trade theory (NTT) is a collection of economic models in international trade which focuses on the role of increasing returns to scale and network effects, which were developed in the late 1970s and early 1980s.

New trade theorists relaxed the assumption of constant returns to scale, and some argue that using protectionist measures to build up a huge industrial base in certain industries will then allow those sectors to dominate the world market.

Less quantitative forms of a similar "infant industry" argument against totally free trade have been advanced by trade theorists since at least 1848 (see: History of free trade).

The Theory's Impact

The value of protecting "infant industries" has been defended at least since the 18th century; for example, Alexander Hamilton proposed in 1791 that this be the basis for US trade policy. What was "new" in new trade theory was the use of mathematical economics to model the increasing returns to scale, and especially the use of the network effect to argue that the formation of important industries was path dependent in a way which industrial planning and judicious tariffs might control.

The models developed predicted the national specialization-by-industry observed in the industrial world (movies in Hollywood, watches in Switzerland, etc.). The model also showed how path-dependent industrial concentrations can sometimes lead to monopolistic competition or even situations of oligopoly.

Some economists, such as Ha-Joon Chang, had argued that protectionist policies had facilitated the development of the Japanese auto industries in the 1950s, when quotas and regulations prevented import competition. Japanese companies were encouraged to import foreign production technology but were required to produce 90% of parts domestically within five years. Japanese consumers suffered in the short term by being unable to buy superior vehicles produced by the world market, but eventually gained by having a local industry that could out-compete their international rivals.

Econometric Testing

The econometric evidence for NTT was mixed, and highly technical. Due to the timescales required, and the particular nature of production in each 'monopolizable' sector, statistical judgements were hard to make. In many ways, the available data have been too limited to produce a reliable test of the hypothesis, which doesn't require arbitrary judgements from the researchers.

Japan is cited as evidence of the benefits of "intelligent" protectionism, but critics of NTT have argued that the empirical support post-war Japan offers for beneficial protectionism is unusual, and that the NTT argument is based on a selective sample of historical cases. Although many examples (like Japanese cars) can be cited where a 'protected' industry subsequently grew to world status, regressions on the outcomes of such "industrial policies" (which include failures) have been less conclusive; some findings suggest that sectors targeted by Japanese industrial policy had decreasing returns to scale and did not experience productivity gains.

History of the Theory's Development

The theory was initially associated with Paul Krugman in the late 1970s; Krugman claims that he heard about monopolistic competition from Robert Solow. Looking back in 1996 Krugman wrote that International economics a generation earlier had completely ignored *returns to scale*. "The idea that trade might reflect an overlay of increasing-returns specialization on comparative advantage was not there at all: instead, the ruling idea was that increasing returns would simply alter the pattern of comparative advantage." In 1976, however, MIT-trained economist Victor Norman had worked out the central elements of what came to be known as the Helpman–Krugman theory. He wrote it up and showed it to Avinash Dixit. However, they both agreed the results were not very significant. Indeed, Norman never had the paper typed up, much less published. Norman's formal stake in the race comes from the final chapters of the famous Dixit–Norman book.

James Brander, a PhD student at Stanford at the time, was undertaking similarly innovative work using models from industrial organisation theory—cross-hauling—to explain two-way trade in similar products.

"New" New Trade Theory

Marc Melitz and Pol Antràs started a new trend in the study of international trade. While new trade theory put emphasis on the growing trend of intermediate goods, this new trend emphasizes firm level differences in the same industry of the same country and this new trend is frequently called 'new' new trade theory (NNTT). NNTT stresses the importance of firms rather than sectors in understanding the challenges and the opportunities countries face in the age of globalization.

As international trade is increasingly liberalized, industries of comparative advantage are expected to expand, while those of comparative disadvantage are expected to shrink, leading to an uneven spatial distribution of the corresponding economic activities. Within the very same industry, some firms are not able to cope with international competition while others thrive. The resulting intra-industry reallocations of market shares and productive resources are much more pronounced than inter-industry reallocations driven by comparative advantage.

Theoretical Foundations

New trade theory and "new" new trade theory (NNTT) need their own trade theory. New trade theories are often based on assumptions such as monopolistic competition and increasing returns to scale. One of the typical explanation, given by P. Krugman, depends on the assumption that all firms are symmetrical, meaning that they all have the same production coefficients. This is too strict as an assumption and deprived general applicability of Krugman's explanation. Shiozawa, based on much more general model, succeeded in giving a new explanation on why the traded volume increases for intermediates goods when the transport cost decreases.

"New" new trade theory (NNTT) also needs new theoretical foundation. Melitz and his followers concentrate on empirical aspects and pay little interest on theoretical aspects of NNTT. Shiozawa's new construction, or Ricardo-Sraffa trade theory, enables Ricardian trade theory to include choice of techniques. Thus the theory can treat a situation where there are many firms with different production processes. Based on this new theory, Fujimoto and Shiozawa analyze how different production sites, either of competing firms or of the same firms locating in the different countries, compete.

Criticism

New trade theory has been criticised as not providing an efficient allocation of resources. The criticism follows the line that if a nation has to protect infant industries, then the protection suggests a lack of comparative advantage, and the nation would be better shifting resources into an industry where it does have comparative advantage and can dominate without protectionism. This would represent the most efficient utilisation of global resources.

Prebisch–Singer Hypothesis

In economics, the Prebisch–Singer hypothesis (also called the Prebisch–Singer thesis) argues that the price of primary commodities declines relative to the price of manufactured goods over the long term, which causes the terms of trade of primary-product-based economies to deteriorate. As of 2013, recent statistical studies have given moderate support for the idea. The idea was initially developed by Hans Singer in 1948–49 and expanded by Raúl Prebisch shortly thereafter; since that time, it has served as a major pillar of dependency theory and policies such as import substitution industrialization (ISI).

Theory

A common explanation for this supposed phenomenon is that manufactured goods have a greater income elasticity of demand than primary products, especially food. Therefore, as incomes rise, the demand for manufactured goods increases more rapidly than demand for primary products. In addition, primary products have a low price elasticity of demand, so a decline in their prices tends to reduce revenue rather than increase it.

This theory implies that the very structure of the global market is responsible for the persistent inequality within the world system. This provides an interesting twist on Wallerstein's neo-Marxist interpretation of the international order which faults differences in power relations between 'core' and 'periphery' states as the chief cause for economic and political inequality (However, the Singer–Prebisch thesis also works with different bargaining positions of labour in developed and developing countries). As a result, the hypothesis enjoyed a high degree of popularity in the 1960s and 1970s with neo-Marxist developmental economists and even provided a justification for an expansion of the role of the commodity futures exchange as a tool for development.

Singer and Prebisch noticed a similar statistical pattern in long-run historical data on relative prices, but such regularity is consistent with a number of different explanations and policy stances. Later in his career, Prebisch argued that, due to the declining terms of trade primary producers face, developing countries should strive to diversify their economies and lessen dependence on primary commodity exports by developing their manufacturing industry.

The hypothesis has lost some of its relevance in the last 30 years, as exports of simple manufactures have overtaken exports of primary commodities in most developing countries outside of Africa. For this reason, much of the recent research focuses less on the relative prices of primary products and manufactured goods, and more on the relationship between the prices of simple manufactures produced by developing countries and of complex manufactures produced by advanced economies.

In 1998, Singer argued that the thesis he pioneered has joined the mainstream:

One indication of this is that the PST is now incorporated, both implicitly and explicitly, in the advice given by the Bretton Woods Institutions to developing countries. They are warned to be prudent even when export prices are temporarily favourable and to guard against currency overvaluation and Dutch Disease, with all the unfavourable impact on the rest of the economy and all the dangers of macroeconomic instability which a sudden boom in a major export sector could imply. They are warned to remember that the outlook for commodity prices is not favourable and that windfalls will tend to be temporary, with the subsequent relapse likely to be greater than the temporary windfall. This is exactly the warning which the PST would give.

Evidence

Recent statistical research has given the idea qualified support.

During the 2000s commodities boom, the terms of trade of most developing countries improved, while east Asia (which exports mostly manufactured goods) saw deteriorating terms of trade—the opposite of what the hypothesis generally predicts. However, the boom was a relatively brief event compared to the timeframes covered by most studies.

History

In February 1949, Hans Singer, then working in the United Nations Department of Economic Affairs in New York City, published a paper titled "Post-war Price Relations between Under-developed and Industrialized Countries", which suggested that the terms of trade of underdeveloped countries had declined significantly between 1876 and 1948. Inspired by this, Raúl Prebisch presented a paper of his own discussing the decline at the United Nations Economic Commission for Latin America and the Caribbeans second annual meeting, in Havana in May 1949.

Therefore, the initial statistical argument about the long-term trend in terms of trade of underdeveloped countries must be attributed to Singer. However, both seem to have independently invented similar explanations, stressing that the terms of trade moved against the 'borrowing' (i.e., underdeveloped) and in favour of the 'investing' (i.e., developed) countries. However, Prebisch specifically deals with the economic cycle and highlights to a greater extent than Singer the reasons for the different behaviour of wages in developed and underdeveloped countries, and received much greater recognition for his work, in part because of efforts by industrialized countries like the United States to distance themselves from his work.

International Trade Theory

International trade theory is a sub-field of economics which analyzes the patterns of international trade, its origins, and its welfare implications.

Adam Smith's Model

Adam Smith describes trade taking place as a result of countries having absolute advantage in production of particular goods, relative to each other.

Ricardian Model

The law of comparative advantage was first proposed by David Ricardo.

The Ricardian model focuses on comparative advantage, which arises due to differences in technology or natural resources. The Ricardian model does not directly consider factor endowments, such as the relative amounts of labor and capital within a country.

The Ricardian model is based on the following assumptions:

- Labor is the only primary input to production.
- The relative ratios of labor at which the production of one good can be traded off for another differ between countries.

Heckscher–ohlin Model

In the early 1900s, a theory of international trade was developed by two Swedish economists, Eli Heckscher and Bertil Ohlin. This theory has subsequently became known as the Heckscher–Ohlin model (H–O model). The results of the H–O model are that the pattern of international trade is determined by differences in factor endowments. It predicts that countries will export those goods that make intensive use of locally abundant factors and will import goods that make intensive use of factors that are locally scarce.

The H–O model makes the following core assumptions:

- Labor and capital flow freely between sectors.
- The amount of labor and capital in two countries differ (difference in endowments).
- Technology is the same among countries (a long-term assumption).
- Tastes are the same.

Applicability

In 1953, Wassily Leontief published a study in which he tested the validity of the Heckscher-Ohlin theory. The study showed that the United States was more abundant in capital compared to other countries, therefore the United States would export capital-intensive goods and import labor-intensive goods. Leontief found out that the United States' exports were less capital intensive than its imports. The result became known as Leontief's paradox.

After the appearance of Leontief's paradox, many researchers tried to save the Heckscher-Ohlin theory, either by new methods of measurement, or by new interpretations.

Specific Factors Model

In the specific factors model, labor mobility among industries is possible while capital is assumed to be immobile in the short run. Thus, this model can be interpreted as a short-run version of the Heckscher-Ohlin model. The "specific factors" name refers to the assumption that in the short run, specific factors of production such as physical capital are not easily transferable between industries. The theory suggests that if there is an increase in the price of a good, the owners of the factor of production specific to that good will profit in real terms.

New Trade Theory

New Trade Theory tries to explain empirical elements of trade that comparative advantage-based models above have difficulty with. These include the fact that most trade is between countries with similar factor endowment and productivity levels, and the large amount of multinational production (i.e., foreign direct investment) that exists. New Trade theories are often based on assumptions such as monopolistic competition and increasing returns to scale. One result of these theories is the home-market effect, which asserts that, if an industry tends to cluster in one location because of returns to scale and if that industry faces high transportation costs, the industry will be located in the country with most of its demand, in order to minimize cost.

Gravity Model

The Gravity model of trade presents a more empirical analysis of trading patterns. The gravity model, in its basic form, predicts trade based on the distance between countries and the interaction of the countries' economic sizes. The model mimics the Newtonian law of gravity which also considers distance and physical size between two objects. The model has been shown to have significant empirical validity.

Ricardian Theory of International Trade (Modern Development)

The Ricardian theory of comparative advantage became a basic constituent of neoclassical trade theory. Any undergraduate course in trade theory includes a presentation of Ricardo's example of a two-commodity, two-country model.

Many Countries, Many Goods

This model has been expanded to many-country and many-commodity cases. Major general results were obtained by McKenzie and Jones. Ricardo's idea was even expanded to the case of continuum of goods by Dornbusch, Fischer, and Samuelson This formulation is employed for example by Matsuyama and others. These theories use a special property that is applicable only for the two-country case.

Traded Intermediate Goods

Ricardian trade theory ordinarily assumes that the labor is the unique input. This is a significant deficiency for Ricardian trade theory since intermediate goods comprise a major part of world international trade.

McKenzie and Jones emphasized the necessity to expand the Ricardian theory to the cases of traded inputs. McKenzie (1954, p. 179) pointed that "A moment's consideration will convince one that Lancashire would be unlikely to produce cotton cloth if the cotton had to be grown in England." Paul Samuelson coined a term *Sraffa bonus* to name the gains from trade of inputs.

John S. Chipman observed in his survey that McKenzie stumbled upon the questions of intermediate products and postulated that "introduction of trade in intermediate product necessitates a fundamental alteration in classical analysis". It took many years until Shiozawa succeeded in removing this deficiency. The Ricardian trade theory was now constructed in a form to include intermediate input trade for the most general case of many countries and many goods. Chipman called this the Ricardo-Sraffa trade theory.

Based on an idea of Takahiro Fujimoto, who is a specialist in automobile industry and a philosopher of the international competitiveness, Fujimoto and Shiozawa developed a discussion in which how the factories of the same multi-national firms compete between them across borders. International *intra-firm competition* reflects a really new aspect of international competition in the age of so-called *global competition*.

Concertina Model

The concertina model, sometimes referred to as the concertina rule or "concertina method", is an international trade liberalisation strategy, which consists in removing the highest tariffs first. Amiti (2004, p. 3) traces this "idea back to Meade (1955, Trade and Welfare) who concluded that the welfare gains will be larger if tariffs on those goods with the highest tariffs are reduced first. This result was formalized by a number of authors, including Bertrand and Vanek (1971) and Falvey (1988) for a small, open, perfectly competitive economy." The concertina method consists in a piecemeal approach to trade reforms, however, with a clear quantitative priority setting. The concertina model is also highlighted briefly in Dani Rodrik's book One Economics, Many Recipes and Max Corden's textbook *Trade Policy and Economic Welfare*. Haussmann, Rodrik and Velasco (HRV)(Growth Diagnostics, 2004) refer to the concertina method as a simple trade and more specifically, tariff reform, second best strategy. The concertina method is a general rule of thumb, which consists in eliminating the highest tariffs first, and so on, until ideally all tariffs are eliminated. "HRV" see 5 possible reform strategies: 1. Wholesale reform ("augmented Washington Consensus": getting prices and institutions right) 2. Do as much and as best as you can (opportunistic approach, e.g. picking low "hanging fruits", etc.) 3. Sophisticated second-best reform (many trade offs)4. Target the largest distortions ("concertina rule") and 5. Focus on the most binding constraints. Targeting the largest distortions first in the overall economic reform agenda is not very practical as many important distortions (e.g. with respect to institutions) cannot be easily quantified, hence a deeper qualitative analysis is needed. Focussing on the binding constrainst is seen by these "HRV" as the best practical reform agenda. It is superior to the "concertina rule" and also to the so-called "augmented Washington Consensus" which is an impossibly broad and ambitious reform agenda that is insufficiently differentiated according to the needs of different countries. The Concertina policy approach can be seen as a simple rule of thumb approach for an easy quantifiable problem. Reforming implies planning. However planning has clear limits due to limits to rationality ("bounded rationality" see Simon (1957) and Lindblom (1979)). The HRV approach again is an approach based on rationality. Human interactions often defy a clear rationality or rationality changes with respect to the number of peoples or interest groups involved (see Olson, Mancur's Logic of Collective Action).

Development Theory

Development theory is a conglomeration or a collective vision of theories about how desirable change in society is best achieved. Such theories draw on a variety of social science disciplines and approaches. In this article, multiple theories are discussed, as are recent developments with regard to these theories.

Modernization Theory

Modernization theory is used to analyze in which modernization processes in societies take place. The theory looks at which aspects of countries are beneficial and which constitute obstacles for economic development. The idea is that development assistance targeted at those particular aspects can lead to modernization of 'traditional' or 'backward' societies. Scientists from various research disciplines have contributed to modernization theory.

Sociological and Anthropological Modernization Theory

The earliest principles of modernization theory can be derived from the idea of progress, which stated that people can develop and change their society themselves. Marquis de Condorcet was involved in the origins of this theory. This theory also states that technological advancements and economic changes can lead to changes in moral and cultural values. The French sociologist Émile Durkheim stressed the interdependence of institutions in a society and the way in which they interact with cultural and social unity. His work 'The Division of Labor in Society' was very influential. It described how social order is maintained in society and ways in which primitive societies can make the transition to more advanced societies.

Other scientists who have contributed to the development of modernization theory are: David Apter, who did research on the political system and history of democracy; Seymour Martin Lipset, who argued that economic development leads to social changes which tend to lead to democracy; David McClelland, who approached modernization from the psychological side with his motivations theory; and Talcott Parsons who used his pattern variables to compare backwardness to modernity.

Linear Stages of Growth Model

The linear stages of growth model is an economic model which is heavily inspired by the Marshall Plan which was used to revitalize Europe's economy after World War II. It assumes that economic growth can only be achieved by industrialization. Growth can be restricted by local institutions and social attitudes, especially if these aspects influence the savings rate and investments. The constraints impeding economic growth are thus considered by this model to be internal to society.

According to the linear stages of growth model, a correctly designed massive injection of capital coupled with intervention by the public sector would ultimately lead to industrialization and economic development of a developing nation.

The Rostow's stages of growth model is the most well-known example of the linear stages of growth model. Walt W. Rostow identified five stages through which developing countries had to pass to reach an advanced economy status: (1) Traditional society, (2) Preconditions for take-off, (3) Take-off, (4) Drive to maturity, (5) Age of high mass consumption. He argued that economic development could be led by certain strong sectors; this is in contrast to for instance Marxism which states that sectors should develop equally. According to Rostow's model, a country needed to follow some rules of development to reach the take-off: (1) The investment rate of a country needs to be increased to at least 10% of its GDP, (2) One or two manufacturing sectors with a high rate of growth need to be established, (3) An institutional, political and social framework has to exist or be created in order to promote the expansion of those sectors.

The Rostow model has serious flaws, of which the most serious are: (1) The model assumes that development can be achieved through a basic sequence of stages which are the same for all countries, a doubtful assumption; (2) The model measures development solely by means of the increase of GDP per capita; (3) The model focuses on characteristics of development, but does not identify the causal factors which lead development to occur. As such, it neglects the social structures that have to be present to foster development.

Economic modernisation theories such as Rostow's stages model have been heavily inspired by the Harrod-Domar model which explains in a mathematical way the growth rate of a country in terms of the savings rate and the productivity of capital. Heavy state involvement has often been considered necessary for successful development in economic modernization theory; Paul Rosenstein-Rodan, Ragnar Nurkse and Kurt Mandelbaum argued that a big push model in infrastructure investment and planning was necessary for the stimulation of industrialization, and that the private sector would not be able to provide the resources for this on its own. Another influential theory of modernization is the dual-sector model by Arthur Lewis. In this model Lewis explained how the traditional stagnant rural sector is gradually replaced by a growing modern and dynamic manufacturing and service economy.

Because of the focus on the need for investments in capital, the Linear Stages of Growth Models are sometimes referred to as suffering from 'capital fundamentalism'.

Critics of Modernization Theory

Modernization theory observes traditions and pre-existing institutions of so-called "primitive" societies as obstacles to modern economic growth. Modernization which is forced from outside upon a society might induce violent and radical change, but according to modernization theorists it is generally worth this side effect. Critics point to traditional societies as being destroyed and slipping away to a modern form of poverty without ever gaining the promised advantages of modernization.

Structuralism

Structuralism is a development theory which focuses on structural aspects which impede the economic growth of developing countries. The unit of analysis is the transformation of a country's economy from, mainly, a subsistence agriculture to a modern, urbanized manufacturing and service economy. Policy prescriptions resulting from structuralist thinking include major government intervention in the economy to fuel the industrial sector, known as import substitution industrialization (ISI). This structural transformation of the developing country is pursued in order to create an economy which in the end enjoys self-sustaining growth. This can only be reached by ending the reliance of the underdeveloped country on exports of primary goods (agricultural and mining products), and pursuing inward-oriented development by shielding the domestic economy from that of the developed economies. Trade with advanced economies is minimized through the erection of all kinds of trade barriers and an overvaluation of the domestic exchange rate; in this way the production of domestic substitutes of formerly imported industrial products is encouraged. The logic of the strategy rests on the infant industry argument, which states that young industries initially do not have the economies of scale and experience to be able to compete with foreign competitors and thus need to be protected until they are able to compete in the free market. The Prebisch–Singer hypothesis states that over time the terms of trade for commodities deteriorate compared to those for manufactured goods, because the income elasticity of demand of manufactured goods is greater than that of primary products. If true, this would also support the ISI strategy.

Structuralists argue that the only way Third World countries can develop is through action by the state. Third world countries have to push industrialization and have to reduce their dependency on trade with the First World, and trade among themselves.

The roots of structuralism lie in South America, and particularly Chile. In 1950, Raul Prebisch went to Chile to become the first director of the Economic Commission for Latin America. In Chile, he cooperated with Celso Furtado, Anibal Pinto, Osvaldo Sunkel, and Dudley Seers, who all became influential structuralists.

Dependency Theory

Dependency theory is essentially a follow up to structuralist thinking, and shares many of its core ideas. Whereas structuralists did not consider that development would be possible at all unless a strategy of delinking and rigorous ISI was pursued, dependency thinking could allow development with external links with the developed parts of the globe. However, this kind of development is considered to be "dependent development", i.e., it does not have an internal domestic dynamic in the developing country and thus remains highly vulnerable to the economic vagaries of the world market. Dependency thinking starts from the notion that resources flow from the 'periphery' of poor and underdeveloped states to a 'core' of wealthy countries, which leads to accumulation of wealth in the rich states at the expense of the poor states. Contrary to modernization theory, dependency theory states that not all societies progress through similar stages of development. Primitive states have unique features, structures and institutions of their own and are the weaker with regard to the world market economy, while the developed nations have never been in this follower position in the past. Dependency theorists argue that underdeveloped countries remain economically vulnerable unless they reduce their connectedness to the world market.

Dependency theory states that poor nations provide natural resources and cheap labor for developed nations, without which the developed nations could not have the standard of living which they enjoy. Also, developed nations will try to maintain this situation and try to counter attempts by developing nations to reduce the influence of developed nations. This means that poverty of developing nations is not the result of the disintegration of these countries in the world system, but because of the way in which they are integrated into this system.

In addition to its structuralist roots, dependency theory has much overlap with Neo-Marxism and World Systems Theory, which is also reflected in the work of Immanuel Wallerstein, a famous dependency theorist. Wallerstein rejects the notion of a Third World, claiming that there is only one world which is connected by economic relations (World Systems Theory). He argues that this system inherently leads to a division of the world in core, semi-periphery and periphery. One of the results of expansion of the world-system is the commodification of things, like natural resources, labor and human relationships.

Basic Needs

The basic needs approach was introduced by the International Labor Organization in 1976, mainly in reaction to prevalent modernization- and structuralism-inspired development approaches, which were not achieving satisfactory results in terms of poverty alleviation and combating inequality in developing countries. It tried to define an absolute minimum of resources necessary for long-term physical well-being. The poverty line which follows from this, is the amount of income needed to satisfy those basic needs. The approach has been applied in the sphere of development assistance, to determine what a society needs for subsistence, and for poor population groups to rise above the poverty line. Basic needs theory does not focus on investing in economically productive activities. Basic needs can be used as an absolute.

Proponents of basic needs have argued that elimination of absolute poverty is a good way to make people active in society so that they can provide labor more easily and act as consumers and savers. There have been also many critics of the basic needs approach. It would lack theoretical rigour, practical precision, be in conflict with growth promotion policies, and run the risk of leaving developing countries in permanent.

Neoclassical Theory

Neoclassical development theory has it origins in its predecessor: classical economics. Classical economics was developed in the 18th and 19th centuries and dealt with the value of products and on which production factors it depends. Early contributors to this theory are Adam Smith and David Ricardo. Classical economists argued - as do the neoclassical ones - in favor of the free market, and against government intervention in those markets. The 'invisible hand' of Adam Smith makes sure that free trade will ultimately benefit all of society. John Maynard Keynes was a very influential classical economist as well, having written his General Theory of Employment, Interest, and Money in 1936.

Neoclassical development theory became influential towards the end of the 1970s, fired by the election of Margaret Thatcher in the UK and Ronald Reagan in the USA. Also, the World Bank shifted from its Basic Needs approach to a neoclassical approach in 1980. From the beginning of the 1980s, neoclassical development theory really began to roll out.

Structural Adjustment

One of the implications of the neoclassical development theory for developing countries were the Structural Adjustment Programmes (SAPs) which the World Bank and the International Monetary Fund wanted them to adapt. Important aspects of those SAPs include:

- Fiscal austerity (reduction in government spending).
- Privatization (which should both raise money for governments and improve efficiency and financial performance of the firms involved).
- Trade liberalization, currency devaluation and the abolition of marketing boards (to maximize the static comparative advantage the developing country has on the global market).
- Retrenchment of the government and deregulation (in order to stimulate the free market).

These measures are more or less reflected by the themes which were identified by the Institute of International Economics which were believed to be necessary for the recovery of Latin America from the economic and financial crises of the 1980s. These themes are known as the Washington consensus, a termed coined in 1989 by the economist John Williamson.

Recent Trends

Postdevelopment Theory

Postdevelopment theory is a school of thought which questions the idea of national economic development altogether. According to postdevelopment scholars, the goal of improving living standards leans on arbitrary claims as to the desirability and possibility of that goal. Postdevelopment theory arose in the 1980s and 1990s.

According to postdevelopment theorists, the idea of development is just a 'mental structure' (Wolfgang Sachs) which has resulted in an hierarchy of developed and underdeveloped nations, of which the underdeveloped nations desire to be like developed nations. Development thinking has been dominated by the West and is very ethnocentric, according to Sachs. The Western lifestyle may neither be a realistic nor a desirable goal for the world's population, postdevelopment theorists argue. Development is being seen as a loss of a country's own culture, people's perception of themselves and modes of life. According to Majid Rahnema, another leading postdevelopment scholar, things like notions of poverty are very culturally embedded and can differ a lot among cultures. The institutes which voice the concern over underdevelopment are very Western-oriented, and postdevelopment calls for a broader cultural involvement in development thinking.

Postdevelopment proposes a vision of society which removes itself from the ideas which currently dominate it. According to Arturo Escobar, postdevelopment is interested instead in local culture and knowledge, a critical view against established sciences and the promotion of local grassroots movements. Also, postdevelopment argues for structural change in order to reach solidarity, reciprocity, and a larger involvement of traditional knowledge.

Sustainable Development

Sustainable development is development that meets the needs of the present without compromising the ability of future generations to meet their own needs. (Brundtland Commission) There exist more definitions of sustainable development, but they have in common that they all have to do with the carrying capacity of the earth and its natural systems and the challenges faced by humanity. Sustainable development can be broken up into environmental sustainability, economic sustainability and sociopolitical sustainability. The book 'Limits to Growth', commissioned by the Club of Rome, gave huge momentum to the thinking about sustainability. Global warming issues are also problems which are emphasized by the sustainable development movement. This led to the 1997 Kyoto Accord, with the plan to cap greenhouse-gas emissions.

Opponents of the implications of sustainable development often point to the environmental Kuznets curve. The idea behind this curve is that, as an economy grows, it shifts towards more capital and knowledge-intensive production. This means that as an economy grows, its pollution output increases, but only until it reaches a particular threshold where production becomes less resource-intensive and more sustainable. This means that a pro-growth, not an anti-growth policy is needed to solve the environmental problem. But the evidence for the environmental Kuznets curve is quite weak. Also, empirically spoken, people tend to consume more products when their income increases. Maybe those products have been produced in a more environmentally friendly way, but on the whole the higher consumption negates this effect. There are people like Julian Simon however who argue that future technological developments will resolve future problems.

Human Development Theory

Human development theory is a theory which uses ideas from different origins, such as ecology, sustainable development, feminism and welfare economics. It wants to avoid normative politics and is focused on how social capital and instructional capital can be deployed to optimize the overall value of human capital in an economy.

Amartya Sen and Mahbub ul Haq are the most well-known human development theorists. The work of Sen is focused on capabilities: what people can do, and be. It is these capabilities, rather than the income or goods that they receive (as in the Basic Needs approach), that determine their well being. This core idea also underlies the construction of the Human Development Index, a human-focused measure of development pioneered by the UNDP in its Human Development Reports. The economic side of Sen's work can best be categorized under welfare economics, which evaluates the effects of economic policies on the well-being of peoples. Sen wrote the influential book 'Development as freedom' which added an important ethical side to development economics.

Technology Gap

The technology gap theory a model by Posner 1961, describes an advantage enjoyed by the country that introduces new goods in a market. As a consequence of research activity and entrepreneurship, new goods are produced and the innovating country enjoys a monopoly until the other countries learn to produce these goods: in the meantime they have to import them. It is based on two forms of lags, that is, demand lag and imitation lag. Demand lag refers to the time it takes from creating a new product, up to when it is accepted locally, at this point, exports are equal to zero and there is test marketing as well as product activation. This lag also reaches up to a point when the importing countries slowly accept the newly developed product due to lack of awareness. Imitation lag refers to the time when the product is now fully accepted by the importing country and there will be a rise in exports, hence producers in the importing country will start imitating the new product. This process' length depends on the innovativeness and the amount of R&D the importing country spends on developing the product. Thus, international trade is created for the time necessary to imitate the new goods (*imitation lag*).

This lag has several components, that Posner (1961) classifies (from the point of view of the importing country) in the following categories:

1. *Foreign reaction lag*. This is the time between the successful utilization of the innovation by entrepreneurs in the innovating country and the new goods becoming regarded, by some firms in the importing country, as a likely competitor for their products.

2. *Domestic reaction lag*, which is the time required for all firms in the importing country to become aware of the competition from the new good.

3. *Learning period*, which is the time required for the importing country's firms to learn to produce the new good, and actually produce and begin selling it on the domestic market.

According to Posner, to get the total net lag, one should subtract from the imitation lag a *demand lag*, that is, the time elapsing between the introduction of the new good in the innovating country and the appearance of a demand for it in other countries (some time elapses before the other countries' consumers come to know of the new good and acquire a taste for it). Imports of the new good will therefore take place only in the period of time resulting from the difference between the imitation lag and the demand lag.

References

- Khun, Alex (2008-08-06). "Inform Educate Action: Critical Review of Modernisation Theory". Ourdevelopment.blogspot.nl. Retrieved 09, February 2020
- Richman, Raymond; Howard Richman; Jesse Richman (2014). "Balanced Trade: Ending the Unbearable Costs of America's Trade Deficits". Lexington Books. Retrieved 16, April 2020
- Balding, C., & Dauchy, E. P. (2013). Asymmetric Trade Estimator in Modified Gravity: Corporate Tax Rates and Trade in OECD Countries. Available at SSRN 2249536

4

Theorems of International Trade

Heckscher-Ohlin Theorem, Factor Price Equalization Theorem, Stopler-Samuelson Theorem and Rybczynski Theorem are the theorems covered in this chapter. These theorems are based on various factors like the theory of comparative advantage, endowment changes and changes in product prices. This chapter has been carefully written to provide an easy understanding of these concepts and theories.

Heckscher-Ohlin Theory

The structure of the modern theory of international trade rests fundamentally upon the theory developed by Eli Heckscher and Bertil Ohlin. This theory has almost completely replaced the classical and neo-classical theories related to international trade. But it does not mean that there is some real conflict between the Hecksher-Ohlin approach and the comparative costs approach or that the former, in any way, invalidates the latter.

In fact, the Heckscher-Ohlin approach supplements the traditional approach in a powerful manner. It goes behind the comparative costs doctrine to investigate the basic cause of the relative differences in costs. Heckscher and Ohlin have traced the cause of cost differences to relative factor endowments and relative factor intensities. That is why this theory is also known as Factor- Proportions-Factor-Intensity Theory. According to this theory, countries which are rich in labour will export labour-intensive goods and those rich in capital will export capital-intensive goods.

Assumptions of the Heckscher-Ohlin Theory

The H.O. theory is based upon the following assumptions:

- This theory considers a two-country, two- commodity and two factor (labour and capital) case. It is possible, however, to extend the theory to a multi-factor and multi-commodity case. But such an extension can be done only if the number of factors and number of commodities are equal.
- The factors of production are perfectly mobile within their respective countries but they are immobile between the countries.

- There is a state of perfect competition both in the product and factor markets.
- There is full employment of the factors of production in both the countries.
- Production functions pertaining to both the commodities are linearly homogenous. It implies that the production is governed by constant returns to scale.
- The techniques of production in both the countries remain unchanged. In such a situation, the input-output co-efficient in production functions will remain unchanged.
- The consumer's taste pattern and therefore the demand functions for different goods are identical in both the countries.
- The factors endowments, in absolute terms, remain constant in both the countries but the relative endowments of the two factors are disproportionate in the two countries. Suppose country A has an abundance of capital while B has an abundance of labour. In qualitative terms, however, the factors are homogenous in the two countries.
- The production functions are such that the two commodities show different factor intensities—one commodity is capital-intensive and the other is labour-intensive. Although production functions for different commodities are different, yet the production functions for each commodity are the same in both the countries.
- The factor intensities are not reversible.
- The trade between two countries is free and unrestricted.
- There is an absence of transport costs so that product prices are related exclusively to factor costs.
- There is incomplete specialisation in the trading countries.

Factor Endowments

It is an incontrovertible fact that regions or countries differ from one another in respect of endowments or availability of factors. In country A, there may be an abundance of capital and labour may be scarce. On the opposite, there may be an abundance of labour in country B, while capital may be scarce. The terms 'relative factor abundance,' in H-O model can be defined in terms of two criteria:

- The physical criterion of relative factor abundance.
- The price criterion of relative factor abundance.

Physical Criterion

According to this criterion, a country is said to be relatively capital abundant, if and only if, it is endowed with a higher proportion of capital to labour than the other country. The country A can be called as relatively capital abundant, if the following condition is satisfied:

$$\frac{\overline{K}_A}{\overline{L}_A} > \frac{\overline{K}_B}{\overline{L}_B}$$

where K and L refer to capital and labour respectively. Bars over K and L signify the fixed factor quantities in each country. The subscripts A and B refer to countries A and B. Similarly the relative scarcity of labour, in physical terms, in country A can be expressed as:

$$\frac{\overline{L}_A}{\overline{K}_A} > \frac{\overline{L}_B}{\overline{K}_B}$$

For country B, relative labour-abundance can be indicated by:

$$\frac{\overline{L}_B}{\overline{K}_B} > \frac{\overline{L}_A}{\overline{K}_A}$$

And capital-scarcity in this country can be denoted by:

$$\frac{\overline{K}_B}{\overline{L}_B} > \frac{\overline{K}_A}{\overline{L}_A}$$

Given the above conditions, H-O theory lays down that country A will produce capital-intensive commodity (say machines) and country B will have a bias in producing labour-intensive commodity (say, cloth). If both the countries produce machines and cloth in the same proportion and production occurs along OR in Figure, the country A would be producing at C and country B at D. The points C and D lie on the respective production possibility curves PQ and P_1Q_1 of these two countries.

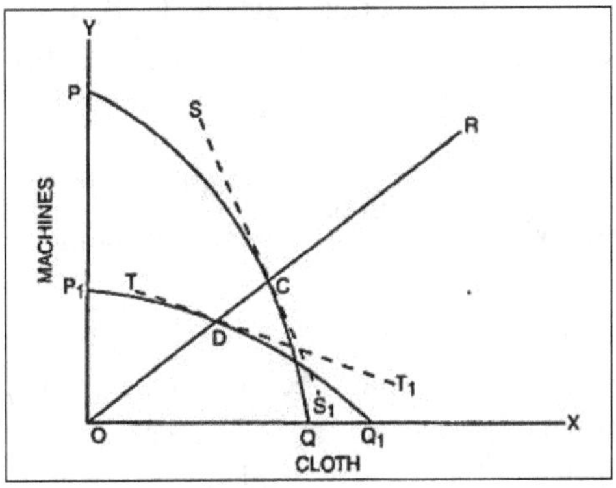

Since at point C, the slope of country A's production possibility curve is more steep than the slope of the production possibility curve of country B at D, this will imply that MC of producing cloth in country A is higher than the MC of producing cloth in country B. So if the production takes place at points C and D, machines can be produced more cheaply in country A and cloth can be produced more cheaply in country B.

Since country A is capital-abundant and the production of machines is capital-intensive, country A will tend to extend the production of machines. Country B, at the same time being labour-abundant, will tend to extend the production of cloth, which is relatively labour-intensive.

The Heckscher-Ohlin theorem can, however, be valid on the basis of this physical criterion and give the above conclusion only if the consumption pattern in both the countries is identical and the income elasticity of demand for each commodity equals unity. If the demand conditions are different in two countries, the conclusion that capital-abundant countries will export capital-intensive commodity and vice-versa cannot be sustained. This can be shown through Figure.

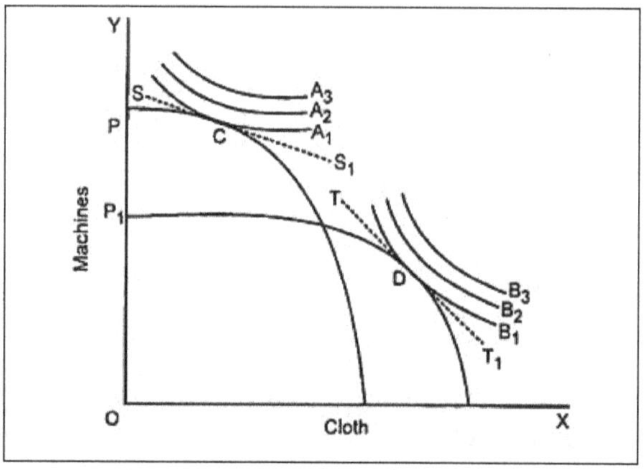

Even in Figure, the opportunity cost curves PQ and P1Q1 indicate that country A is capital-abundant and country B is labour-abundant. The pattern of demand is different in the two countries. The community indifference curves A_1, A_2 and A_3 indicate demand pattern in country A and the indifference curves B_1, B_2 and B_3 indicate the demand pattern in country B. The iso-revenue curve SS_1 related to country A is less steep than the iso-revenue curve TT_1 for country B, therefore:

$$\frac{\text{Price of Cloth}}{\text{Price of machine}} \text{ in A} > \frac{\text{Price of Cloth}}{\text{Price of Machine}} \text{ in B.}$$

Now demand conditions indicate that machines are costly in country A while cloth is costly in country B. Therefore, country A may decide to export cloth and country B may export machines. So the pattern of demand may off-set the Heckscher-Ohlin generalisation that capital-abundant country will export capital-intensive commodity and vice-versa.

Price Criterion

The alternative criterion for defining relative factor-abundance is the price criterion. The criterion lays down that a country having capital relatively cheap and labour relatively costly is capital-abundant and vice-versa, irrespective of the physical quantities of capital and labour that they have.

Country A can be called as relatively capital-abundant if $(P_{KA}/P_{LA}) < (P_{KB}/P_{LB})$. Here P denotes prices. K and L signify capital and labour respectively. A and B indicate countries A and B respectively. Similarly country A can be regarded as labour- abundant and capital-scarce, if $(P_{LA}/P_{KA}) < (P_{LB}/P_{KB})$.

Now suppose country A is capital-abundant and labour-scarce, the interest rates will be relatively low and wage rates will be relatively higher when compared with interest rates and wage rates in country B. Therefore, country A will decide to produce and export capital-intensive commodity (say, machine) and import labour-intensive commodity (say, cloth). Now this generalization can be proved through Figure.

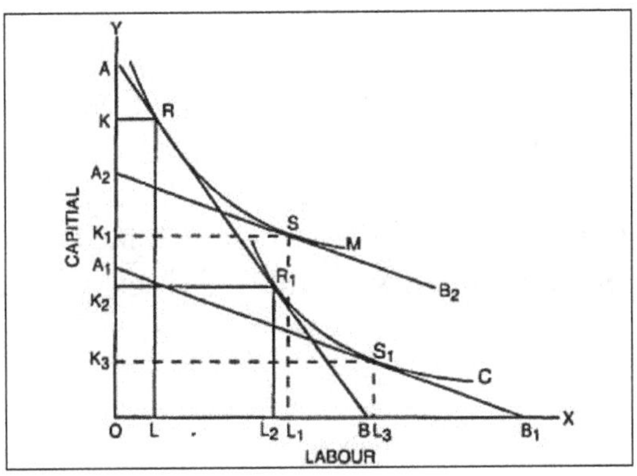

AB is the factor-price line for country A and A_1B_1 is the factor price line for country B. As the slope of AB is greater than that of A_1B_1, capital is relatively cheap in country A and labour is relatively cheap in country B. It signifies that $(P_{KA}/P_{LA}) < (P_{KB}/P_{LB})$.

Now the factor price line AB is tangent to the isoquant M of the capital-intensive commodity machine at R. It means country A can produce certain number of units of machine, say 100 machines, by employing OK units of capital and OL units of labour. OL amount of labour is equal to AK amount of capital. In other words, the cost of producing 100 machines in country A in terms of capital is OA.

The factor price line A_2B_2 of country B is parallel to A_1B_1. It is tangent to the isoquant M at S. It signifies that country B can produce 100 machines by employing OK_1 units of capital and OL_1 units of labour. It means A_2K_1 units of capital are equal to OL_1 units of labour and the total cost of producing 100 machines in country B is OA_2 in terms of capital. From this, the conclusion can be derived that the production of machine is more capital-intensive in country A than in country B.

Similarly in the production of one unit of cloth (say, 1000 metres) in country A, OL_2 units of labour and OK_2 units of capital are employed at R_1, the point of tangency between country A's factor price line AB and the isoquant for cloth C representing 1000 meters of cloth. Given this factor combination, OK_2 units of capital are equal to BL_2 units of labour and the cost of producing 1000 metres of cloth in country A in terms of labour is OB.

In country B, given the factor price line A_1B_1, the point of tangency between A_1B_1 and isoquant C is S_1. Country B employs OK_3 units of capital and OL_3 units of labour for producing 1000 metres of cloth. Now the quantity of capital OK_3 equals B_1L_3 units of labour.

The cost of producing 1000 metres of cloth in labour terms is OB_1 in country B. This shows that labour-abundant country B makes more use of labour in producing 1000 metres of cloth than country A. B will specialise in the production and export of cloth while country A will export more capital-intensive commodity machine.

Factor Intensities

The Heckscher-Ohlin theory attributed the comparative differences in costs also to the factor intensities which have been defined by Ellsworth as "relative use made of each one of the two (or more) factors when combined in production." Alternatively, factor intensity means the relative proportions in which two factors, say labour and capital, are combined at each point on a given isoquant. This is explained through figure below.

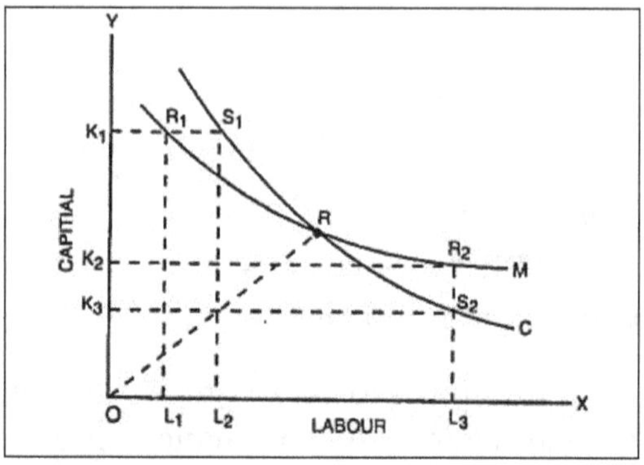

C and M in figure represent the isoquants of cloth and machine respectively. They are not identical otherwise they would have coincided. They intersect each other at R. That indicates equal factor proportions in producing a given number of units of the two commodities. The portion to the left and above R is capital-intensive and the portion below and to the right of R is labour-intensive. Along isoquant M, the quantities of capital and labour used at R1 are OK_1 and OL_1 respectively. At R_2, these inputs are OK_2 and OL_3 to have the same output of machines.

Thus above and to the left of R, the factor combinations involve larger input of capital than labour. The opposite is true on the combinations below and to the right of R. The same applies even in the case of isoquant C. If OK_1 quantity of capital is used, one unit of machine requires the labour input of OL1 but one unit of cloth requires OL_2 units of labour along with OK_1 units of capital at point S_1.

Similarly if OK_2 units of capital are employed, one machine can be turned out when labour input is OL_3. At S_2, one unit of cloth needs OL_3 labour input along with a smaller capital input OK_3. It clearly shows that machine is a capital- intensive and cloth is a labour-intensive commodity, throughout the length of isoquants M and C except of course at the point of intersection R.

So the relative factor abundance and factor intensity together determine the comparative differences in costs and accordingly the countries will decide about specialisation and export of specific commodities. On the basis of factor proportions, factor intensities and factor prices, Heckscher and Ohlin made the generalisation that capital-abundant countries will export capital-intensive commodities and labour-abundant countries will export labour-intensive commodities.

Superiority of Heckscher-Ohlin Theory over the Classical Theory

Heckscher-Ohlin theory does not contradict the Ricardian theory. It rather supplements it as it attempts to investigate the basic forces determining the comparative advantage of one country over the other. However, H-O theory makes some departures from the traditional theory and in the process, effects significant improvements upon the latter in following respects:

Based on General Theory of Value

While the classical theory is based upon the labour theory of value, Heckscher-Ohlin model, on the other hand, is necessarily based upon a more general theory of value. It takes into amount both demand and supply forces for determining specialisation and pattern of trade. In contrast, Ricardian theory was very deficient and one-sided. It had relied exclusively upon the supply factors and overlooked completely the demand factors.

No Need for Separate Theory

Ricardo had made a distinction between internal and international trade. On account of factor immobility among different countries, he felt the need for a separate theory of international trade. Even though Heckscher and Ohlin too believe that there are obstacles to international mobility of factors, yet the greater mobility of products tends to neutralise the factor immobility.

In their opinion, the immobility of factors remains only a matter of degree and not of kind and any distinction between international or inter-regional trade is only superficial. In the words of Ohlin, "International trade is but a special case of inter-local or inter-regional trade and there is not substantial difference between domestic trade and foreign trade. The basis of inter-regional specialisation also follows the principle of comparative cost."

Ultimate Cause of Trade

The classical theory failed to explain the cause of comparative difference in costs. Heckscher and Ohlin provided a highly plausible cause of comparative differences in costs and consequent international specialisation in production.

Permanent Basis of Trade

The classical theory implicitly relates the comparative differences in costs to differences in skill and efficiency of labour. Over a long period, there can be international transmission of technical knowledge from one country to another and all differences in costs due to skill, efficiency and technology are likely to be eliminated. It implies that the trade between two countries may come to an end in the long run.

Kelvin Lancaster has, however, pointed out that the trade between countries is not likely to come to an end even if there is perfect transmission of knowledge and techniques because the differences in factor endowments will continue to persist even in the long run. Since the factor movements from one country to the other cannot take place on such a scale that the factor endowment gap can be completely bridged, the comparative cost differences will continue to exist and hence there can be permanent exchange of commodities. It shows that H-O model lays down a permanent basis for international trade.

Two Factors of Production

In the classical comparative costs theory, it was supposed that production involves only one factor of production—labour. The H-O theory, on the opposite, maintains that in a two-country and two- commodity model, production involves two factors of production—labour and capital.

Stress on Relative Product or Factor Prices

A highly significant difference between the classical and H-O theories is that the former approach consists primarily of propositions related to the relative product prices. The latter, on the contrary, deals with propositions related to the relative factor prices.

Emphasis on Gains vs. Bases of Trade

The traditional theory emphasises upon the gains accruing to countries from foreign trade. Therefore, the classical theory has useful welfare implication. The Heckscher-Ohlin theory on the opposite, stresses on the analysis of bases of trade between two countries and makes contribution mainly to positive economics.

Qualitative vs. Quantitative Differences in Factors

The classical theory takes into account only the single factor, labour, and attributes the comparative differences in costs to qualitative differences in labour. The H-O theory, on the other hand, deals with two factors—labour and capital. It assumes an absence of qualitative differences in them. The international trade and specialisation results on account of quantitative differences in factor proportions and factor intensities.

Production Function

The classical trade theory is based on the differences in the production of specified commodities between the two trading countries. In contrast, the H-O theory gives prominence to differences in their production functions.

Product Specialisation

The comparative costs theory maintains that the comparative advantages of trading countries may or may not lead to complete specialisation in the production and export of respective commodities. On the opposite, the H-O theorem explicitly states that the factor proportions and factor intensities lead to complete specialisation in the production of a specific commodity in the first country and another commodity in the second country. From this viewpoint, the latter theory is more specific and realistic.

Locational Theory

Haberler points out that the H-O theory gives prominence to the space factor in the international trade through factor endowments of trading countries. He prefers to call this theory as a locational theory. In contrast, the Ricardian-Mill theory treats different countries as a spaceless market. Even from this angle, the H-O theory is an improvement upon the classical theory.

Distributions of Income and Welfare

Since the classical theory takes into account a single factor of production, the distribution of income remains unchanged. It implies that the welfare of every individual unequivocally increases with trade or else no one is worse off than before. The Heckscher-Ohlin theorem does not make such an unqualified and unrealistic statement about welfare.

Integration between the Theory of Value and Theory of International Trade

The classical theory relies upon the forces of demand and supply in their value theory. But when they come to the trade theory there is a complete neglect of demand factors. So classical approach fails to integrate the theories of value and trade. The Heckscher-Ohlin theory brought about a successful integration between the theories of value and trade.

From the above facts, it becomes clear that the modern theory of international trade does not only make a highly significant break from the traditional analysis but also registers a considerable improvement upon it.

Criticism of Heckscher-Ohlin Theory

No doubt, the Heckscher-Ohlin theory has been found to be more exact, precise, scientific and analytically superior to the earlier approaches to the theory of international trade, still it has certain deficiencies for which it has been criticized by many a writer.

Partial Equilibrium Analysis

Haberler although recognized Ohlin's theory as less abstract, yet it has failed to develop a general equilibrium concept. It remains, by and large, a part of the partial equilibrium analysis. This theory seeks to explain the pattern of trade only on the basis of factor proportions and factor intensities, while ignoring several other influences such as transport costs, economies of scale, external economies etc., which too exert influence on the cost of production.

In such a situation, Ellsworth states that "with several causes operating simultaneously upon costs, it becomes a matter of adding up the influence of all cost-reducing and increasing forces to arrive at a net result."

Oversimplifying Assumptions

This theory is based upon highly over-simplifying assumptions of perfect competition, full employment of resources, identical production function, constant returns to scale, absence of transport costs and absence of product differentiation. Given this set of assumptions, the whole model becomes quite unrealistic.

Static Analysis

The Heckscher-Ohlin model assumes fixed quantities of factors of production, given production functions, incomes and costs. It means the theory investigates the pattern of international trade in a static setting. The conclusions drawn from such an analysis are simply not relevant to a dynamic economic system.

Identical Factors

This theory maintains that there are no qualitative differences in factors and that these factors are capable of exact measurement so that factor endowment ratios can be calculated. In the real world, however, qualitative factor differences exist. Moreover, there are more than one variety of each factor. This creates serious complications in the measurement and comparison of costs and the determinations of trade pattern.

Neglect of Product Differentiation

The theory overlooks the role played by product differentiation in international trade. Even when the production agents are identical in two countries, the international trade may still take place due to product differentiation. For instance, the Japanese machines are sold out in the U.S.A. and the American machines are sold in Japan. In this context, Wijanholds opines that factor prices do not determine cost. It is rather the commodity prices that determine factor prices.

Prices of goods are determined by their utility to the buyers (the force of demand) and prices of factors like raw materials, labour etc., are ultimately dependent on the demand and prices of final goods because the demand for them is the derived demand. So Wijanholds states that "prices are the only things we may accept as data. Everything else to be derived therefrom." He regards both Ricardian theory and Heckscher-Ohlin theory as faulty as they related cost to factor prices and neglected the influence of product differentiation on international trade.

Factor Proportions and Specialisation

The H-O theory suggests that the relative factor proportions (or factor endowments) determine the specialisation in exports of different countries. The capital-abundant countries export capital-intensive goods and labour-abundant countries export the labour-intensive goods. It implies that trade will not take place between such countries or regions as have similar relative factor proportions. But this is not true.

A large part of world trade is between the U.S.A. and the countries of Western Europe despite the fact that all of them have a relative greater capital- abundance and scarcity of labour. The H-O theory cannot provide a complete and satisfactory explanation of trade in such cases. In fact, the specialisation is governed not only by factor proportions but also by several other factors like cost and price differences, transport costs, economies of scale, external economies etc. The H-O theory was clearly wrong in overlooking these factors.

Neglect of Factor Demand

The H-O theory assumes that the factor prices are determined by the relative factor endowments of a country. It means the rate of interest should be relatively low and wage rates relatively high in a capital-abundant but a labour-scarce country. On this basis, the United States should have a lower structure of interest rate but it is in fact higher because even in that capital-surplus country, the demand for capital too is very strong. In fact, the relative factor prices are influenced not only by their supply but also by the demand for them. The H-O theory failed to take into account the influence of demand for factors on their prices.

Factor Mobility

This theory assumes that there is absence of international mobility of factors. This assumption is not valid. The writers like Williams and Levin have pointed out that the international mobility of factors is actually even more than the inter-regional mobility within the same countries. This is evident from international capital flows from advanced countries to such export sectors in the LDC's as petroleum, minerals, plantations etc.

Similarly the large-scale movement of labour from the Third World countries to the advanced countries has assisted the latter in enlarging their production and export. It is, therefore, clear that H-O theory takes an unrealistic assumption of international immobility of factors.

Neglect of Technological Change

The H-O model assumes identical production function. It implies that the technological conditions in a given country remain unchanged. This assumption again is invalid. There has been continuous improvement in techniques of production both in the advanced and the less developed countries. The neglect of technological change in H-O theory makes this model quite inconsistent with actual reality.

Factor-intensity

This theory gives much prominence to the concept of factor intensity. It is assumed in this model that one good is capital- intensive and the other is labour-intensive. The capital-intensive good remains capital-intensive in both the counties and the labour-intensive good remains labour-intensive in both the countries. It means there can be no reversal of factor-intensity i.e., the same good is capital-intensive in one country while labour-intensive in the other. The empirical evidence on this issue is conflicting. However, if there is reversal of factor-intensity, the whole structure of H-O theory will collapse.

Neglect of By-products

Sometimes byproducts are even more important than the main final product. The Heckscher-Ohlin theorem, however, provides no explanation how the terms of trade are determined in the case of by-products.

Possibility of Trade Even under Identical Proportions

The factor proportions theory implies that there can be no possibility of international trade when factor proportions between two countries are identical. In fact the identical factor proportions may not close the possibility of trade if consumer preferences are not identical due to differences in income distribution in two countries. This can be explained through figure.

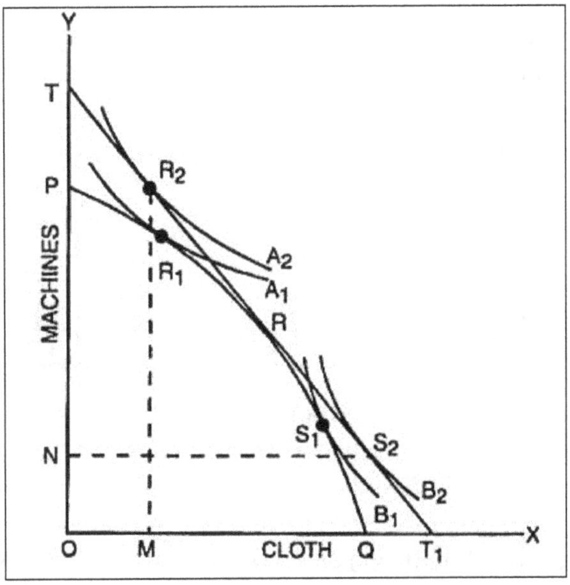

Given the identical factor proportions in two countries A and B, there is the same production possibility curve PQ for both the countries. A_1 and A_2 are the community indifference curves of A. B_1 and B_2 are the indifference curves of B. In the absence of international trade, consumption points of the two countries are respectively R_1 and S_1. It shows that country A has a stronger consumer preference for machines and country B has a greater preference for cloth.

As international trade takes place, TT_1 is the international exchange ratio line. Now both the countries get superior alternatives at R_2 and S_2 respectively. At R_2, country A consumes R_2M of machines and OM of cloth. On the other hand, country B consumes S2N quantity of cloth and ON quantity of machines at S_2. The consumption in excess of production is met through mutual imports. Thus even when the factor proportions are identical, the international trade may still occur and that vitiates the Heckscher-Ohlin theory.

Vague Theory

No doubt H-O theorem attempted to explain the basis reason for comparative advantage of the trading countries, yet the theory is vague and conditional. It depends upon several restrictive and unrealistic assumptions. In the words of Haberler,

"With many factors of production, some of which are qualitatively incommensurable as between different countries, and with dissimilar production functions in different countries, no sweeping a priori generalisations concerning the composition of trade are possible."

Undoubtedly, this theory is based upon some unrealistic assumptions, yet Lancaster regards it as of central importance in the theory of international trade because of it's objectively and simplicity. According to him, "model occupies the very centre of international trade theory, for reasons unconnected with its realism, and indeed strengthened by the very properties which have been subject to so much criticism." He goes on further to comment, "It is in fact, the simple model of international trade just as two-commodity indifference curve is the simple model of consumer's behaviour."

Factor Price Equalization Theorem

The factor price equalisation theory is an important corollary of the H-O theory of trade. If there is a free international movement of factors, the prices of the factors of production undisputably get equalised. However, the classical theorists as well as Heckscher and Ohlin had assumed an international immobility of factors. This led to the crucial question of how the international trade would affect the prices of the factors of production.

Heckscher, on the one hand, suggested that international trade in commodities would act as a substitute for the international mobility of factors leading to a complete equalisation of the costs or factor prices. Ohlin, on the other hand, recognised that the international trade might result in only an incomplete or partial equalisation of prices of factors.

The factor price equalisation theory picks up the argument that the labour-abundant country specialises in the export of the labour-intensive commodity because labour is a relatively cheaper factor compared with capital. On the other hand, the capital-abundant country specialises in the export of capital-intensive commodity on account of capital being a relatively cheaper factor there. The pressure of international demand renders the abundant factor scarce and its price starts rising.

At the same time, the import of the commodities that require more input of scarce factor relieves the domestic pressure of demand for that factor, resulting in a fall in its price. The process of change in prices of factors will ultimately bring about equality in the prices of factors. It is in this sense that free international trade in commodities acts as a substitute for the international mobility of factors.

Samuelson's Analysis of Factor-Price Equalisation Theorem

Samuelson's analysis of the factor price equalisation is based upon the following assumptions:

- There are two countries, say A and B.
- These countries produce two commodities, say X and Y.
- The production of these commodities requires only two factors of production—labour and capital.
- There is free competition both in the product and labour markets.
- There is an absence of tariff and transport costs.
- The production function related to each commodity is identical and homogeneous of degree first. It implies the production is governed by constant returns of scale.
- The factor-intensities are different for the two commodities. For instance, the commodity X is labour-intensive, while commodity Y is capital- intensive. It means there is an absence of reversal of factor intensity.
- Capital and labour are qualitatively identical in the two countries.
- The availability of factors is quantitatively different in the two countries. The country A is supposed to be labour-abundant whereas country B is capital-abundant.
- There is absence of complete specialisation. It means both the countries continue to produce both the commodities even after trade takes place between them.
- The factor supplies are fixed in the two countries.
- In each country, there is full employment of both the factors.
- There is no mobility of factors between the countries.
- The marginal-physical product of each factor is diminishing.
- The tastes are identical in the two countries.

Before trade, there is low capital-labour ratio in country A and a high capital-labour ratio in country B. As trade commences, the labour-abundant country A exports the labour-intensive commodity X and country B exports the capital-intensive commodity Y. The export of labour-intensive commodity X by A creates relative scarcity of labour and consequent rise in wage rate. It also leads to a rise in capital- labour ratio.

On the opposite, the export of capital- intensive commodity by country B will result in its scarcity there. It will cause a rise in the price of capital (rate of interest) and a consequent fall in the capital-labour ratio. These relative changes in K-L ratio will continue until the K-L ratios in both the countries become exactly equal. Along with it, the prices of the two factors also undergo changes (rise in wage rate in country A and rise in interest rate of country B) in such a manner that there is ultimate equalisation of prices of two factors in both the countries.

Hicksian Analysis of Factor Price Equalisation Theorem

J.R. Hicks attempted to provide a proof for the absolute factor price equalisation. He remained all the assumptions taken by Samuelson. It is assumed that price of labour is low in the labour- abundant country, while it is higher in country B which is capital-abundant. On the contrary, the price of capital is high in country A but it is low in country B.

After trade, country A exports labour- intensive commodity X and B exports capital-intensive commodity Y. l_x and l_y are the labour co-efficients for X and Y commodities and k_x and k_y are the capital co-efficient, w_a and w_b are the wage rates in the two countries, r_a and r_b are the rates of interest in these two countries. It is assumed that the unit cost of producing X and Y commodities becomes equal in the two countries after the determination of trade equilibrium.

Unit Cost of Commodity X:

$$l_x.w_a + k_x r_a = l_x.w_b + k_x r_b$$

Dividing both sides by k_x:

$$(l_x/k_x) + r_a = (l_x/k_x)\, w_b + r_b$$

$$r_a - r_b = (l_x\text{-}k_x)\, w_b - (l_x/k_x)\, w_a$$

$$r_a - r_b = (l_x/k_x)\, [w_b - w_a]$$

Unit Cost of Commodity Y:

$$L_y.w_a + k_y r_a = l_y.w_b + k_y r_b$$

Dividing both sides by k_y:

$$(I_y/k_y)\, w_a + r_a = (l_y/k_y)\, w_a$$

$$r_a - rb = w_b (l_y/k_y) - (l_y/k_y)\, w_a$$

$$r_a - r_b = (l_y/k_y)(w_b - w_a)$$

$$r_a - r_b = (I_x/k_x)(w_b - w_a) = (l_y/k_y)(w_b - w_a)$$

From above both equations:

$$r_a - r_b = (I_x/k_x)(w_b - w_a) = (l_y/k_y)(w_b - w_a)$$

If trade results in equalisation of factor-intensity in the two products X and Y and $r_a = r_b$, there will also be $w_a = w_b$. It shows that after-trade equilibrium results in the equalisation of factor prices.

The relative factor price equalisation can be explained on the assumption that the value of marginal product (MP) of each factor within each country is equal before trade under the conditions of prefect competition in product and factor markets and constant return to scale.

Country A:

$$MPL_{ax} \cdot P_{ax} = MPL_{ay} \cdot P_{ay}$$

$$\therefore \frac{P_{ax}}{P_{ay}} = \frac{MPL_{ay}}{MPL_{ax}}$$

And,

$$MPK_{ax} \cdot P_{ax} = MPK_{ay} \cdot P_{ay}$$

$$\therefore \frac{P_{ax}}{P_{ay}} = \frac{MPK_{ay}}{MPK_{ax}}$$

Country B:

$$MPK_{bx} \cdot P_{bx} = MPK_{by} \cdot P_{by}$$

$$\therefore \frac{P_{bx}}{P_{by}} = \frac{MPL_{by}}{MPL_{bx}}$$

After trade takes place, there is equalisation of MPL and MPK in both the countries.

$$MPL_{ax} = MPL_{bx}, MPL_{ay} = MPL_{by}$$

$$MPK_{ax} = MPK_{bx}, MPK_{ay} = MPK_{by}$$

Hence $(P_{ax} / P_{ay}) = (P_{bx} / P_{by})$ respect of both the commodities in the two countries. The relative equalisation of factor prices can be explained also through figure below.

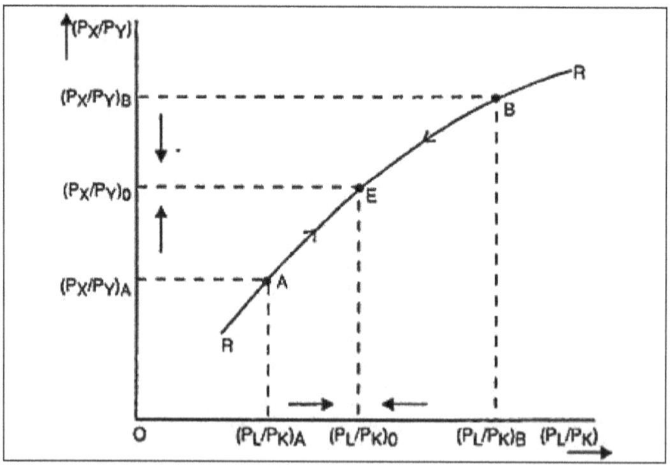

In Figure above, the factor-price ratio is measured along the horizontal scale and the commodity-price ratio is measured along the vertical scale. RR is the curve expressing the relation between the commodity price ratio and the factor-price ratio. Before trade, the labour-abundant country A is at the point A on the curve RR where the factor-price ratio P_L/P_K is low at $(P_L/P_K)_A$ and the commodity price ratio is also low at $(P_X/P_Y)_A$ because the labour-intensive commodity X is cheaper than the capital-intensive commodity Y.

On the other hand, the capital- abundant country B is originally at point B on the curve RR. At this point, both the commodity-price ratio and factor-price ratio are high at $(P_X/P_Y)_B$ and $(P_L/P_K)_B$ respectively. Country A has comparative advantage in commodity X and B has comparative advantage in commodity Y. Country A will export the labour-intensive commodity X and B will export the capital-intensive commodity Y.

The trade will lead to a rise in K-L ratio in country A and a fall in K-L ratio in country B. The increase in demand for labour relative to capital in A causes a rise in both the ratio of PL to PK and the ratio of P_X to P_Y. On the other hand, export of capital-intensive commodity Y by country B causes an increase in the demand for capital relative to labour. It brings about a fall in the ratio of P_L to P_K and also a fall in the ratio of P_X to P_Y.

These changes in factor-price ratio and commodity-price ratio continue until both the countries reach the point E on the curve RR. At this point, the factor- price ratio in both the countries becomes equal at $(P_L/P_K)_o$ and the commodity-price ratio gets equalized at $(P_X/P_Y)_o$. Thus trade results in the equalisation of relative factor prices in the two trading countries.

The relative factor price equalisation can be explained through the use of Edgeworth-type box diagram. First of all the effect of trade on factor- intensity and factor price ratio is analysed in the case of the labour-surplus country A.

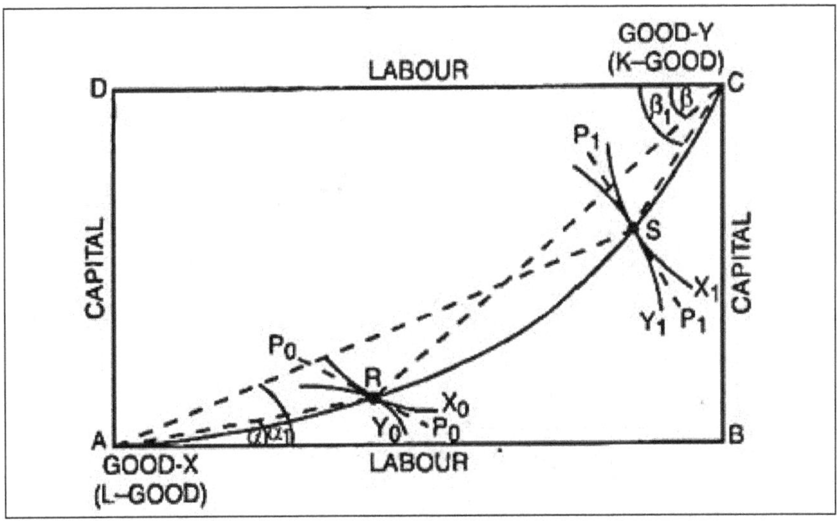

In Figure, the box ABCD is related to the labour-abundant country A. The longer horizontal scale and relatively short vertical scale signifies that country A is labour-abundant and capital-scarce. AC is the non-linear contract curve. Good X is labour-intensive good (L-good) and good Y is the capital-intensive good (K-good). A is the point of origin for the L-good X and C is the origin for K-good Y. X_0 and X_1 are isoquants related to good X and Y_0 and Y_1 are the isoquants related to good Y. Before trade, equilibrium takes place at R, which is the point of tangency between X_0. Y_0 and the factor-price line P_0P_0.

K-L Ratio in X = Slope of line AR = Tan α

K-L Ratio in Y = Slope of line RC = Tan β

As trade takes place, this country would specialise in the production and export of labour- intensive commodity X. The isoquant related to X commodity shifts to X_1. The equilibrium takes place at S where X_1, Y_1 and the factor price line P_1P_1 are tangent to one another.

K-L Ratio in X = Slope of line AS = Tan α_1

K-L Ratio in Y = Slope of line SC = Tan α_1

Since Tan α_1 > Tan α and Tan β_1 > Tan β it signifies that trade results in an increase K-L ratio in this labour-abundant country in respect of both the commodities. After trade, increased pressure of demand for labour results in an increase in price of labour relative to capital. This is shown by greater steepness of factor price line P1P1 than the original factor price line P_0P_0. The changes in K-L ratio and factor price ratio in a capital-abundant country can be shown through Figure below.

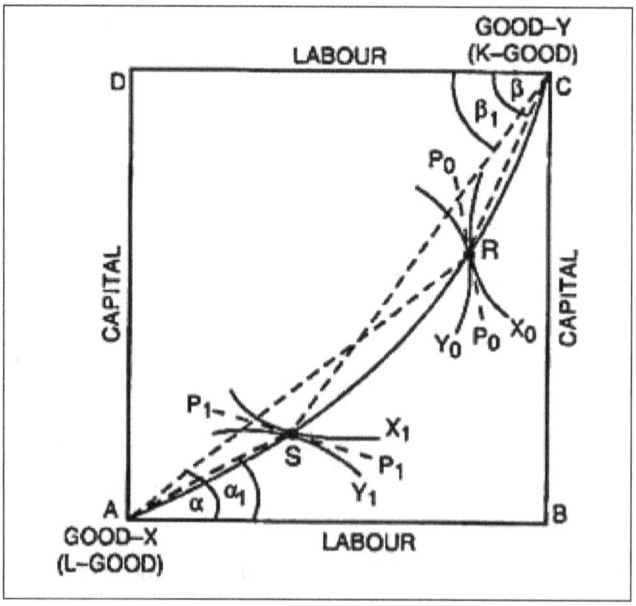

In figure the box ABCD shows the capital-abundance of the country B. The vertical scale is longer than the horizontal scale. AC is the nonlinear contract curve. Before trade, the original equilibrium occurs at R where the isoquant X_0 of good X and Y_0 of good Y are tangent to the factor price line P_0P_0.

The capital-intensity of two commodities at R is measured as:

K-L Ratio in X = Slope of line AR = Tan α

K-L Ratio in Y = Slope of line RC = Tan β

When trade takes place, this capital-abundant country specializes in the production and export of the K-good Y. As the production of Y is increased, the isoquant concerning this commodity shifts to Y_1. The equilibrium now takes place at S where the isoquants Y_1, X_1 and the factor price line P_1P_1 are tangent to one another. The capital-intensity of two commodities at S is measured as:

K-L Ratio in X = Slope of line AS = Tan α_1

K-L Ratio in Y = Slope of line SC = Tan β_1

Since Tan α_1 < Tan α and Tan β_1 < Tan β, it signifies that trade results in a decrease in K-L ratio in respect of both the commodities. After trade, increased pressure of demand for capital causes an increase in the price of capital. This is reflected through the reduced steepness of the factor-price line P_1P_1 than the original factor price line P_0P_0. The factor price equalisation after trade can be explained through figure.

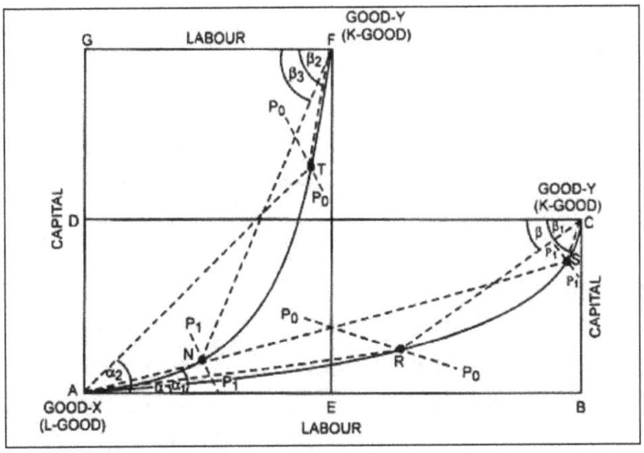

In Figure ABCD is the box related to the labour-abundant country A and AEFG is the box related to the capital-abundant country B. Before trade, the production takes place in country A at R and in country B at T. The capital-intensity of two commodities is measured below.

Before Trade:

K-L Ratio of X in country A=Slope of Line AR=Tan α.

K-L Ratio of Y in country A=Slope of Line RC=Tan β.

K-L Ratio of X in country B=Slope of Line AT=Tan $\alpha 2$.

K-L Ratio of Y in country B=Slope of Line TF=Tan β_2.

When trade commences, the production in country A takes place at S. In country B, it takes place at N. The capital-intensity of two commodities in two countries can be measured as: After Trade:

K-L Ratio of X in country A=Slope of Line AS=Tan $\propto_1$.

K-L Ratio of X in country A=Slope of Line SC=Tan β_1.

K-L Ratio of X in country B=Slope of Line AN=Tan a_1.

K-L Ratio of X in country B=Slope of Line NF=Tan β_3.

Since Tan α_1 > Tan α and Tan β_1 > Tan β, the K-L ratio increases in both the commodities in country A. At the same time Tan α_1 < Tan α_2 and Tan β_3 < Tan β_2, there is a decrease in K-L ratio in both the commodities in country B.

After trade, K-L ratio in X commodity becomes exactly equal in both the countries because it is measured by the same Tan α_1. It happens because the points S and N lie upon the same line. In case of Y commodity too the capital-intensity is equal in both the countries because the line NF is parallel to the line SC. It means trade leads to equalization of capital-intensity of both X and Y in the two countries.

The increase in capital-intensity in country A occurs because of a rise in the price of labour relative to capital. On the opposite, the decrease in the capital-intensity in country B takes place because the price of capital rises relative to labour. Such changes in prices of the two factors bring about equality in the factor price ratios in the two countries. In country A, originally the factor price ratio is represented by the slope of the factor price line PoPo which is less steep.

After trade, it becomes steeper as shown by the factor price line P_1P_1. It signifies that there is an increase in price of labour relative to capital. In country B, the factor price line P1P1 after trade becomes less steep compared with the original factor price line PoPo. It is on account of the fact that capital becomes costly relative to labour. Since the slope of factor price line P_1P_1 at S is exactly equal to the slope of factor price line P_1P_1 at N (these factor price lines are parallel), the factor price ratios have been equalized through trade.

Lerner's Analysis of Factor Price Equalisation Theorem

Lerner has attempted an analysis about the factor price equalisation theorem on the basis of a series of assumptions:

- There are two countries A and B.
- Each country can produce two goods X and Y, given the factor endowments and techniques of production.
- There are two factors of production— labour and capital.
- The production functions are linear homogenous in both the countries.
- Country A is labour-abundant and B is capital-abundant.
- There are the conditions of perfect competition in both the countries.
- There is absence of transport costs.
- Commodity X is labour-intensive while commodity Y is capital-intensive.
- There is no factor-intensity reversal.

In the labour-abundant country A, originally price of labour is lower relative to that of capital. On the opposite, the price of capital is lower in country B than that of labour. Consequently, country A will produce and export labour-intensive commodity X. As there will be greater substitution of labour for capital, the price of labour will rise and that of capital will decline resulting in equalisation of factor prices.

Similarly the capital- abundant country B will specialise in production and export of capital-intensive commodity Y. The substitution of capital in place of labour will increase the price of capital in this country. Ultimately, the factor prices ratio in this country will also get equalised.

However, if there is factor-intensity reversal i.e., X is labour-intensive in country A but capital- intensive in country B, both the countries will produce it through different techniques. But as they cannot export the same product to each other, the factor price equalisation will fail to take place.

Kindelberger's Analysis of Factor Price Equalisation Theorem

Kindelberger has explained the factor price equalisation by involving factor proportions, product prices and factor prices. In this regard, he has relied upon the figure given below.

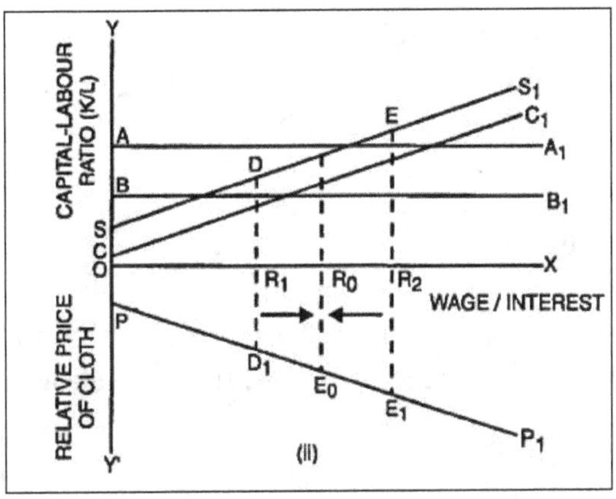

In Figure above Part (i), wages and interest are measured along the horizontal scale and capital- labour ratio (K/L) is measured along the vertical scale. The horizontal line AA_1 and BB_1 measure factor proportions in the capital-abundant country A and labour-abundant country B respectively. SS_1 is the schedule related to capital-intensive good steel and CC_1 is the schedule related to labour- intensive good cloth. In Part (ii) of the Figure, relative price of cloth is measured along the vertical scale.

The curve PP_1 measures relative price of cloth. The domestic demand conditions determine the production of steel and cloth before trade. Wage rate is lower in country B than in country A, whereas the rate of interest is higher in B than in A. The relative price of cloth in A is R_1D_1 and it is R_2E_1 in country B. As trade takes place, the wage rate will rise in country A and fall in country B. The interest rate, on the other hand, will fall in country A but rise in country B. The relative price of cloth in both the countries will tend to approximate to R_0E_0, when wage-interest ratio becomes equal at R_0.

Sodersten's Analysis of Factor Price Equalisation Theorem

Bo Sodersten recognises that the free trade can lead to the equalisation of relative factor prices in two countries. Neither country specialises completely. It can be explained through Figure below. In this figure, factor price ratio (w/r) is measured along the horizontal scale. In Part (i) of the Fig, the commodity price ratio (P_x/P_y) is measured along the vertical scale. In part (ii) of the Fig, the factor intensity (K/L) is measured along the vertical scale.

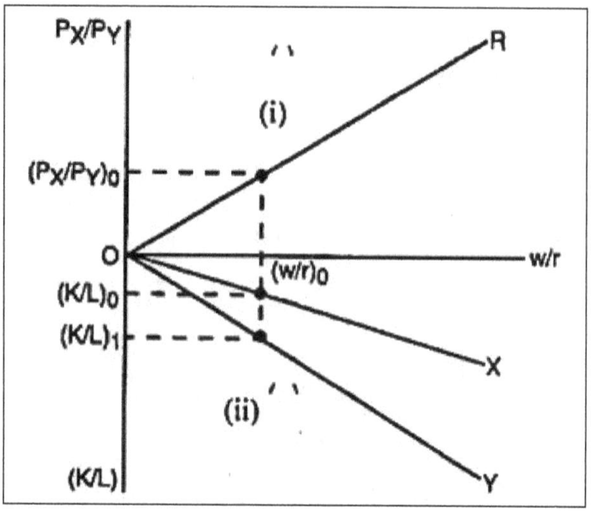

If there is complete specialisation in one or both the countries, there cannot be equalisation of absolute or relative factor prices. It can be shown through figure below.

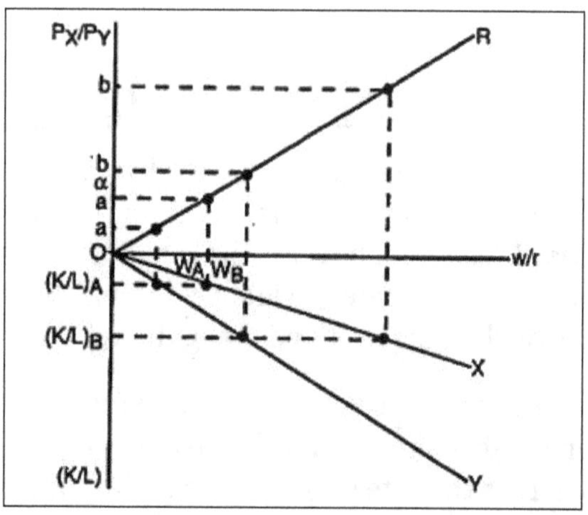

Under autarchy, the range of relative commodity prices for country A is indicated by aa. In case of country B, the range of relative commodity prices is denoted by bb. These two ranges do not overlap; therefore, at least one of the two countries must specialize completely. As both countries specialise completely, the free trade commodity price ratio is α which lies outside the autarchy price ranges.

The relative wage rate in country A cannot rise above w_A, whereas that of country B cannot fall below w_B. In such conditions, there cannot be relative factor price equalisation. So there cannot also be absolute factor price equalisation.

Obstacles to Factor Price Equalisation Theory

The factor price equalisation theory developed by Samuelson has been found to be deficient by several economists including Meade and Ellsworth. They raised serious doubts about the validity of this theory on account of highly restrictive and unrealistic assumptions. They believe that there can only be partial equalisation of factor prices. There are serious obstacles to a complete equalisation of factor prices in the trading countries.

- Tariff and Non-Tariff Barriers: The theory rests upon the assumption that there are no tariff and non-tariff barriers to trade. In actual reality, such barriers do exist. It was on account of them that Ohlin ruled out the possibility of complete equalisation of factor prices.
- Transport Costs: The factor price equalisation theory takes another unrealistic assumption that transport costs are absent. In fact, the import and export of commodities do involve transport costs, which not only have restrictive effect on the product mobility but may also affect the comparative advantages of the trading countries. The existences of transport costs are likely to prevent the equalisation of factor prices.
- Complete Specialisation: This theory assumes that the trading countries are engaged in the production of both the commodities. In other words, there is only partial or incomplete specialisation. When the trading countries are of unequal size, there is possibility that there is complete specialisation in at least the smaller country. In the event of complete specialisation, there is little possibility of complete factor price equalisation.
- Identical Production Function: Samuelson's factor price equalisation theory assumes that production functions are identical in the two trading countries. Even if the two countries have the same resources, yet their productive capacities are different because of natural, technical and sociological differences between them. The diversities in their production functions may create hindrance in the equalisation of factor prices.
- Absence of Perfect Competition: This theory rests upon the assumption that there are the conditions of prefect competition in the product and factor markets. In actual reality, the prefect competition does not exist. In the real market situations like oligopoly or monopolistic competition, there are rigidities in the product and factor markets that prevent the possibility of equalisation of factor prices.
- Increasing Returns to Scale: The factor price equalisation theorem assumes that there is a first-degree homogeneous production function, which implies that the production is governed by the constant returns to scale. If the economies of scale are present, according to Meade, the theory will become invalid for two reasons. Firstly, it will result in the emergence of monopolies and consequent

breakdown of the apparatus based on the assumption of perfect competition. Secondly, the increasing returns to scale will lead to complete specialisation, which again rules out the possibility of equalisation of factor prices.

- Changes in Factor Supplies: The theorem takes the assumption that the factor supplies remain fixed in the trading countries. In actual reality, however, there are changes in factor supplies and these changes will create difficulties in the equalisation of factor prices.
- Dynamic Conditions: The factor price equalisation theory assumes static conditions such as fixed factor endowments, techniques and same taste pattern in the trading countries. In the actual dynamic conditions, the continuous changes take place in all the relevant factors and variables and many often it is found that the differences in factor prices get widened rather than being eliminated.

Such a trend has been confirmed by economists like Kindelberger, Myrdal and Sodresten. In the words of Kindelberger, "trade between developed and less developed countries widens the gap in living standards (the factor prices such as wages) rather than narrows, and it is evident after centuries of trade that there are still poor as well as rich countries.

- Multi-Country, Multi-Commodity and Multi-Factor Trade: The theorem can deal efficiently only in respect of trade involving two countries, two commodities and two factors. The theory is likely to become indeterminate in the multi-country, multi-commodity and multi-factor trade situation. If the number of productive factors exceeds the number of commodities, the theory breaks down completely.
- Factor-Intensity Reversal: This theory assumes that there is an absence of factor intensity reversal. It means the labour-surplus country will export only labour-intensive commodity and the capital-surplus country will export the capital- intensive commodity. If there is reversal of factor intensity, the factor price equalisation theorem will fail to hold. If the labour-surplus country A specialises in the labour-intensive commodity X, the absolute and relative wage rates will rise in this country.

If country B specialises in commodity Y but produces it thorough labour-intensive method, the demand for labour will increase even in this country resulting in a rise in the absolute and relative wage rate. As the wage rates rise in the two countries, whether the difference in absolute and relative wage rates will rise, fall or remain unchanged, will depend on the rates at which wages increase in the two countries. Thus the factor-intensity reversal can result in the invalidation of the factor price equalisation theory.

The above arguments suggest that factor price equalisation cannot take place in actual dynamic realities. It, however, does not mean that the theorem is completely invalid. It only means that the assumptions of this theorem, being unrealistic, lead to an unrealistic conclusion.

There is little doubt that the movement of products from one country to another can at least reduce the factor price differentials. In the absence of trade, such differences are likely to be considerably large. In the words of Robert Heller, "the effect of international trade may be considered as a 'leaning against the wind' in that factor price differentials would be even larger in the absence of trade."

Stolper-Samuelson Theorem

The Stolper-Samuelson theorem is one of the central results of Heckscher-Ohlin theory, itself one of the principal theories of international trade. It provides a definite answer to a central question in applied economics: What is the effect of changes in the prices of goods, caused for example by changes in tariffs, on the prices of factors of production? As first presented by Wolfgang Stolper and Paul A. Samuelson, it dealt with a very special framework with many restrictive assumptions, most notably that the economy consists of only two broad sectors, and that production uses only two factors (often labeled capital and labor). However, subsequent theoretical work has shown that essential features of the theorem hold much more generally. It has also been applied to a range of empirical issues, including the effects of increased globalization on income distribution in developed countries, and the long-run political allegiances of classes and interest groups.

The Stolper-Samuelson theorem in its original setting can be explained intuitively as follows. Suppose that one sector produces exports and the other produces goods which compete directly with imports. Suppose in addition that the import-competing sector is relatively "labor-intensive," meaning that it uses a higher ratio of labor to capital than the export sector. Now ask what will be the effect of a tariff or some other change, which raises the relative price of the import-competing sector's output. Clearly this will encourage that sector to expand. Provided that the economy is at or close to full employment of both factors, this expansion must come at the expense of the export sector. The combined expansion of the relatively labor-intensive sector and contraction of the relatively capital-intensive sector raises the aggregate demand for labor relative to capital, and so puts upward pressure on the wage. Because the price of exports has not changed, a higher wage must imply an absolute fall in the return to capital. This in turn implies that the wage must rise by even more than the price of imports. Thus, when import-competing goods are relatively labor-intensive, wage earners gain and capital owners lose, irrespective of which bundle of goods they consume. Put simply, in this case, protection unambiguously raises real wages.

The starkness and elegance of the theorem in its simplest form prompted much study of its robustness to relaxing the key assumptions. Wilfred Ethier and Ronald W. Jones and José Scheinkman highlighted the central prediction of the theorem which survives such relaxations: With many goods and factors, a tariff change will always raise the real return of at least one factor and lower the real return of at least one other factor. This generalization of the Stolper-Samuelson theorem does not contradict the basic prediction of international trade theory that economies facing fixed world prices will gain overall from tariff reductions. However, it highlights the potential for distributional conflict over trade policy. Unless compensation for income losses is actually paid, there are always both winners and losers from any change in trade policy.

Another key assumption is that all factors are fully mobile between sectors. Relaxing this for one of the two factors in the simplest case yields the specific-factors model, which provides an illuminating contrast with the Heckscher-Ohlin model. In line with the general results of the last paragraph, protection continues to raise the real return of one factor, the one specific to the import-competing sector, and to lower the real return of another factor, that specific to the export sector. However, its effect on the real return of the mobile factor is now ambiguous. The specific-factors model can also be viewed as depicting a short-run equilibrium. Over time, the specific factors lose their distinctiveness and become intersector-ally mobile, so the Stolper-Samuelson predictions are restored.

Among many applications, the Stolper-Samuelson theory has been used to address the "trade and wages" debate. This asks to what extent globalization in general, and increased imports from low-wage countries in particular, are responsible for widening the differential between skilled and unskilled wages in developed countries. With the two factors reinterpreted as skilled and unskilled labor, the simple version of the model is consistent with a widening differential, and Edward E. Leamer presents some evidence in favor of a Stolper-Samuelson chain of causation, though most authors have preferred to explain the fall in demand for unskilled labor by skill-biased technological progress. However, technology and trade are interlinked. Robert Feenstra and Ronald W. Jones develop a theory consistent with the empirical evidence and has a strong Stolper-Samuelson flavor. Improved communications have allowed large firms to fragment their operations, moving more unskilled-labor-intensive stages of production to countries where unskilled wages are low, so lowering unskilled wages in developed countries while simultaneously raising skilled wages in developing countries.

Finally, the Stolper-Samuelson theorem has also been used to explain the political economy of responses to changes in countries' exposure to trade, most notably by Ronald Rogowski. Using an extended model with three factors—labor, land, and capital—he deployed a wide range of historical evidence to show how differences in factor endowments could explain cross-country variations in the impact of trade on nations' internal political cleavages.

Rybczynski Theorem

In both Heckscher-Ohlin theory and the factor- price equalisation theory, the assumption was taken that the factor endowments were fixed. T.M. Rybczynski, published a paper in 1955 to investigate the effect of an increase in the quantity of a factor of production upon production, consumption and the terms of trade.

This theorem states that the increase in the supply of one of the factor of production, other factors remaining the same, causes the output of the good using the accumulating factor intensively to increase and the output of the other good to decrease in absolute amount, provided that commodity and factor prices remain unchanged. Suppose in a labour- surplus country, the supply of labour gets increased. It will lead to an increased output of the labour- intensive commodity, say cloth, and reduced output of the capital-intensive commodity, say steel.

Assumptions of the Rybczynski Theorem

The Rybczynski theorem is based upon the following main assumptions:

- The trade takes place between two countries.
- The given country is labour-abundant and capital-scarce.
- This country produces two commodities— cloth and steel.
- The production of these commodities requires two factors—labour and capital.
- Capital and labour are perfectly mobile, perfectly divisible and substitutable in some degree.
- Cloth is labour-intensive good and steel is a capital-intensive good.
- There are the conditions of perfect competition in the product and factor markets.
- The production functions related to both the commodities are homogenous of the first degree. That implies constant returns to scale in production.
- The factor and commodity prices are constant.
- The supply of the factor labour expands while that of capital remains the same.

It is now clear that Rybczynki makes departure from H-O theorem and factor-price equalisation theorem in respect of his abandoning the assumption of fixed factor supplies. He discusses the effect of an increased supply of the factor in which the country is abundant upon production, factor and commodity prices and the terms of trade. His theorem is explained through figure.

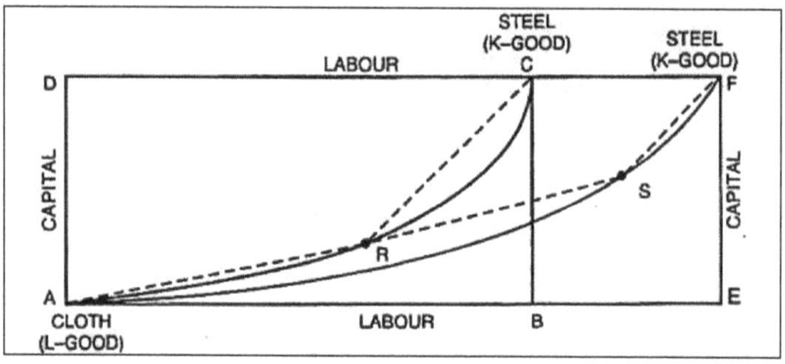

ABCD is the Edgeworth box concerning the given country. It shows that this country is labour- abundant and capital-scarce. A is the origin of the commodity cloth which is labour- intensive (L-good). C is the origin for the good steel which is capital- intensive (K-good). AC is the non-linear contract curve sagging downwards. The production takes place at R. The K-L ratio in cloth is measured by the slope of the line AR and K-L ratio in steel is measured by the slope of the line RC.

It is now supposed that the supply of labour is increased by BE, capital stock remaining the same, so that the new box diagram is AEFD. Now A and F are the points of origin for the goods cloth and steel respectively. AF is the non-linear contract curve. A is the origin for the L-good cloth and F is the origin for K-good steel. Production, in this case, takes place at S. The K-L ratio in cloth is measured by the slope of the line AS and the K-L ratio in steel is measured by the slope of the line SF.

The factor-intensity in the two commodities remains unchanged at the points R and S. Since R and S lie on the same straight line AS, the K-L ratio in cloth remains unchanged. On the other hand, the line RC is parallel to SF. Since the slope of RC and SF are equal, there is no change also in the K-L ratio in the capital-intensive commodity steel.

When the factor- intensity in both the commodities remains the same, there will be no change in the prices of the two factors. It shows that the Rybczynaski theorem refutes the possibility of factor price equalisation. As the increase in the supply of labour in the labour-abundant country and increase in capital stock in the capital-abundant country leaves the prices of two factors unchanged, there can be no equalisation in the factor prices.

When there is no change in the prices of the factors of production, the prices of two commodities will also remain the same as before. The most significant effect of an increase in the supply of factor will be upon the volume of production. The distance of the point of production equilibrium from origin measures the quantity produced of a commodity. In case of cloth, the original production is measured by the distance AR. Subsequently, it is measured by the distance AS. Since AS is greater than AR, it signifies an increase in the production of cloth after there is an increase in the supply of labour.

In case of steel, the production at R was originally indicated by the distance RC and subsequently it is measured by the distance SF. Since SF is shorter than RC, it follows that the production of K-good steel decreases after there is an expansion in the supply of labour in this country. Thus the conclusion can be drawn that the increased supply of one factor, keeping the other unchanged, will raise in absolute amount the production of good intensive in the increasing factor, while the production of the other good will get reduced in absolute amount.

The above analysis suggests that the commodity prices of the two commodities remain constant. This can happen only if the prices of two factors remain constant. It implies that the capital- labour ratio in the two industries remains constant. But how can all this be possible when the quantity of one of the two factors goes on increasing.

In this connection, it may be stated that increase in the supply of labour will result in the entire additional labour going into the labour-intensive industry. There will also be diversion of labour from the capital- intensive industry (steel). Along with the diversion of labour, some amount of capital will also be diverted from the steel industry to the labour-intensive cloth industry.

Consequently, the production of cloth expands and that of steel contracts but the K-L ratios in two industries, factor prices and commodity prices still remain unchanged. If the labour force continues to expand indefinitely, the country will soon become completely specialised in the production of cloth.

The constancy of the commodity prices implies that the terms of trade will remain unaffected. However, the equilibrium with constant prices, when supply of one factor has been increasing, is not compatible with general equilibrium. It may be possible if one of the two commodities, particularly the commodity intensive in the other factor (capital) is inferior. But neither of the two commodities— cloth and steel, can be considered inferior.

The general equilibrium in such a situation can be possible only if the price of the commodity intensive in the expanding factor decreases. It means the terms of trade are likely to become worse for the country in which one factor has been expanding. This is explained through Figure.

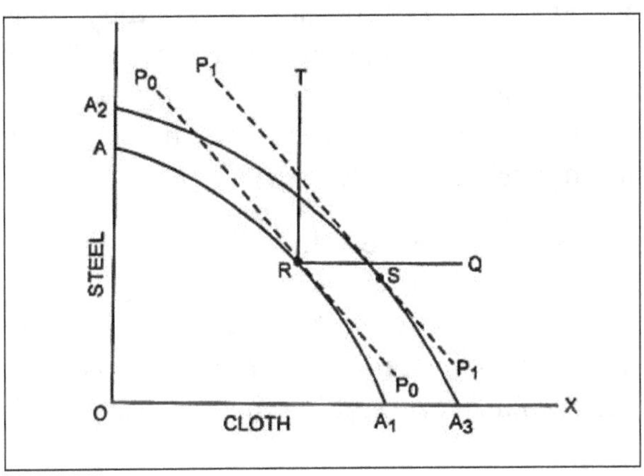

In Figure, the labour-intensive commodity cloth is measured along the horizontal scale and the capital-intensive commodity steel is measured along the vertical scale. The production possibility curve AA_1 is derived from the box ABCD shown in Figure. The international terms of trade are denoted by the slope of P_0P_0. The production equilibrium is determined at R.

The expanded supply of labour along with diversion of labour and capital from steel industry to cloth industry gives the new production possibility curve A_2A_3 derived from Box AEFD in Figure. If the prices of two commodities remain the same, the terms of trade line P_1P_1 is parallel to P_0P_0. The production equilibrium takes place now at S where P_1P_1 is tangent to A_2A_3.

The point S shows a larger production of labour-intensive commodity cloth and reduced output of the capital-intensive commodity steel. This can happen only if steel is an inferior commodity. The expansion in labour force and shift in the production possibility curve to the right imply an increase in national income.

In such a situation, barring the inferior goods, the demand for both the goods must increase. Therefore, the new position of equilibrium must lie on that part of the production possibility curve A_2A_3 that lies between the lines RQ and RT. The slope of this segment on the curve A_2A_3 is less steep than the slope of AA_1 at R. It implies that the price of cloth will be relatively lower and that of steel is relatively higher. A lower price of exportable commodity cloth and a higher price of importable commodity steel mean that there is deterioration of terms of trade subsequent to an increase in the supply of labour.

About the pattern of consumption, Rybczynski explained that the pattern of consumption may remain unaltered, or change in favour of one good or the other despite the change in the relative prices of the two commodities. If the marginal propensity to consume of the product intensive in the accumulated factor is equal to or greater than the average propensity to consume, the production and the consumption pattern will change in the direction of the product intensive in that factor.

When the marginal propensity to consume falls short of the average propensity to consume, the new production and consumption pattern may still change in favour of the commodity using much of the factor increased, or may remain unchanged or move in the direction of the other good. This depends upon the relative magnitudes of the average and marginal propensities to consume.

From the above analysis, it is obvious that the Rybczynski theorem has several implications related to production, factor and commodity prices, and terms of trade and consumption pattern. However, its implication related to the factor price equalisation is most clear-cut. When the supply of the abundant factor increases rapidly, the factor price ratio may remain unchanged preventing the equalisation of factor prices among the trading countries.

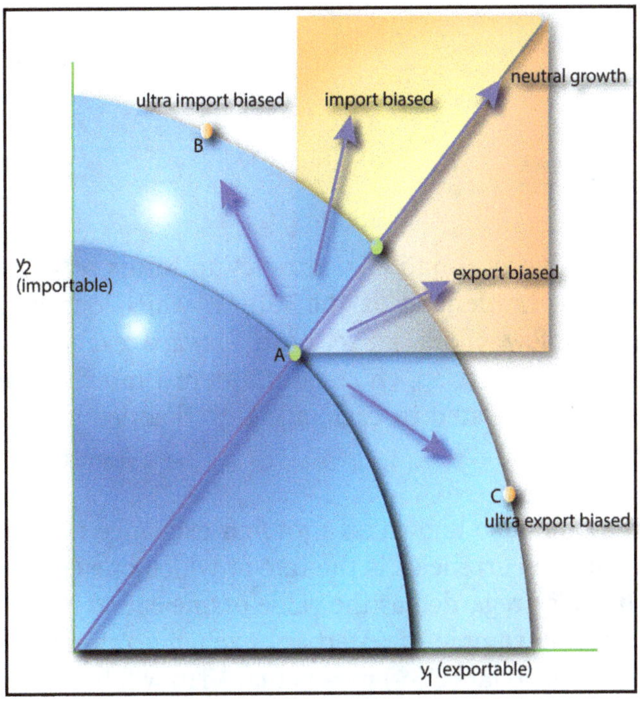

Ultra-export biased growth.

5

Exchange Rate

An exchange rate is the value of a nation's currency in terms of another nation or economic zone. It can also be defined as the rate at which one currency will be exchanged for another. A few of its aspects are forward exchange rate, foreign exchange spot, forward exchange swap, cross rates, interest rate arbitrage, triangular arbitrage, etc. All the aspects related to exchange rate theories have been carefully analyzed in this chapter.

In finance, an exchange rate (also known as a foreign-exchange rate, forex rate, ER, FX rate or Agio) between two currencies is the rate at which one currency will be exchanged for another. It is also regarded as the value of one country's currency in relation to another currency. For example, an interbank exchange rate of 119 Japanese yen (JPY, ¥) to the United States dollar (US$) means that ¥119 will be exchanged for each US$1 or that US$1 will be exchanged for each ¥119. In this case it is said that the price of a dollar in relation to yen is ¥119, or equivalently that the price of a yen in relation to dollars is $1/119.

USD, EUR and Romanian leu.

Exchange rates are determined in the foreign exchange market, which is open to a wide range of different types of buyers and sellers, and where currency trading is continuous: 24 hours a day except weekends, i.e. trading from 20:15 GMT on Sunday until 22:00 GMT Friday. The spot exchange rate refers to the current exchange rate. The forward exchange rate refers to an exchange rate that is quoted and traded today but for delivery and payment on a specific future date.

In the retail currency exchange market, different buying and selling rates will be quoted by money dealers. Most trades are to or from the local currency. The buying rate is the rate at which money dealers will buy foreign currency, and the selling rate is the rate at which they will sell that currency. The quoted rates will incorporate an allowance for a dealer's margin (or profit) in trading, or else the margin may be recovered in the form of a commission or in some other way. Different rates may also be quoted for cash (usually notes only), a documentary form (such as traveler's cheques) or electronically (such as a credit card purchase). The higher rate on documentary transactions has been justified as compensating for the additional time and cost of clearing the document. On the other hand, cash is available for resale immediately, but brings security, storage, and transportation costs, and the cost of tying up capital in a stock of banknotes (bills).

The Retail Exchange Market

Currency for international travel and cross-border payments is predominantly purchased from banks, foreign exchange brokerages and various forms of bureaux de change. These retail outlets source currency from the inter-bank markets, which are valued by the Bank for International Settlements at 5.3 trillion US dollars per day. The purchase is made at the spot contract rate. Retail customers will be charged, in the form of commission or otherwise, to cover the provider's costs and generate a profit. One form of charge is the use of an exchange rate that is less favourable than the wholesale spot rate. The difference between retail buying and selling prices is referred to as the bid-ask spread.

Quotations

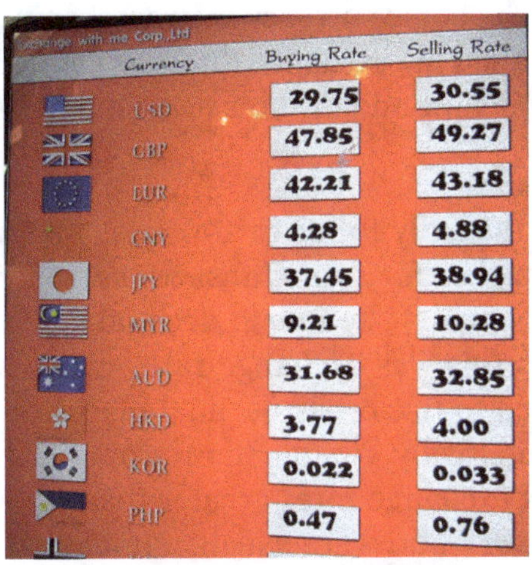

Exchange rates display in Thailand.

In the foreign exchange market, a currency pair is the quotation of the relative value of a currency unit against the unit of another currency. The quotation EUR/USD 1.3225 means that 1 Euro will buy 1.3225 US dollars. In other words, this is the price of a unit of Euro in US dollars. Here, EUR is called the "Fixed currency", while USD is called the "Variable currency".

There is a market convention that determines which is the fixed currency and which is the variable currency. In most parts of the world, the order is: EUR – GBP – AUD – NZD – USD – others. Accordingly, in a conversion from EUR to AUD, EUR is the fixed currency, AUD is the variable currency and the exchange rate indicates how many Australian dollars would be paid or received for 1 Euro. Cyprus and Malta, which were quoted as the base to the USD and others, were recently removed from this list when they joined the Eurozone.

In some areas of Europe and in the retail market in the United Kingdom, EUR and GBP are reversed so that GBP is quoted as the fixed currency to the euro. In order to determine which is the fixed currency when neither currency is on the above list (i.e. both are "other"), market convention is to use the fixed currency which gives an exchange rate greater than 1.000. This reduces rounding issues and the need to use excessive numbers of decimal places. There are some exceptions to this rule: for example, the Japanese often quote their currency as the base to other currencies.

Quotation using a country's home currency as the price currency (for example, EUR 0.8989 = USD 1.00 in the Eurozone) is known as direct quotation or price quotation (from that country's perspective) and is used in most countries.

Quotation using a country's home currency as the unit currency (for example, USD 1.11 = EUR 1.00 in the Eurozone) is known as indirect quotation or quantity quotation and is used in British newspapers ; it is also common in Australia, New Zealand and the Eurozone.

Using direct quotation, if the home currency is strengthening (that is, appreciating, or becoming more valuable) then the exchange rate number decreases. Conversely, if the foreign currency is strengthening and the home currency is depreciating, the exchange rate number increases.

Market convention from the early 1980s to 2006 was that most currency pairs were quoted to four decimal places for spot transactions and up to six decimal places for forward outrights or swaps. (The fourth decimal place is usually referred to as a "pip"). An exception to this was exchange rates with a value of less than 1.000 which were usually quoted to five or six decimal places. Although there is no fixed rule, exchange rates numerically greater than around 20 were usually quoted to three decimal places and exchange rates greater than 80 were quoted to two decimal places. Currencies over 5000 were usually quoted with no decimal places (for example, the former Turkish Lira). e.g. (GBPOMR : 0.765432 - : 1.4436 - EURJPY : 165.29). In other words, quotes are given with five digits. Where rates are below 1, quotes frequently include five decimal places.

In 2005, Barclays Capital broke with convention by quoting spot exchange rates with five or six decimal places on their electronic dealing platform. The contraction of spreads (the difference between the bid and ask rates) arguably necessitated finer pricing and gave the banks the ability to try and win transactions on multibank trading platforms where all banks may otherwise have been quoting the same price. A number of other banks have now followed this system.

Exchange Rate Regime

Each country determines the exchange rate regime that will apply to its currency. For example, the currency may be free-floating, pegged (fixed), or a hybrid.

If a currency is free-floating, its exchange rate is allowed to vary against that of other currencies and is determined by the market forces of supply and demand. Exchange rates for such currencies are likely to change almost constantly as quoted on financial markets, mainly by banks, around the world.

A movable or adjustable peg system is a system of fixed exchange rates, but with a provision for the revaluation (usually devaluation) of a currency. For example, between 1994 and 2005, the Chinese yuan renminbi (RMB) was pegged to the United States dollar at RMB 8.2768 to $1. China was not the only country to do this; from the end of World War II until 1967, Western European countries all maintained fixed exchange rates with the US dollar based on the Bretton Woods system. But that system had to be abandoned in favor of floating, market-based regimes due to market pressures and speculation, according to President Richard M. Nixon in a speech on August 15, 1971, in what is known as the Nixon Shock.

Still, some governments strive to keep their currency within a narrow range. As a result, currencies become over-valued or under-valued, leading to excessive trade deficits or surpluses.

Fluctuations in Exchange Rates

A market-based exchange rate will change whenever the values of either of the two component currencies change. A currency will tend to become more valuable whenever demand for it is greater than the available supply. It will become less valuable whenever demand is less than available supply (this does not mean people no longer want money, it just means they prefer holding their wealth in some other form, possibly another currency).

Increased demand for a currency can be due to either an increased transaction demand for money or an increased speculative demand for money. The transaction demand is highly correlated to a country's level of business activity, gross domestic product (GDP), and employment levels. The more people that are unemployed, the less the public as a whole will spend on goods and services. Central banks typically have little difficulty adjusting the available money supply to accommodate changes in the demand for money due to business transactions.

Speculative demand is much harder for central banks to accommodate, which they influence by adjusting interest rates. A speculator may buy a currency if the return (that is the interest rate) is high enough. In general, the higher a country's interest rates, the greater will be the demand for that currency. It has been argued that such speculation can undermine real economic growth, in particular since large currency speculators may deliberately create downward pressure on a currency by shorting in order to force that central bank to buy their own currency to keep it stable. (When that happens, the speculator can buy the currency back after it depreciates, close out their position, and thereby take a profit).

For carrier companies shipping goods from one nation to another, exchange rates can often impact them severely. Therefore, most carriers have a CAF charge to account for these fluctuations.

Purchasing Power of Currency

The real exchange rate (RER) is the purchasing power of a currency relative to another at current exchange rates and prices. It is the ratio of the number of units of a given country's currency necessary to buy a market basket of goods in the other country, after acquiring the other country's currency in the foreign exchange market, to the number of units of the given country's currency that would be necessary to buy that market basket directly in the given country. There are various ways to measure RER.

Thus the real exchange rate is the exchange rate times the relative prices of a market basket of goods in the two countries. For example, the purchasing power of the US dollar relative to that of the euro is the dollar price of a euro (dollars per euro) times the euro price of one unit of the market basket (euros/goods unit) divided by the dollar price of the market basket (dollars per goods unit), and hence is dimensionless. This is the exchange rate (expressed as dollars per euro) times the relative price of the two currencies in terms of their ability to purchase units of the market basket (euros per goods unit divided by dollars per goods unit). If all goods were freely tradable, and foreign and domestic residents purchased identical baskets of goods, purchasing power parity (PPP) would hold for the exchange rate and GDP deflators (price levels) of the two countries, and the real exchange rate would always equal 1.

The rate of change of the real exchange rate over time for the euro versus the dollar equals the rate of appreciation of the euro (the positive or negative percentage rate of change of the dollars-per-euro exchange rate) plus the inflation rate of the euro minus the inflation rate of the dollar.

Bilateral vs. Effective Exchange Rate

Bilateral exchange rate involves a currency pair, while an effective exchange rate is a weighted average of a basket of foreign currencies, and it can be viewed as an overall measure of the country's external competitiveness. A nominal effective exchange rate (NEER) is weighted with the inverse of the asymptotic trade weights. A real effective exchange rate (REER) adjusts NEER by appropriate foreign price level and deflates by the home country price level. Compared to NEER, a GDP weighted effective exchange rate might be more appropriate considering the global investment phenomenon.

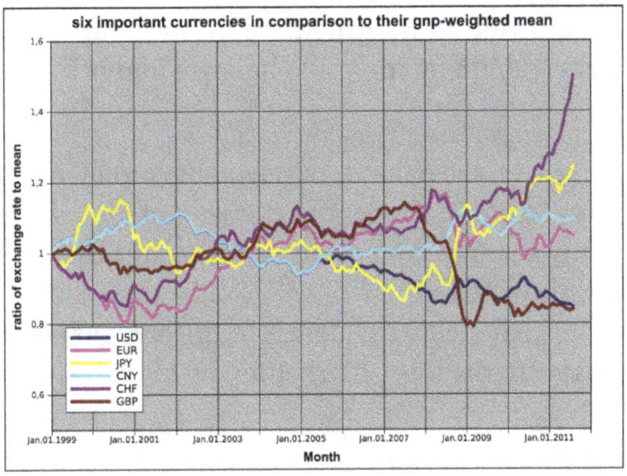

Example of GNP-weighted nominal exchange rate history of a basket of 6 important currencies (US Dollar, Euro, Japanese Yen, Chinese Renminbi, Swiss Franks, Pound Sterling.

Parallel Exchange Rate

In many countries there is a distinction between the official exchange rate for permitted transactions and a parallel exchange rate that responds to excess demand for foreign currency at the official exchange rate. The degree by which the parallel exchange rate exceeds the official exchange rate is known as the parallel premium.

Uncovered Interest Rate Parity

Uncovered interest rate parity (UIRP) states that an appreciation or depreciation of one currency against another currency might be neutralized by a change in the interest rate differential. If US interest rates increase while Japanese interest rates remain unchanged then the US dollar should depreciate against the Japanese yen by an amount that prevents arbitrage (in reality the opposite, appreciation, quite frequently happens in the short-term, as explained below). The future exchange rate is reflected into the forward exchange rate stated today. In our example, the forward exchange rate of the dollar is said to be at a discount because it buys fewer Japanese yen in the forward rate than it does in the spot rate. The yen is said to be at a premium.

UIRP showed no proof of working after the 1990s. Contrary to the theory, currencies with high interest rates characteristically appreciated rather than depreciated on the reward of the containment of inflation and a higher-yielding currency.

Balance of Payments Model

The balance of payments model holds that foreign exchange rates are at an equilibrium level if they produce a stable current account balance. A nation with a trade deficit will experience a reduction in its foreign exchange reserves, which ultimately lowers (depreciates) the value of its currency. A cheaper (undervalued) currency renders the nation's goods (exports) more affordable in the global market while making imports more expensive. After an intermediate period, imports will be forced down and exports to rise, thus stabilizing the trade balance and bring the currency towards equilibrium.

Like purchasing power parity, the balance of payments model focuses largely on tradeable goods and services, ignoring the increasing role of global capital flows. In other words, money is not only chasing goods and services, but to a larger extent, financial assets such as stocks and bonds. Their flows go into the capital account item of the balance of payments, thus balancing the deficit in the current account. The increase in capital flows has given rise to the asset market model effectively.

Asset Market Model

World banknotes

The increasing volume of trading of financial assets (stocks and bonds) has required a rethink of its impact on exchange rates. Economic variables such as economic growth, inflation and productivity are no longer the only drivers of currency movements. The proportion of foreign exchange transactions stemming from cross border-trading of financial assets has dwarfed the extent of currency transactions generated from trading in goods and services.

The asset market approach views currencies as asset prices traded in an efficient financial market. Consequently, currencies are increasingly demonstrating a strong correlation with other markets, particularly equities.

Like the stock exchange, money can be made (or lost) on trading by investors and speculators in the foreign exchange market. Currencies can be traded at spot and foreign exchange options markets. The spot market represents current exchange rates, whereas options are derivatives of exchange rates.

Manipulation of Exchange Rates

A country may gain an advantage in international trade if it controls the market for its currency to keep its value low, typically by the national central bank engaging in open market operations in the foreign exchange market. In the early twenty-first century it was widely asserted that the People's Republic of China had been doing this over a long period of time.

Other nations, including Iceland, Japan, Brazil, and so on have had a policy of maintaining a low value of their currencies in the hope of reducing the cost of exports and thus bolstering their economies. A lower exchange rate lowers the price of a country's goods for consumers in other countries, but raises the price of imported goods and services for consumers in the low value currency country.

In general, exporters of goods and services will prefer a lower value for their currencies, while importers will prefer a higher value.

Standard Forex Exchange Quotations

PiP is the acronym for "price interest point". A pip is the smallest unit by a currency quotations can change. For example, let us assume that on a given day, a bank quotes spot USDINR quote is INR 48.75. The minimum value this rate can change is either INR 48.74 or INR 48.76. In other words, for USD/INR quote, the pip value is 0.01. Pip in foreign currency quotation is similar to the tick size in share quotations.

However, in an interbank market, USDINR rate is quoted upto 4 decimal point. Hence minimum value change will be in the tune of 0.0001.

In a similar manner, minimum value a Euro/USD quote can change is 0.0001 as EuroUSD is quoted upto 4 decimal point.

The difference between bid-ask spread is also quoted in pip terms. For example Spot EURUSD is quoted at a bid price of 1.0213 and an ask price of 1.0219. The difference is USD 0.0006 equal to 6 "pips".

On a forward contract or position, the value of a pip can easily be calculated. We know that the EURUSD is quoted with four decimals; value of 1 pip is 0.0001. Thus, on a EURUSD 100,000 contract, one pip is USD 10. On a USDJPY 100,000 contract, one pip is equal to 1000 yen, because USDJPY is quoted with only two decimals (Yen 107.98/USD).

Forward Exchange Rate

The forward exchange rate (also referred to as forward rate or forward price) is the exchange rate at which a bank agrees to exchange one currency for another at a future date when it enters into a forward contract with an investor. Multinational corporations, banks, and other financial institutions enter into forward contracts to take advantage of the forward rate for hedging purposes. The forward exchange rate is determined by a parity relationship among the spot exchange rate and differences in interest rates between two countries, which reflects an economic equilibrium in the foreign exchange market under which arbitrage opportunities are eliminated. When in equilibrium, and when interest rates vary across two countries, the parity condition implies that the forward rate includes a premium or discount reflecting the interest rate differential. Forward exchange rates have important theoretical implications for forecasting future spot exchange rates. Financial economists have put forth a hypothesis that the forward rate accurately predicts the future spot rate, for which empirical evidence is mixed.

The forward exchange rate is the rate at which a commercial bank is willing to commit to exchange one currency for another at some specified future date. The forward exchange rate is a type of forward price. It is the exchange rate negotiated today between a bank and a client upon entering into a forward contract agreeing to buy or sell some amount of foreign currency in the future. Multinational corporations and financial institutions often use the forward market to hedge future payables or receivables denominated in a foreign currency against foreign exchange risk by using a forward contract to lock in a forward exchange rate. Hedging with forward contracts is typically used for larger transactions, while futures contracts are used for smaller transactions. This is due to the customization afforded to banks by forward contracts traded over-the-counter, versus the standardization of futures contracts which are traded on an exchange. Banks typically quote forward rates for major currencies in maturities of one, three, six, nine, or twelve months, however in some cases quotations for greater maturities are available up to five or ten years.

Relation to Covered Interest Rate Parity

Covered interest rate parity is a no-arbitrage condition in foreign exchange markets which depends on the availability of the forward market. It can be rearranged to give the forward exchange rate as a function of the other variables. The forward exchange rate depends on three known variables: the spot exchange rate, the domestic interest rate, and the foreign interest rate. This effectively means that the forward rate is the price of a forward contract, which derives its value from the pricing of spot contracts and the addition of information on available interest rates.

The following equation represents covered interest rate parity, a condition under which investors eliminate exposure to foreign exchange risk (unanticipated changes in exchange rates) with the use of a forward contract – the exchange rate risk is effectively *covered*. Under this condition, a domestic investor would earn equal returns from investing in domestic assets or converting currency at the spot exchange rate, investing in foreign currency assets in a country with a different interest rate, and exchanging the foreign currency for domestic currency at the negotiated forward exchange rate. Investors will be indifferent to the interest rates on deposits in these countries due to the equilibrium resulting from the forward exchange rate. The condition allows for no arbitrage opportunities because the return on domestic deposits, $1+i_d$, is equal to the return on foreign deposits, $[S/F](1+i_f)$. If these two returns weren't equalized by the use of a forward contract, there would be a potential arbitrage opportunity in which, for example, an investor could borrow currency in the country with the lower interest rate, convert to the foreign currency at today's spot exchange rate, and invest in the foreign country with the higher interest rate.

$$(1+i_d) = \frac{S}{F}(1+i_f)$$

where

F is the forward exchange rate

S is the current spot exchange rate

i_d is the interest rate in domestic currency (base currency)

i_f is the interest rate in foreign currency (quoted currency)

This equation can be arranged such that it solves for the forward rate:

$$F = S\frac{(1+i_f)}{(1+i_d)}$$

Forward Premium or Discount

The equilibrium that results from the relationship between forward and spot exchange rates within the context of covered interest rate parity is responsible for eliminating or correcting for market inefficiencies that would create potential for arbitrage profits. As such, arbitrage opportunities are fleeting. In order for this equilibrium to hold under differences in interest rates between two countries, the forward exchange rate must generally differ from the spot exchange rate, such that a no-arbitrage condition is sustained. Therefore, the forward rate is said to contain a premium or discount, reflecting the interest rate differential between two countries. The following equations demonstrate how the forward premium or discount is calculated.

The forward exchange rate differs by a premium or discount of the spot exchange rate:

$$F = S(1+P)$$

where

P is the premium (if positive) or discount (if negative)

The equation can be rearranged as follows to solve for the forward premium/discount:

$$P = \frac{F}{S} - 1$$

In practice, forward premiums and discounts are quoted as annualized percentage deviations from the spot exchange rate, in which case it is necessary to account for the number of days to delivery as in the following example.

$$P_N = (\frac{F}{S} - 1)\frac{360}{d}$$

where

N represents the maturity of a given forward exchange rate quote

d represents the number of days to delivery

For example, to calculate the 6-month forward premium or discount for the euro versus the dollar deliverable in 30 days, given a spot rate quote of 1.2238 $/€ and a 6-month forward rate quote of 1.2260 $/€:

$$P_6 = (\frac{1.2260}{1.2238} - 1)\frac{360}{30} = 0.021572 = 2.16\%$$

The resulting 0.021572 is positive, so one would say that the euro is trading at a 0.021572 or 2.16% premium against the dollar for delivery in 30 days. Conversely, if one were to work this example in euro terms rather than dollar terms, the perspective would be reversed and one would say that the dollar is trading at a discount against the Euro.

Forecasting Future Spot Exchange Rates

Unbiasedness Hypothesis

The unbiasedness hypothesis states that given conditions of rational expectations and risk neutrality, the forward exchange rate is an unbiased predictor of the future spot exchange rate. Without introducing a foreign exchange risk premium (due to the assumption of risk neutrality), the following equation illustrates the unbiasedness hypothesis.

$$F_t = E_t(S_{t+k})$$

where

- F_t is the forward exchange rate at time t.
- $E_t(S_{t+k})$ is the expected future spot exchange rate at time $t + k$.
- k is the number of periods into the future from time t.

The empirical rejection of the unbiasedness hypothesis is a well-recognized puzzle among finance researchers. Empirical evidence for cointegration between the forward rate and the future spot rate is mixed. Researchers have published papers demonstrating empirical failure of the hypothesis by conducting regression analyses of the realized changes in spot exchange rates on forward premiums and finding negative slope coefficients. These researchers offer numerous rationales for such failure. One rationale centers around the relaxation of risk neutrality, while still assuming rational expectations, such that a foreign exchange risk premium may exist that can account for differences between the forward rate and the future spot rate.

The following equation represents the forward rate as being equal to a future spot rate and a risk premium:

$$F_t = E_t(S_{t+1}) + P_t$$

The current spot rate can be introduced so that the equation solves for the forward-spot differential (the difference between the forward rate and the current spot rate):

$$F_t - S_t = E_t(S_{t+1} - S_t) + P_t$$

Eugene Fama concluded that large positive correlations of the difference between the forward exchange rate and the current spot exchange rate signal variations over time in the premium component of the forward-spot differential $F_t - S_t$ or in the forecast of the expected change in the spot exchange rate. Fama suggested that slope coefficients in the regressions of the difference between the forward rate and the future spot rate $F_t - S_{t+1}$, and the expected change in the spot rate $E_t(S_{t+1} - S_t)$, on the forward-spot differential $F_t - S_t$ which are different from zero imply variations over time in both components of the forward-spot differential: the premium and the expected change in the spot rate. Fama's findings were sought to be empirically validated by a significant body of research, ultimately finding that large variance in expected changes in the spot rate could only be accounted for by risk aversion coefficients that were deemed "unacceptably high." Other researchers have found that the unbiasedness hypothesis has been rejected in both cases where there is evidence of risk premia varying over time and cases where risk premia are constant.

Other rationales for the failure of the forward rate unbiasedness hypothesis include considering the conditional bias to be an exogenous variable explained by a policy aimed at smoothing interest rates and stabilizing exchange rates, or considering that an economy allowing for discrete changes could facilitate excess returns in the forward market. Some researchers have contested empirical failures of the hypothesis and have sought to explain conflicting evidence as resulting from contaminated data and even inappropriate selections of the time length of forward contracts. Economists demonstrated that the forward rate could serve as a useful proxy for future spot exchange rates between currencies with liquidity premia that average out to zero during the onset of floating exchange rate regimes in the 1970s. Research examining the introduction of endogenous breaks to test the structural stability of cointegrated spot and forward exchange rate time series have found some evidence to support forward rate unbiasedness in both the short and long term.

Forward Quotations on Point Basis

Except the spot quotation which is expressed as "outright", forex dealers normally quote forward rates in points. In terms of points, these quotations are known as "cash rates" or "swap rates" or "basis points". The cash/swap rates are nothing but the difference between the forward rate and the spot rate.

Suppose a forex exchange dealer is giving the following quotations as listed in Table 3.1. The spot rate is expressed in outright form and the forward rates are point form. In earlier days when most of the forex transactions were undertaken through telephone, to reduce the effort to quote full figure forex quotes, operators started quoting in point form. Conversation between two dealers highlights how forex quotations via telephone are mostly done in point forms to save time as well as reduce error while quoting. As there is a higher probability of the dealer making a mistake in quoting in outright form, quotations based point form evolved and gained popularity.

Table 3.1: Cash/ Swap rates in points

USD/INR	Bid in points	Ask in points
Spot	47.0725	47.0745
1 week	25	30
2 weeks	70	90
1 month	115	145
2 months	175	220

Now how do we arrive at the actual forward rates?

The cash/swap rates are either added or subtracted from the spot rates to get the forward rates in "outright" form.

Now the question is when these points are to be added and when to be subtracted? There is a thumb rule to decide when points are added or deleted.

If "Bid in points" > "Ask in points"	Points are subtracted from the spot
If "Bid in points" < "ask in points"	Points are added to the spot

The above thumb rule, is also know as "High-Low" or "Low-High" rule.

High-Low Rule: If the bid points are higher (than the ask points), the spot rate has to be made lower (by subtracting bid-ask points from spot bid-ask rates) to find the forward rate.

Low-High Rule: If the bid points are lower (than the ask points), the spot rate has to be made high (by adding bid-ask points to spot bid-ask rates) to arrive at the forward bid-ask rates.

In the Table 3.1, as the "bid in points" < "ask in points". Hence these points are to be added to the spot rate to arrive at the forward rates. When these points are added, the outright quotations will be same.

Table 3.2 Forward Quotations in outright and percentage form

USDINR	Outright Quotations	
	Bid Rate	Ask Rate
Spot	47.0725	47.0745
1 week	47.0750	47.0775
2 weeks	47.0795	47.0835
1 month	47.0840	47.0890
2 months	47.0900	47.0965

Now suppose, a forex dealer gives the following quotations.

Table3.3: Cash/Swap rates in points

USDINR	Bid Rate	Ask Rate
Spot	47.0725	47.0745
1 week	35	30
2 weeks	40	33
1 month	60	45
2 months	75	55

In the Table 3.3, as the "bid in points" > "ask in points", these points are subtracted from the spot rate to arrive at the forward rates. When these points are subtracted, the outright quotations will be same as the details given in Table 3.4.

The outright quotations will be.

Table. 3.4: Outright Quotations		
USDINR	**Bid Rate**	**Ask Rate**
Spot	47.0725	47.0745
1 week	47.0690	47.0710
2 weeks	47.0685	47.0712
1 month	47.0665	47.0700
2 months	47.0650	47.0690

Forward quotations given in Table 3.3 and Table 3.5 indicate the market collective opinion about the future exchange rate movement.

Forex dealers normally quote rates in outright form to retail customers and in point form for other kinds of customers. In fact, forex dealers may either be quoting bid rate or ask rate as a retail trader may be interested either buy or sell foreign currency but not both at a given point of time.

The relationship between spot bid-ask spread, forward points and forward bid-ask spread can be summarized as:

- Bid-ask spreads of the forward price should always be greater than the spot price. It is obvious as the forex dealer is taking more risk in a forward contract than a spot contract. As given in Table 14.4, spot bid-ask spread is INR0.0020/USD while for 1-week and 2-week forward it is INR0.0025/USD and INR0.0040/USD respectively.
- Sum of the bid-ask spreads of the spot price and forward points should equal the spread of the forward price. The spot bid-ask spread is 0.0020. 1-week forward point bid-ask spread is 0.0005. Sum of these two is 0.0025. Hence, bid-ask spread for 1 week forward should equal to 0.0025.

Relationship between spot bid-ask spread, forward points and forward bid-ask spread:

- Bid-ask spreads of the forward rate is always greater than the spot bid-ask spread.
- Sum of the bid-ask spreads of the spot rate and forward points should equal the bid-ask spread of the forward rate.

Forward Rates

Forex dealers normally quote forward rates at regular intervals like one month or three months. For example, dealers normally quote 1-week, 2-week, 1,2,3 6 months forward rate. However, depending on customer's requirement, these delaers quote forward rate on a specific future date that is not an exact multiple of months. Such kinds of forwards quotes are known as broken period quotes.

Banks normally quote broken period rates by method of interpolation. Let us take an example to understand this.

However a corporate customer wants to buy 100,000 USD on October 21st. The bank has to quote a forward rate for this date.

Table 3.5: Cash/Swap rates in points

USDINR	Maturity Date	Bid Rate	Ask Rate
Spot	July 14th	47.0725	47.0745
1 Month	August 14th	135	130
2 Month	September 14th	140	133
3 month	October 14th	160	145
4 months	November 14th	175	155

The interpolation method is used as follows:

- The forward rate points applicable are (160 to 175) for bid and (145-155) for ask.
- For 31 days (October 14th to November 14th), the bid spread is 15 points (175 to 160).
- For 7 days, the spread in bid point $=\frac{15}{31}*7=3.89$ So the spread applicable for October 21st is 160 + 3.89 = 163.89.
- Similarly, for 31 days (October 14th to November 14th), the ask spread is 10 points (155 to 145). For 7 days, the spread in bid point $=\frac{10}{31}*7=2.26$ So the spread applicable for October 21st is 145 + 2.26 = 147.26.
- The applicable bid rate for 31 days (October 14th to November 14th), the ask spread is 15 points (175 to 160). For 7 days, the spread in ask point $=\frac{15}{31}*7=3.89.$ So the ask spread applicable for October 21st is 160 + 2.26 = 163.89.
- So the applicable bid rate will be = 47.0725 - 0.014726 = 47.0577.
- Ask spread is = 47.0745- 0.016389=47.0581.

Table 3.6: Interpolated Bid-Ask Spread (USDINR)

Maturity Date	Bid Rate	Ask Rate
October 21st	47.0576	47.0581

For a forward contract maturing on October 21st, the bank would quote a rate (47.0576-47.0581) given in Table 3.6. As the company wants to buy USD 100,000, the bank will offer USD at a rate of INR 47.0581. If the company would like to sell USD, then applicable rate would be INR 47.0576.

As forward contracts are OTC contracts, in real life, most of the contracts would be for a broken periods.

Premium & Discount on Forward Quotations

Forward quotations can be expressed as percentage premium or discount to the spot rate. Table 3.7 details the forward quotations expressed as percentage premium/discount to forward quotations.

Table 3.7 Forward Quotations in Outright and Percentage form

USDINR	Outright Quotations		USD Percentage Premium/Discount (*)	
	Bid Rate	Ask Rate	Bid Rate	Ask Rate
Spot	47.0725	47.0745		
1 week	47.0750	47.0775	0.28%	0.33%
2 weeks	47.0795	47.0835	0.40%	0.52%
1 month	47.0840	47.0890	0.29%	0.37%
2 months	47.0900	47.0965	0.22%	0.28%

(*) : Annualized premium/discount.

The forward rate (1 week) is expressed as a percentage premium/discount in relation to spot in the following manner.

Compared to spot and 1 week forward, forward bid price of USD is more expensive by 0.0025.

$$\%\,\text{Premium / Discount} = \frac{\text{n day forward bid} - \text{spot bid}}{\text{spot bid}} * \frac{365}{\text{n day forward rate}} * 100$$

$$= \frac{47.0750 - 47.0725}{47.0725} * \frac{365}{7} * 100 = 0.28\%$$

The above equation indicates that forward 1 week USD is at premium.

Similarly % premium/discount in forward ask rate (1 week) can be calculated in the above manner by comparing 1 week ask rate with the spot ask rate.

As the forward rates (for different maturities) are higher than the spot rates, the forward rates are at a premium. In other words, as USD is expected appreciate (as INR is expected to depreciate), forward USD is at premium.

To find out the % premium/discount of INR, we need to find out the bid-ask spread with INR as base currency. Table 3.8 lists the INRUSD bid-ask spread.

Table 3.8 Forward Quotations in outright and percentage form

INRUSD	Outright Quotations		INR Percentage Premium/Discount (*)	
	Bid Rate	Ask Rate	Bid Rate	Ask Rate
Spot	0.021243	0.021244		
1 week	0.021242	0.021243	-0.25%	-0.25%
2 weeks	0.021239	0.021241	-0.49%	-0.37%
1month	0.021236	0.021239	-0.40%	-0.28%
2 months	0.021233	0.021236	-0.28%	-0.23%

As the forward rates (for different maturities) are lesser than the spot rates, INR is expected to depreciate as USD is expected to appreciate). Hence, forward INR is at discount to USD.

To sum up, when forward quote/variable currency appreciates (depreciates), the base currency is at discount (premium).

Factors Affecting Forward Rates

By now, we are familiar with the intricacies of bid-ask quotations, broken period quotation, forward rate premium/discount aspects. But how do the banks/dealers quote these forward rates? What factors do they take into consideration for quoting a forward rate.

Besides supply, demand factors, the most important factor which governs the forward point quotation is the prevailing interest rates in two currencies.

$$\text{Forward point} = \frac{\text{Spot} * \left[\frac{I_V - I_B}{100}\right] * \frac{D}{360}}{1 + \left(\frac{I_B}{100} * \frac{D}{360}\right)}$$

Where: S = spot rate

I_V = Interest rate in Variable/Quote/Term currency.

I_B = Interest rate in Base currency.

D= Actual No. of days between the spot and forward date.

360= No. of days in year. Different countries use different day count conventions. It can also be 365.

If the forward point is positive, it is added to the spot rate otherwise, it is subtracted form the spot rate.

Let us take an example to understand this aspect: A bank wants to quote forward rate for 6 month from the spot date. The details are:

S = Rs. 46.60/USD.

I_V = Interest rate in India is 8% per annum.

I_B = Interest rate in US is 4% per annum.

D = 182 days.

360= No. of days in year.

$$\text{Forward point} = \frac{\text{Spot} * \left[\frac{I_V - I_B}{100}\right] * \frac{D}{360}}{1 + \left(\frac{I_B}{100} * \frac{D}{360}\right)}$$

$$\text{Forward point} = \frac{46.60 * \left[\frac{8-4}{100}\right] * \frac{182}{360}}{1 + \left(\frac{4}{100} * \frac{182}{360}\right)} = 0.485 = 48.5 \text{ points.}$$

Forward point calculated in the above manner is also known as forward swap points

Hence the 6-month forward rate would be = 46.60 +0.485= INR 47.085/ USD.

Now suppose, the interest rate in India is 3% while in USA it is 5%. The forward point would be calculated as,

$$\text{Forward point} = \frac{46.60 * \left[\frac{3-5}{100}\right] * \frac{182}{360}}{1 + \left(\frac{5}{100} * \frac{182}{360}\right)} = 0.459 = 45.9 \text{ points.}$$

Hence the 6-month forward rate would be = 46.60 - 0.459= INR 46.141/ USD.

Foreign Exchange Spot

A foreign exchange spot transaction, also known as FX spot, is an agreement between two parties to buy one currency against selling another currency at an agreed price for settlement on the spot date. The exchange rate at which the transaction is done is called the spot exchange rate. As of 2010, the average daily turnover of global FX spot transactions reached nearly 1.5 trillion USD, counting 37.4% of all foreign exchange transactions. FX spot transactions increased by 38% to 2.0 trillion USD from April 2010 to April 2013.

Settlement Date

The standard settlement timeframe for foreign exchange spot transactions is $T + 2$ days; i.e., two business days from the trade date. Notable exceptions are USD/CAD, USD/TRY, USD/PHP, USD/RUB, USD/KZT and USD/PKR currency pairs, which settle at $T + 1$.

Execution Methods

Common methods of executing a spot foreign exchange transaction include the following:

- *Direct* – Executed between two parties directly and not intermediated by a third party. For example, a transaction executed via direct telephone communication or direct electronic dealing systems such as Reuters Conversational Dealing.
- *Electronic broking systems* – Executed via automated order matching system for foreign exchange dealers. Examples of such systems are EBS and Reuters Matching 2000/2.
- *Electronic trading systems* – Executed via a single-bank proprietary platform or a multibank dealing system. These systems are generally geared towards customers. Examples of multibank systems include Integral, FXall, HotSpotFX, Currenex, LMAX Exchange, FX Connect, Prime Trade, Globalink, Seamless FX, and eSpeed.
- *Voice broker* – Executed via telephone with a foreign exchange voice broker.

Foreign Exchange Swap

In finance, a foreign exchange swap, forex swap, or FX swap is a simultaneous purchase and sale of identical amounts of one currency for another with two different value dates (normally spot to forward) and may utilize foreign exchange derivatives. An FX swap allows sums of a certain currency to be used to fund charges designated in another currency without acquiring foreign exchange risk. It permits companies that have funds in different currencies to manage them efficiently.

Structure

A foreign exchange swap has two legs - a spot transaction and a forward transaction - that are executed simultaneously for the same quantity, and therefore offset each other.

Forward foreign exchange transactions occur if both companies have a currency the other needs. It prevents negative foreign exchange risk for either party. Foreign exchange spot transactions are similar to forward foreign exchange transactions in terms of how they are agreed upon; however, they are planned for a specific date in the very near future, usually within the same week.

It is also common to trade "forward-forward" where both transactions are for (different) forward dates.

Uses

The most common use of foreign exchange swaps is for institutions to fund their foreign exchange balances.

Once a foreign exchange transaction settles, the holder is left with a positive (or "long") position in one currency and a negative (or "short") position in another. In order to collect or pay any overnight interest due on these foreign balances, at the end of every day institutions will close out any foreign balances and re-institute them for the following day. To do this they typically use "tom-next" swaps, buying (or selling) a foreign amount settling tomorrow, and then doing the opposite, selling (or buying) it back settling the day after.

The interest collected or paid every night is referred to as the cost of carry. As currency traders know roughly how much holding a currency position will make or cost on a daily basis, specific trades are put on based on this; these are referred to as carry trades.

Companies may also use them to avoid foreign exchange risk.

Example:

> A British Company may be long EUR from sales in Europe but operate primarily in Britain using GBP. However, they know that they need to pay their manufacturers in Europe in 1 month.
>
> They could of course SPOT Sell their EUR and buy GBP to cover their expenses in Britain, and then in one month SPOT Buy EUR and sell GBP to pay their business partners in Europe.
>
> However, this exposes them to FX risk. If Britain has financial trouble and the EUR/GBP exchange rate moves against them, they may have to spend a lot more GBP to get the same amount of EUR.
>
> Therefore they create a 1M Swap, where they Sell EUR and Buy GBP on SPOT and simultaneously Buy EUR and Sell GBP on a 1 Month (1M) forward. This significantly reduces their risk. The company knows they will be able to purchase EUR reliably while still being able to use currency for domestic transactions in the interim.

Pricing

The relationship between spot and forward is known as the interest rate parity, which states that,

$$F = S\left(\frac{1 + r_d \cdot T}{1 + r_f \cdot T}\right),$$

where

- F = forward rate
- S = spot rate
- r_d = simple interest rate of the term currency
- r_f = simple interest rate of the base currency
- T = tenor (calculated according to the appropriate day count convention)

The forward points or swap points are quoted as the difference between forward and spot, *F* - *S*, and is expressed as the following:

$$F - S = S\left(\frac{1 + r_d \cdot T}{1 + r_f \cdot T} - 1\right) = \frac{S(r_d - r_f) \cdot T}{1 + r_f \cdot T} \approx S(r_d - r_f)T,$$

if $r_f \cdot T$ is small. Thus, the value of the swap points is roughly proportional to the interest rate differential.

Related Instruments

A foreign exchange swap should not be confused with a currency swap, which is a rarer long-term transaction governed by different rules.

Currency Pair

A currency pair is the quotation of the relative value of a currency unit against the unit of another currency in the foreign exchange market. The currency that is used as the reference is called the counter currency, quote currency or currency and the currency that is quoted in relation is called the base currency or transaction currency.

Currency pairs are sometimes then written by concatenating the ISO currency codes (ISO 4217) of the base currency and the counter currency, separating them with a slash character. Often the slash character is omitted, alternatively the slash may be replaced by and etc. A widely traded currency pair is the relation of the euro against the US dollar, designated as EUR/USD. The quotation *EUR/USD 1.2500* means that one euro is exchanged for 1.2500 US dollars. Here, EUR is the base currency and USD is the quote currency(counter currency). This means that 1 Euro can be exchangeable to 1.25 US Dollars.

The most traded currency pairs in the world are called the *Majors*. They involve the currencies euro, US dollar, Japanese yen, pound sterling, Australian dollar, Canadian dollar, and the Swiss franc.

Syntax and Quotation

Currency quotations use the abbreviations for currencies that are prescribed by the International Organization for Standardization (ISO) in standard ISO 4217. The major currencies and their designation in the foreign exchange market are the US dollar (USD), euro (EUR), Japanese yen (JPY), British pound (GBP), Australian dollar (AUD), Canadian dollar (CAD), and the Swiss franc (CHF).

As has been mentioned previously, the quotation *EUR/USD 1.2500* (or EURUSD 1.2500) means that one euro is exchanged for 1.2500 US dollars. If the quote changes from EUR/USD 1.2500 (or EURUSD 1.2500) to 1.2510, the euro has increased in relative value, because either the dollar buying strength has weakened or the euro has strengthened, or both. On the other hand, if the EUR/USD (or EURUSD) quote changes from 1.2500 to 1.2490 the euro has become relatively weaker than the dollar.

Base Currency

Most traded currencies by value
Currency distribution of global foreign exchange market turnover

Rank	Currency	ISO 4217 code (symbol)	% daily share (April 2016)
1	United States dollar	USD ($)	87.6%
2	Euro	EUR (€)	31.4%
3	Japanese yen	JPY (¥)	21.6%
4	Pound sterling	GBP (£)	12.8%
5	Australian dollar	AUD (A$)	6.9%
6	Canadian dollar	CAD (C$)	5.1%
7	Swiss franc	CHF (Fr)	4.8%
8	Renminbi	CNY (元)	4.0%
9	Swedish krona	SEK (kr)	2.2%
10	New Zealand dollar	NZD (NZ$)	2.1%
11	Mexican peso	MXN ($)	1.9%
12	Singapore dollar	SGD (S$)	1.8%
13	Hong Kong dollar	HKD (HK$)	1.7%

14	Norwegian krone	NOK (kr)	1.7%
15	South Korean won	KRW (₩)	1.7%
16	Turkish lira	TRY	1.4%
17	Russian ruble	RUB	1.1%
18	Indian rupee	INR	1.1%
19	Brazilian real	BRL (R$)	1.0%
20	South African rand	ZAR (R)	1.0%
		Other	7.1%
		Total	200.0%

The rules for formulating standard currency pair notations result from accepted priorities attributed to each currency.

From its inception in 1999 and as stipulated by the European Central Bank, the euro has first precedence as a base currency. Therefore, all currency pairs involving it should use it as their base, listed first. For example, the US dollar and euro exchange rate is identified as EUR/USD.

Although there is no standards-setting body or ruling organization, the established priority ranking of the major currencies is:

- Euro,
- Pound sterling,
- Australian dollar,
- New Zealand dollar,
- United States dollar,
- Canadian dollar,
- Swiss franc,
- Japanese yen.

Historically, this was established by a ranking according to the relative values of the currencies with respect to each other, but the introduction of the euro and other market factors have broken the original price rankings. For example, while historically Japanese yen would rank above Mexican peso, the quoting convention for these is now MXNJPY, i.e. Mexican peso has higher priority than Japanese yen.

Other currencies (the *Minors*) are generally quoted against USD. Quotes against currencies other than USD are referred to as currency crosses, or simply crosses. The most common crosses are EUR, JPY, and GBP crosses, but may be against any other currency. The rates are almost universally derived, however, by taking the first currency's rate against the USD and multiplying/dividing by the second currency's rate against the USD.

Sometimes the term *base currency* may also refer to the [functional currency] of a bank or company; usually their domestic currency. For example, a British bank may use GBP as a base currency for accounting, because all profits and losses are converted to sterling. If a EUR/USD position is closed out with a profit in USD by a British bank, then the *rate-to-base* will be expressed as a GBP/USD rate. This ambiguity leads many market participants to use the expressions *currency 1* (CCY1) and *currency 2* (CCY2), where one unit of CCY1 equals the quoted number of units of CCY2.

The Majors

The most traded pairs of currencies in the world are called the *Majors*. They constitute the largest share of the foreign exchange market, about 85%, and therefore they exhibit high market liquidity.

The Majors are: EUR/USD, USD/JPY, GBP/USD, AUD/USD, USD/CHF, NZD/USD and USD/CAD.

Nicknames

In everyday foreign exchange market trading and news reporting, the currency pairs are often referred to by nicknames rather than their symbolic nomenclature. These are often reminiscent of national or geographic connotations. The GBP/USD pairing is known by traders as *cable* (also *the cable*), which has its origins from the time when a communications cable under the Atlantic Ocean synchronized the GBP/USD quote between the London and New York markets. GBP is also referred to by traders as *quid*. The following nicknames are common: "Swissy" or "Euro-Swissy" for EUR/CHF, *Fiber* for EUR/USD, *Chunnel* for EUR/GBP, *Loonie* and *The Funds* for USD/CAD, *Aussie* for AUD/USD, *Gopher* for USD/JPY, *Guppy* for GBP/JPY, *Yuppy* for EUR/JPY, and *Kiwi* or *The Bird* for the New Zealand Dollar NZD/USD pairing. New innovations include *Barney* for USD/RUB and *Betty* for EUR/RUB after the fictional characters the Rubbles in The Flintstones. Additionally, exotic pairs have earned more esoteric nicknames such as "Glock" for COP/SGN after the service pistol often carried by police officers (the ticker can be viewed as (Cop's G(u)n)). Nicknames vary between the trading centers in New York, London, and Tokyo. Care should be taken with the use of 'Betty, for EUR/RUB as, in London markets 'Betty' is used as cockney slang for Cable as in Betty Grable = Cable = GBP/USD.

Cross Pairs

The currency pairs that do not involve USD are called *cross currency pairs*, such as GBP/JPY. Pairs that involve the euro are often called *euro crosses*, such as EUR/GBP.

Trading

Currencies are traded in fixed contract sizes, specifically called lot sizes, or multiples thereof. The standard lot size is 100,000 units of the base currency. Many retail trading firms also offer 10,000-unit (mini lot) trading accounts and a few even 1,000-unit (micro lot).

The officially quoted rate is a spot price. In a trading market however, currencies are offered for sale at an offering price (the *ask price*), and traders looking to buy a position seek to do so at their *bid price*, which is always lower or equal to the asking price. This price differential is known as the *spread*. For example, if the quotation of EUR/USD is 1.3607/1.3609, then the spread is USD 0.0002, or 2 pips. In general, markets with high liquidity exhibit smaller spreads than less frequently traded markets.

The spread offered to a retail customer with an account at a brokerage firm, rather than a large international forex market maker, is larger and varies between brokerages. Brokerages typically increase the spread they receive from their market providers as compensation for their service to the end customer, rather than charge a transaction fee. A bureau de change usually has spreads that are even larger.

Example: consider EUR/USD currency pair traded at a quotation of 1.33

In the above case, someone buying 1 EUR will have to pay 1.33 USD; conversely one selling 1 EUR will receive 1.33 USD (assuming no FX spread). Forex traders buy EUR/USD pair if they believe that the Euro would increase in value relative to the US dollar, buying EUR/USD pair; this way is called going long on the pair; conversely, would sell EUR/USD pair, called going short on the pair, if they believe the value of the Euro will go down relative to the US dollar. A pair is depicted only one way and never reversed for the purpose of a trade, but a buy or sell function is used at initiation of a trade. Buy a pair if bullish on the first position as compared to the second of the pair; conversely, sell if bearish on the first as compared to the second.

Cross Rates

Cross rates for spot quotations have been discussed in the Session 13.2. However, at the cost of repetition, the cross rate calculation is given here, as it forms basis for calculation of forward cross rates.

A spot cross rate is a rate which can be calculated from two other spot rates. Suppose USDCAD (US dollar and Canadian Dollar) rate is given along with and an USDAUD (US Dollar and Aussie Dollar) quotation.

USDCAD = 1.1546 (CAD 1.1546 is equal to 1 USD).

CADAUD= 1.0421 (AUD of 1.3421 is equal to 1 CAD).

The USDAUD rate = (CAD1.1546/ USD) * (1.0421AUD/1 CAD) = AUD1.2032/USD.

However, in real life, the dealers give bid-ask spread for currency pair. With bid-ask spread, the cross calculation becomes little complex.

Cross Rate Calculation with bid-ask Spared

USDCAD bid-ask rate is given along with and USDAUD bid-rate is given in in Table 3.9. The rates for CADAUD (or AUDCAD) can be calculated from the above two quotes.

Table 3.9: Spot r Bid-Ask Rates

USDCAD		USDAUD	
Bid	Ask	Bid	Ask
1.1641	1.1646	1.2948	1.2956

From the above quotations, cross rate between AUD/CAD can be calculated as follows

- Bank buys 1USD and pays (sells) 1.1641 CAD.
- Bank sells 1 USD and receives (buys)1.1646 CAD.
- Bank buys 1 USD and pays (sells) 1.2948 AUD.
- Bank sells 1 USD and receives(buys) 1.2956 AU.

To get the bid rate for CADAUD (CAD as base currency and AUD as quote currency), the bank must sell AUD and buy CAD. This is achieved in two steps. That is:

- The bank must sell AUD and buy USD.
- Simultaneously sell USD and buy CAD.

This indicates that 1.1646 CAD = 1.2948 AUD. In other words, 1 CAD = 1.1118 AUD.

To get the ask rate for CADAUD, the bank must sell CAD and buy AUD. This is achieved in two steps ie. the bank must sell CAD buy USD and simultaneously sell USD and buy AUD.

This means that 1.1641 CAD = 1.2956 AUD. In other words, 1 CAD = 1.1129 AUD.

Hence the cross rate, given in Table 3.10 is:

Table 3.10:CADAUD cross rates

Bid	Ask
1.1118	1.1129

Forward Cross Rates

Cross rates for different maturities can be found out in the similar manner like the spot cross rates. The following table, Table 3.11 lists the actual rates(forward contracts rates for) different maturities. From these rates, the cross rates have been calculated and listed in Table 3.12.

Table 3.11 Outright Quotations for USD/INR and USD/ZAR(*)

	USDINR		USDRAND	
	Bid Rate	Ask Rate	Bid Rate	Ask Rate
Spot	47.0725	47.0745	7.5937	7.5950
1 week	47.0750	47.0775	7.5918	7.5938
2 weeks	47.0795	47.0835	7.5887	7.5911
1 month	47.0840	47.0890	7.5812	7.5860
2 months	47.0900	47.0965	7.5775	7.5838

Table 3.12 INR/ZAR(*) Cross Rates for different forward periods

INRRAND	Bid	Ask
spot	0.16131	0.16135
1 week	0.16126	0.16131
2 weeks	0.16118	0.16124
1 month	0.16100	0.16112
2 months	0.16089	0.16105

(*): ZAR is the currency of South Africa. It is known as South African Rand but has a ISO code of ZAR.

Cross rate calculation becomes necessity when two currency pair exchange rate is not quoted by a dealer or bank. For example, an Indian company imports textile yarns from South Africa for which the payment has to be made in ZAR. As none of the Indian banks directly offer, INRZAR quotations, the exporter has to sell INR and buy USD and then sell USD and buy ZAR to make the payment. As most currencies of the world are quoted with either Euro/USD/Pound sterling, these currencies form one leg of trade in any cross currency transaction.

To summarize, for many infrequently traded currencies pairs, cross rates are the only sources of rate quotations as no dealer/bank directly offers quote.

Cross Rates and Triangular Arbitrage

Cross rates are the exchange rates of 1 currency with other currencies, and those currencies with each other. Cross rates are equalized among all currencies through a process called triangular arbitrage. As different forex dealers quote different rates for a given currency pair at a given point of time, it provides forex traders with arbitrage opportunity. Hence this is known as "intermarket arbitrage".

Cross rate calculations helps in identifying the intermarket arbitrage opportunity. The following table, Table 3.13, indicates the list of exchange rates for currency pair. From these pairs, cross rates can be calculated.

TABLE 3.13: Currency Rates

	US $	¥en	Euro	Can $	UK £	Aust $	SFranc
1 US $	1.0	92.1700	0.7161	1.1633	0.6218	1.2924	1.0843
1 ¥en	0.010843	1.0	0.007768	0.012614	0.006741	0.014014	0.011758
1 Euro	1.3958	128.6900	1.0	**1.6244**	0.8682	1.8052	1.5138
1 Can $	0.8592	79.2100	0.6153	1.0	0.5344	1.1106	0.9318
1 UK £	1.6072	148.1600	1.1512	1.8699	1.0	2.0779	1.7429
1 Aust $	0.7732	71.2900	0.5538	0.8997	0.4809	1.0	0.8383
1 SFranc	0.9218	85.0000	0.6602	1.0726	0.5735	1.1919	1.0

Now let us calculate the cross rate for Can$ and US$ by comparing Can$-Euro and Euro-US$ rates.

- 1 Can $ = 0.8592 US $.
- 1 Euro = 1.3958 US$.
- From these two rates, the cross rate for Can $/Euro can be calculated.

Implied Cross Rates:

- 1 Euro = 1.3958 US$.

$$1\text{US\$} = \frac{1}{0.8592}\text{Can\$} = 1.16387\,\text{Can\$}$$

- 1 Euro = 1.3958*1.16387 Can$ = 1.6245 Can$.

Can$1.6245/Euro is known as the implied cross rate.

The implied cross rate calculated in this manner is compared with the actual rate quoted by another dealer or bank. If these two are rates are significantly different, then arbitrage opportunity arises.

The actual Euro/Can$ rate given in Table 3.13 is Can$1.6244/Euro. The implied cross rate is very close to the actual rate. The minor difference arises as the transaction cost and bid-ask spread have not been factored into the calculation of implied cross rates.

Suppose there is a significant difference between the implied cross rate and the actual rate. This will lead to arbitrage profit.

Let us take a numerical example, to understand how triangular arbitrage happens. Three different banks are quoting spot rates for three currency pairs given below.

- Bank of Japan quotes : St = 100 JPY/USD.
- Bank of America quotes: St = 1.60 USD/GBP.
- Bank of England quotes St = 140 JPY/GBP.

If we consider the first two quotes, then JPY/GBP quote should be at 160 JPY/GBP. However bank of England quotes 140 JPY/GBP. It indicates that Bank of England is undervaluing GBP.

The triangular arbitrage happens:

- Borrow 100 USD.
- Convert it to 10000 JPY at Bank of Japan.
- Convert 10,000 JPY to GBP at Bank of England. Receive 71.428 GBP.
- Convert 71.428 GBP to USD at Bank of America. Receive 114.285 USD.

Profit of 14.285 USD before adjusting for USD borrowing cost.

In real life, the rates are quoted with bid-ask spread. The triangular arbitrage with bid and ask spread is given in Table 3.14.

Table 3.14: Bid-ask rates offered by three banks		
	Bid	**Ask**
Bank A (GBP/USD)	1.60	1.61
Bank B (MYR/USD)	0.2	0.202
Bank C (GBP/MYR)	8.10	8.20

MYR : Malaysian Ringgit

With the rate given in Table 3.15, the triangular arbitrage happens in three steps:

- Sell USD 1.61 and Receive 1 GBP at Bank A ask rate.
- Sell 1 GBP and Receive 8.10 MYR at Bank C bid rate.
- Sell 8.10 MYR and receive $ 1.62 at Bank B bid rate.

Arbitrage profit is $0.01 for every 1 USD investments. The investor takes full circle – sell USD to receive USD to get the benefit of triangular arbitrage.

The triangular arbitrage can also happen:

- Sell 1 MYR, receive 0.2 USD.
- Sell 0.2 USD and buy 0.124224 GBP (Sell 1.61USD and receive 1 GBP).
- Sell 0.124224 GBP and receive 1.0062 MYR.

Hence for every 1 MYR investment, the trader would be bale to make a profit of MYR 0.006.

Can arbitrage happen, if the investors starts from GBP? This needs to be found out!

Exploiting Triangular arbitrage opportunity is a favourite hunting ground for forex traders. In fact, forex traders buy software packages which analyses real time bid-ask quotations offered by forex dealers, identify arbitrage opportunity and place order to benefit from the opportunity without any human intervention.

Interest Rate Arbitrage

Arbitrage opportunities available to forex traders are known as the inte rmarket arbitrage. Forex traders regular make arbitrage profit though interest rate differential in two countries. This is known as "interest rate arbitrage".

Interest rate arbitrage works like this:

Spot rate £1 = €1.6140. Interest rate for coming 12 months is 5.5% for Pound Sterling and 3.75% for Euro. Suppose a bank quotes a 3 month forward rate as £1 = €1.5970. Now let us see whether there exist an arbitrage opportunity or not.

For example, a trader borrows £100,000 for 3 months. He has to pay £101,375 after 3-months. He converts £100,000 to € at the spot rate. He receives €161400. Invests €161400 at 3.75% interest rate for 3 months. He earns € 162913. He converts euro proceeding to Pound sterling at the 3 month forward rate of £1 = €1.5970. He earns £102,012. He returns £101,375and makes a arbitrage profit of £636.

This profit opportunity will entice many traders to borrow Pound Sterling, sell Pound sterling to buy Euro, invest in Euro and sell Euro forward to buy Pound Sterling. This will ensure that the arbitrage opportunity vanishes quickly. In fact, with spot bid £1 = €1.6140, interest rate for coming 12 months is 5.5% for Pound Sterling and 3.75% for Euro, the 3month forward rate should have been £1 = €1.6070 and not £1 = €1.5970.

Interest rate arbitrage opportunity forms the core of interest rate parity and covered interest rate arbitrage. This aspect will be discussed in greater detail in later sessions.

Covered Interest Arbitrage

Covered interest arbitrage is an arbitrage trading strategy whereby an investor capitalizes on the interest rate differential between two countries by using a forward contract to *cover* (eliminate exposure to) exchange rate risk. Using forward contracts enables arbitrageurs such as individual investors or banks to make use of the forward premium (or discount) to earn a riskless profit from discrepancies between two countries' interest rates. The opportunity to earn riskless profits arises from the reality that the interest rate parity condition does not constantly hold. When spot and forward exchange rate markets are not in a state of equilibrium, investors will no longer be indifferent among the available interest rates in two countries and will invest in whichever currency offers a higher rate of return. Economists have discovered various factors which affect the occurrence of deviations from covered interest rate parity and the fleeting nature of covered interest arbitrage opportunities, such as differing characteristics of assets, varying frequencies of time series data, and the transaction costs associated with arbitrage trading strategies.

Mechanics of Covered Interest Arbitrage

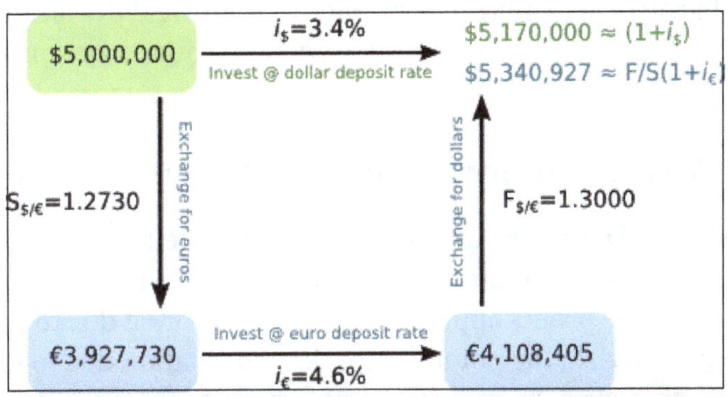

A visual representation of a simplified covered interest arbitrage scenario, ignoring compounding interest. In this numerical example the arbitrageur is guaranteed to do better than would be achieved by investing domestically.

An arbitrageur executes a covered interest arbitrage strategy by exchanging domestic currency for foreign currency at the current spot exchange rate, then investing the foreign currency at the foreign interest rate. Simultaneously, the arbitrageur negotiates a forward contract to sell the amount of the future value of the foreign investment at a delivery date consistent with the foreign investment's maturity date, to receive domestic currency in exchange for the foreign-currency funds.

For example, as per the chart at right consider that an investor with $5,000,000 USD is considering whether to invest abroad using a covered interest arbitrage strategy or to invest domestically. The dollar deposit interest rate is 3.4% in the United States, while the euro deposit rate is 4.6% in the euro area. The current spot exchange rate is 1.2730 $/€ and the six-month forward exchange rate is 1.3000 $/€. For simplicity, the example ignores compounding interest. Investing $5,000,000 USD domestically at 3.4% for six months ignoring compounding, will result in a future value of $5,085,000 USD. However, exchanging $5,000,000 dollars for euros today, investing those euros at 4.6% for six months ignoring compounding, and exchanging the future value of euros for dollars at the forward exchange rate (on the delivery date negotiated in the forward contract), will result in $5,223,488 USD, implying that investing abroad using covered interest arbitrage is the superior alternative.

Effect of Arbitrage

If there were no impediments, such as transaction costs, to covered interest arbitrage, then any opportunity, however minuscule, to profit from it would immediately be exploited by many financial market participants, and the resulting pressure on domestic and forward interest rates and the forward exchange rate premium would cause one or more of these to change virtually instantaneously to eliminate the opportunity. In fact, the anticipation of such arbitrage leading to such market changes would cause these three variables to align to prevent any arbitrage opportunities from even arising in the first place: incipient arbitrage can have the same effect, but sooner, as actual arbitrage. Thus any evidence of empirical deviations from covered interest parity would have to be explained on the grounds of some friction in the financial markets.

Evidence for Covered Interest Arbitrage Opportunities

Economists Robert M. Dunn, Jr. and John H. Mutti note that financial markets may generate data inconsistent with interest rate parity, and that cases in which significant covered interest arbitrage profits appeared feasible were often due to assets not sharing the same perceptions of risk, the potential for double taxation due to differing policies, and investors' concerns over the imposition of foreign exchange controls cumbersome to the enforcement of forward contracts. Some covered interest arbitrage opportunities have appeared to exist when exchange rates and interest rates were collected for different periods; for example, the use of daily interest rates and daily closing exchange rates could render the illusion that arbitrage profits exist. Economists have suggested an array of other factors to account for observed deviations from interest rate parity, such as differing tax treatment, differing risks, government foreign exchange controls, supply or demand inelasticity, transaction costs, and time differentials between observing and executing arbitrage opportunities. Economists Jacob Frenkel and Richard M. Levich investigated the performance of covered interest arbitrage strategies during the 1970s' flexible exchange rate regime by examining transaction costs and differentials between observing and executing arbitrage opportunities. Using weekly data, they estimated transaction costs and evaluated their role in explaining deviations from interest rate parity and found that most deviations could be explained by transaction costs. However, accommodating transaction costs did not explain observed deviations from covered interest rate parity between treasury bills in the United States and United Kingdom. Frenkel and Levich found that executing such transactions resulted in only illusory opportunities for arbitrage profits, and that in each execution the mean percentage of profit decreased such that there was no statistically significant difference from zero profitability. Frenkel and Levich concluded that unexploited opportunities for profit do not exist in covered interest arbitrage.

Using a time series dataset of daily spot and forward USD/JPY exchange rates and same-maturity short-term interest rates in both the United States and Japan, economists Johnathan A. Batten and Peter G. Szilagyi analyzed the sensitivity of forward market price differentials to short-term interest rate differentials. The researchers found evidence for substantial variation in covered interest rate parity deviations from equilibrium, attributed to transaction costs and market segmentation. They found that such deviations and arbitrage opportunities diminished significantly nearly to a point of elimination by the year 2000. Batten and Szilagyi point out that the modern reliance on electronic trading platforms and real-time equilibrium prices appear to account for the removal of the historical scale and scope of covered interest arbitrage opportunities. Further investigation of the deviations uncovered a long-term dependence, found to be consistent with other evidence of temporal long-term dependencies identified in asset returns from other financial markets including currencies, stocks, and commodities.

Economists Wai-Ming Fong, Giorgio Valente, and Joseph K.W. Fung, examined the relationship of covered interest rate parity arbitrage opportunities with market liquidity and credit risk using a dataset of tick-by-tick spot and forward exchange rate quotes for the Hong Kong dollar in relation to the United States dollar. Their empirical analysis demonstrates that positive deviations from covered interest rate parity indeed compensate for liquidity and credit risk. After accounting for these risk premia, the researchers demonstrated that small residual arbitrage profits accrue only to those arbitrageurs capable of negotiating low transaction costs.

Forward Contract

In finance, a forward contract or simply a forward is a non-standardized contract between two communities to buy or to sell an asset at a specified time at a price agreed upon today, making it a type of derivative instrument. The party agreeing to buy the underlying asset in the future assumes a long position, and the party agreeing to sell the asset in the future assumes a short position.

A closely related contract is a futures contract; they differ in certain respects. Forward contracts are very similar to futures contracts, except they are not exchange-traded, or defined on standardized assets. Forwards also typically have no interim partial settlements or "true-ups" in margin requirements like futures – such that the parties do not exchange additional property securing the party at gain and the entire unrealized gain or loss builds up while the contract is open. However, being traded over the counter (OTC), forward contracts specification can be customized and may include mark-to-market and daily margin calls. Hence, a forward contract arrangement might call for the loss party to pledge collateral or additional collateral to better secure the party at gain. In other words, the terms of the forward contract will determine the collateral calls based upon certain "trigger" events relevant to a particular counterparty such as among other things, credit ratings, value of assets under management or redemptions over a specific time frame, e.g., quarterly, annually, etc.

Payoffs

The value of a forward position *at maturity* depends on the relationship between the delivery price (K) and the underlying price (S_T) at that time.

- For a long position this payoff is: $f_T = S_T - K$.
- For a short position, it is: $f_T = K - S_T$.

Since the final value (at maturity) of a forward position depends on the spot price which will then be prevailing, this contract can be viewed, from a purely financial point of view, as *"a bet on the future spot price".*

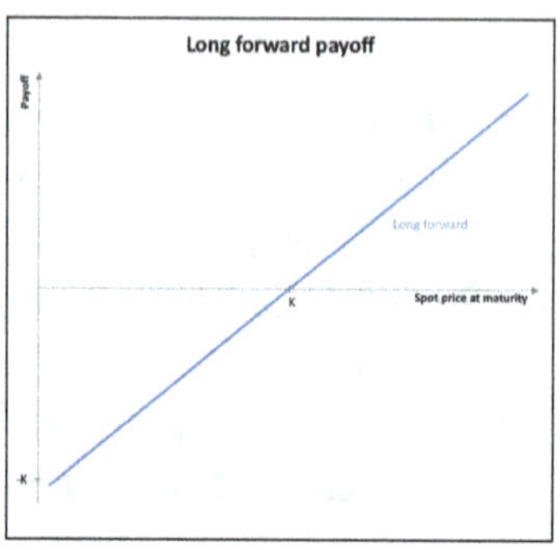

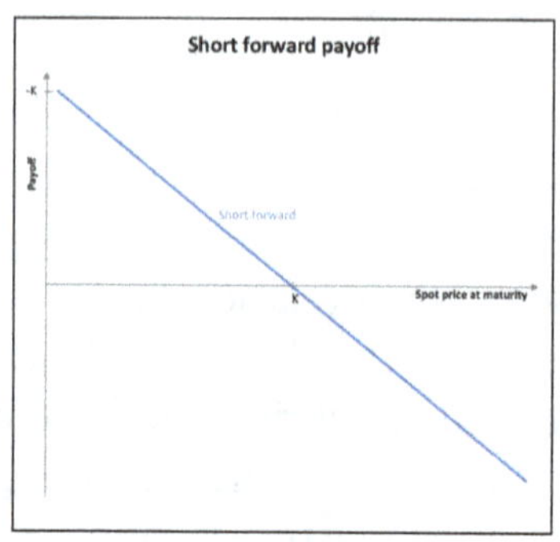

How a Forward Contract Works

Suppose that Bob wants to buy a house a year from now. At the same time, suppose that Andy currently owns a $100,000 house that he wishes to sell a year from now. Both parties could enter into a forward contract with each other. Suppose that they both agree on the sale price in one year's time of $104,000 (more below on why the sale price should be this amount). Andy and Bob have entered into a forward contract. Bob, because he is buying the underlying, is said to have entered a long forward contract. Conversely, Andy will have the short forward contract.

At the end of one year, suppose that the current market valuation of Andy's house is $110,000. Then, because Andy is obliged to sell to Bob for only $104,000, Bob will make a profit of $6,000. To see why this is so, one needs only to recognize that Bob can buy from Andy for $104,000 and immediately sell to the market for $110,000. Bob has made the difference in profit. In contrast, Andy has made a potential loss of $6,000, and an actual profit of $4,000.

The similar situation works among currency forwards, in which one party opens a forward contract to buy or sell a currency (ex. a contract to buy Canadian dollars) to expire/settle at a future date, as they do not wish to be exposed to exchange rate/currency risk over a period of time. As the exchange rate between U.S. dollars and Canadian dollars fluctuates between the trade date and the earlier of the date at which the contract is closed or the expiration date, one party gains and the counterparty loses as one currency strengthens against the other. Sometimes, the buy forward is opened because the investor will actually need Canadian dollars at a future date such as to pay a debt owed that is denominated in Canadian dollars. Other times, the party opening a forward does so, not because they need Canadian dollars nor because they are hedging currency risk, but because they are speculating on the currency, expecting the exchange rate to move favorably to generate a gain on closing the contract.

In a currency forward, the notional amounts of currencies are specified (ex: a contract to buy $100 million Canadian dollars equivalent to, say $75.2 million USD at the current rate—these two amounts are called the notional amount(s)). While the notional amount or reference amount may be a large number, the cost or margin requirement to command or open such a contract is considerably less than that amount, which refers to the leverage created, which is typical in derivative contracts.

Example of How Forward Prices Should be Agreed Upon

Continuing on the example above, suppose now that the initial price of Andy's house is $100,000 and that Bob enters into a forward contract to buy the house one year from today. But since Andy knows that he can immediately sell for $100,000 and place the proceeds in the bank, he wants to be compensated for the delayed sale. Suppose that the risk free rate of return R (the bank rate) for one year is 4%. Then the money in the bank would grow to $104,000, risk free. So Andy would want at least $104,000 one year from now for the contract to be worthwhile for him – the opportunity cost will be covered.

Spot–forward Parity

For liquid assets ("tradeables"), spot–forward parity provides the link between the spot market and the forward market. It describes the relationship between the spot and forward price of the underlying asset in a forward contract. While the overall effect can be described as the *cost of carry*, this effect can be broken down into different components, specifically whether the asset:

- pays income, and if so whether this is on a discrete or continuous basis.
- Incurs storage costs.

- Is regarded as:
    - An *investment asset*, i.e. an asset held primarily for investment purposes (e.g. gold, financial securities).
    - Or a *consumption asset*, i.e. an asset held primarily for consumption (e.g. oil, iron ore etc.)

Investment Assets

For an asset that provides no income, the relationship between the current forward (F_0) and spot (S_0) prices is,

$$F_0 = S_0 e^{rT}$$

where r is the continuously compounded risk free rate of return, and *T* is the time to maturity. The intuition behind this result is that given you want to own the asset at time *T*, there should be no difference in a perfect capital market between buying the asset today and holding it and buying the forward contract and taking delivery. Thus, both approaches must cost the same in present value terms. For an arbitrage proof of why this is the case.

For an asset that pays known income, the relationship becomes:

- Discrete: $F_0 = (S_0 - I)e^{rT}$
- Continuous: $F_0 = S_0 e^{(r-q)T}$

where $I =$ the present value of the discrete income at time $t_0 < T$, and q%p.a. is the continuously compounded dividend yield over the life of the contract. The intuition is that when an asset pays income, there is a benefit to holding the asset rather than the forward because you get to receive this income. Hence the income (I or q) must be subtracted to reflect this benefit. An example of an asset which pays discrete income might be a stock, and an example of an asset which pays a continuous yield might be a foreign currency or a stock index.

For investment assets which are commodities, such as gold and silver, storage costs must also be considered. Storage costs can be treated as 'negative income', and like income can be discrete or continuous. Hence with storage costs, the relationship becomes:

- Discrete: $F_0 = (S_0 + U)e^{rT}$
- Continuous: $F_0 = S_0 e^{(r+u)T}$

where $U =$ the present value of the discrete storage cost at time $t_0 < T$, and u%p.a. is the continuously compounded storage cost where it is proportional to the price of the commodity, and is hence a 'negative yield'. The intuition here is that because storage costs make the final price higher, we have to add them to the spot price.

Consumption Assets

Consumption assets are typically raw material commodities which are used as a source of energy or in a production process, for example crude oil or iron ore. Users of these consumption commodities may feel that there is a benefit from physically holding the asset in inventory as opposed to holding a forward on the asset. These benefits include the ability to "profit from" (hedge against) temporary shortages and the ability to keep a production process running, and are referred to as the *convenience yield*. Thus, for consumption assets, the spot-forward relationship is:

- Discrete storage costs: $F_0 = (S_0 + U)e^{(r-y)T}$
- Continuous storage costs: $F_0 = S_0 e^{(r+u-y)T}$

where y%p.a. is the convenience yield over the life of the contract. Since the convenience yield provides a benefit to the holder of the asset but not the holder of the forward, it can be modelled as a type of 'dividend yield'. However, it is important to note that the convenience yield is a non cash item, but rather reflects the market's expectations concerning future availability of the commodity. If users have low inventories of the commodity, this implies a greater chance of shortage, which means a higher convenience yield. The opposite is true when high inventories exist.

Cost of Carry

The relationship between the spot and forward price of an asset reflects the net cost of holding (or carrying) that asset relative to holding the forward. Thus, all of the costs and benefits above can be summarised as the *cost of carry*, c. Hence,

- Discrete: $F_0 = (S_0 + U - I)e^{(r-y)T}$
- Continuous: $F_0 = S_0 e^{cT}$, where $c = r - q + u - y$.

Relationship between the Forward Price and the Expected Future Spot Price

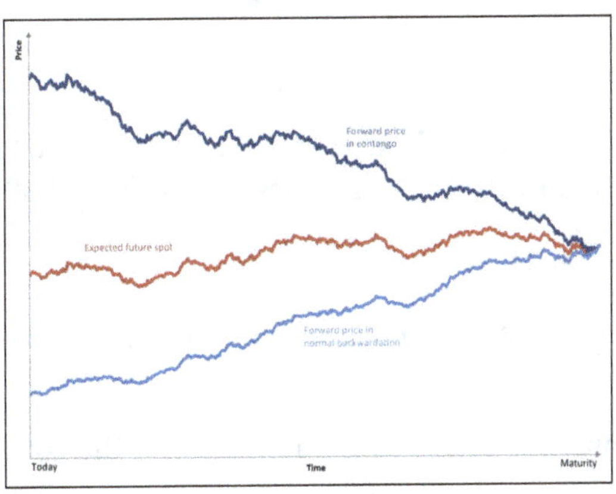

The market's opinion about what the spot price of an asset will be in the future is the *expected future spot price*. Hence, a key question is whether or not the current forward price actually predicts the respective spot price in the future. There are a number of different hypotheses which try to explain the relationship between the current forward price, F_0 and the expected future spot price, $E(S_T)$.

The economists John Maynard Keynes and John Hicks argued that in general, the natural hedgers of a commodity are those who wish to sell the commodity at a future point in time. Thus, hedgers will collectively hold a net short position in the forward market. The other side of these contracts are held by speculators, who must therefore hold a net long position. Hedgers are interested in reducing risk, and thus will accept losing money on their forward contracts. Speculators on the other hand, are interested in making a profit, and will hence only enter the contracts if they *expect* to make money. Thus, if speculators are holding a net long position, it must be the case that the expected future spot price is greater than the forward price.

In other words, the expected payoff to the speculator at maturity is:

$E(S_T - K) = E(S_T) - K$, where K is the delivery price at maturity

Thus, if the speculators expect to profit,

$$E(S_T) - K > 0$$

$$E(S_T) > K$$

$E(S_T) > F_0$, as $K = F_0$ when they enter the contract

This market situation, where $E(S_T) > F_0$, is referred to as normal backwardation. Forward/futures prices converge with the spot price at maturity, as can be seen from the previous relationships by letting T go to 0; then normal backwardation implies that futures prices for a certain maturity are increasing over time. The opposite situation, where $E(S_T) < F_0$, is referred to as contango. Likewise, contango implies that futures prices for a certain maturity are falling over time.

Rational Pricing

If S_t is the spot price of an asset at time t, and r is the continuously compounded rate, then the forward price at a future time T must satisfy $F_{t,T} = S_t e^{r(T-t)}$.

To prove this, suppose not. Then we have two possible cases.

Case 1: Suppose that $F_{t,T} > S_t e^{r(T-t)}$. Then an investor can execute the following trades at time t:

1. go to the bank and get a loan with amount S_t at the continuously compounded rate r;

2. with this money from the bank, buy one unit of asset for S_t;

3. enter into one short forward contract costing 0. A short forward contract means that the investor owes the counterparty the asset at time T.

The initial cost of the trades at the initial time sum to zero.

At time T the investor can reverse the trades that were executed at time t. Specifically, and mirroring the trades 1., 2. and 3. the investor:

1. 'repays the loan to the bank. The inflow to the investor is $-S_t e^{r(T-t)}$;

2. 'settles the short forward contract by selling the asset for $F_{t,T}$. The cash inflow to the investor is now $F_{t,T}$ because the buyer receives S_T from the investor.

The sum of the inflows in 1.' and 2.' equals $F_{t,T} - S_t e^{r(T-t)}$, which by hypothesis, is positive. This is an arbitrage profit. Consequently, and assuming that the non-arbitrage condition holds, we have a contradiction. This is called a cash and carry arbitrage because you "carry" the asset until maturity.

Case 2: Suppose that $F_{t,T} < S_t e^{r(T-t)}$. Then an investor can do the reverse of what he has done above in case 1. But if you look at the convenience yield page, you will see that if there are finite assets/inventory, the reverse cash and carry arbitrage is not always possible. It would depend on the elasticity of demand for forward contracts and such like.

Extensions to the Forward Pricing Formula

Suppose that $FV_T(X)$ is the time value of cash flows *X* at the contract expiration time T. The forward price is then given by the formula:

$$F_{t,T} = S_t e^{r(T-t)} - FV_T(\text{all cash flows over the life of the contract})$$

The cash flows can be in the form of dividends from the asset, or costs of maintaining the asset.

If these price relationships do not hold, there is an arbitrage opportunity for a riskless profit similar to that discussed above. One implication of this is that the presence of a forward market will force spot prices to reflect current expectations of future prices. As a result, the forward price for nonperishable commodities, securities or currency is no more a predictor of future price than the spot price is - the relationship between forward and spot prices is driven by interest rates. For perishable commodities, arbitrage does not have this.

The above forward pricing formula can also be written as:

$$F_{t,T} = (S_t - I_t)e^{r(T-t)}$$

Where I_t is the time *t* value of all cash flows over the life of the contract.

Theories of Why a Forward Contract Exists

Allaz and Vila (1993) suggest that there is also a strategic reason (in an imperfect competitive environment) for the existence of forward trading, that is, forward trading can be used even in a world without uncertainty. This is due to firms having Stackelberg incentives to anticipate their production through forward contracts.

Uncovered Interest Arbitrage

Uncovered interest arbitrage is an arbitrage trading strategy whereby an investor capitalizes on the interest rate differential between two countries. Unlike covered interest arbitrage, uncovered interest arbitrage involves no hedging of foreign exchange risk with the use of forward contracts or any other contract. The strategy involves risk, as an investor exposed to exchange rate fluctuations is speculating that exchange rates will remain favorable enough for arbitrage to be profitable. The opportunity to earn profits arises from the reality that the uncovered interest rate parity condition does not constantly hold—that is, the interest rate on investments in one country's currency does not always equal the interest rate on foreign-currency investments plus the rate of appreciation that is expected for the foreign currency relative to the domestic currency. When a discrepancy between these occurs, investors who are willing to take on risk will not be indifferent between the two possible locations of investment, and will invest in whichever currency is expected to offer a higher rate of return including currency exchange gains or losses (perhaps adjusted for a risk premium).

Mechanics of Uncovered Interest Arbitrage

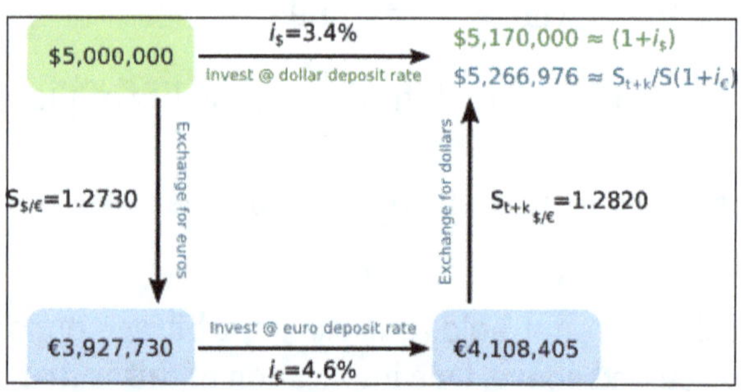

A visual representation of a simplified uncovered interest arbitrage scenario, ignoring compounding interest.

An arbitrageur executes an uncovered interest arbitrage strategy by exchanging domestic currency for foreign currency at the current spot exchange rate, then investing the foreign currency at the foreign interest rate, and at the end of the investment term using the spot foreign exchange market to convert back to the original currency. The risk arises from the fact that the future spot exchange rate for the currencies is not known with certainty when the strategy is chosen.

For example, consider that an investor with $5,000,000 USD is considering whether to invest abroad using an uncovered interest arbitrage strategy or to invest domestically. The dollar deposit interest rate is 3.4% in the United States, while the euro deposit rate is 4.6% in the euro area. The current spot exchange rate is 1.2730 $/€. For simplicity, the example ignores compounding interest. Investing $5,000,000 USD domestically at 3.4% for six months ignoring compounding, will result in a future value of $5,170,000 USD. However, exchanging $5,000,000 dollars for euros today, investing those euros at 4.6% for six months ignoring compounding, and exchanging the future value of euros for dollars at the future spot exchange rate (which for this example is 1.2820 $/€), will result in $5,266,976 USD, implying that investing abroad using uncovered interest arbitrage is the superior alternative if the future spot exchange rate turns out to be favorable.

Triangular Arbitrage

Triangular arbitrage (also referred to as cross currency arbitrage or three-point arbitrage) is the act of exploiting an arbitrage opportunity resulting from a pricing discrepancy among three different currencies in the foreign exchange market. A triangular arbitrage strategy involves three trades, exchanging the initial currency for a second, the second currency for a third, and the third currency for the initial. During the second trade, the arbitrageur locks in a zero-risk profit from the discrepancy that exists when the market cross exchange rate is not aligned with the implicit cross exchange rate. A profitable trade is only possible if there exist market imperfections. Profitable triangular arbitrage is very rarely possible because when such opportunities arise, traders execute trades that take advantage of the imperfections and prices adjust up or down until the opportunity disappears.

Cross Exchange Rate Discrepancies

Triangular arbitrage opportunities may only exist when a bank's quoted exchange rate is not equal to the market's implicit cross exchange rate. The following equation represents the calculation of an implicit cross exchange rate, the exchange rate one would expect in the market as implied from the ratio of two currencies other than the base currency.

$$S_{a/\$} = S_{a/b} S_{b/\$}$$

where

- $S_{a/\$}$ is the implicit cross exchange rate for dollars in terms of currency *a*.
- $S_{a/b}$ is the quoted market cross exchange rate for b in terms of currency *a*.
- $S_{b/\$}$ is the quoted market cross exchange rate for dollars in terms of currency *b*.

If the market cross exchange rate quoted by a bank is equal to the implicit cross exchange rate as implied from the exchange rates of other currencies, then a no-arbitrage condition is sustained. However, if an inequality exists between the market cross exchange rate,, $S_{a/\$}$ and the implicit cross exchange rate,, $_{a/b}\,S_{b/\$}$ then there exists an opportunity for arbitrage profits on the difference between the two exchange rates.

Mechanics of Triangular Arbitrage

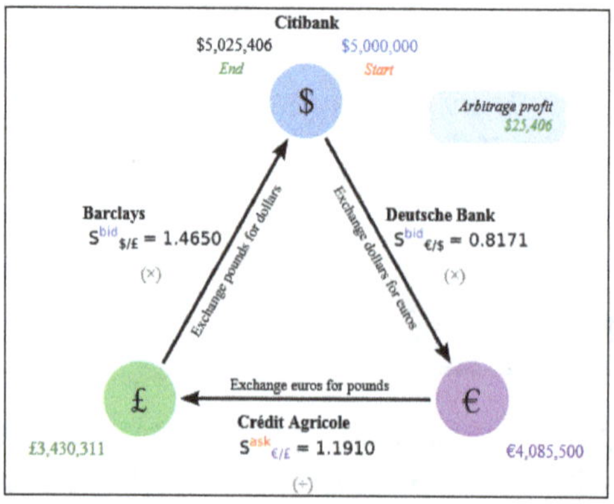

A visual representation of a realistic triangular arbitrage scenario, using sample bid and ask prices quoted by international banks.

Some international banks serve as market makers between currencies by narrowing their bid-ask spread more than the bid-ask spread of the implicit cross exchange rate. However, the bid and ask prices of the implicit cross exchange rate naturally discipline market makers. When banks' quoted exchange rates move out of alignment with cross exchange rates, any banks or traders who detect the discrepancy have an opportunity to earn arbitrage profits via a triangular arbitrage strategy. To execute a triangular arbitrage trading strategy, a bank would calculate cross exchange rates and compare them with exchange rates quoted by other banks to identify a pricing discrepancy.

For example, Citibank detects that Deutsche Bank is quoting dollars at a bid price of 0.8171 €/$, and that Barclays is quoting pounds at a bid price of 1.4650 $/£ (Deutsche Bank and Barclays are in other words willing to buy those currencies at those prices). Citibank itself is quoting the same prices for these two exchange rates. A trader at Citibank then sees that Crédit Agricole is quoting pounds at an ask price of 1.1910 €/£ (in other words it is willing to sell pounds at that price). While the quoted market cross exchange rate is 1.1910 €/£, Citibank's trader realizes that the implicit cross exchange rate is 1.1971 €/£ (by calculating 1.4650 × 0.8171 = 1.1971), meaning that Crédit Agricole has narrowed its bid-ask spread to serve as a market maker between the euro and the pound. Although the market suggests the implicit cross exchange rate should be 1.1971 euros per pound, Crédit Agricole is selling pounds at a lower price of 1.1910 euros. Citibank's trader can hastily exercise triangular arbitrage by exchanging dollars for euros with Deutsche Bank, then exchanging euros for pounds with Crédit Agricole, and finally exchanging pounds for dollars with Barclays. The following steps illustrate the triangular arbitrage transaction.

1. Citibank sells $5,000,000 to Deutsche Bank for euros, receiving €4,085,500. ($5,000,000 × 0.8171 €/$ = €4,085,500).

2. Citibank sells €4,085,500 to Crédit Agricole for pounds, receiving £3,430,311. (€4,085,500 ÷ 1.1910 €/£ = £3,430,311).

3. Citibank sells £3,430,311 to Barclays for dollars, receiving $5,025,406. (£3,430,311 × 1.4650 $/£ = $5,025,406).

4. Citibank ultimately earns an arbitrage profit of $25,406 on the $5,000,000 of capital it used to execute the strategy.

The reason for dividing the euro amount by the euro/pound exchange rate in this example is that the exchange rate is quoted in euro terms, as is the amount being traded. One could multiply the euro amount by the reciprocal pound/euro exchange rate and still calculate the ending amount of pounds.

Evidence for Triangular Arbitrage

Research examining high-frequency exchange rate data has found that mispricings do occur in the foreign exchange market such that executable triangular arbitrage opportunities appear possible. In observations of triangular arbitrage, the constituent exchange rates have exhibited strong correlation. A study examining exchange rate data provided by HSBC Bank for the Japanese yen (JPY) and the Swiss franc (CHF) found that although a limited number of arbitrage opportunities appeared to exist for as many as 100 seconds, 95% of them lasted for 5 seconds or less, and 60% lasted for 1 second or less. Further, most arbitrage opportunities were found to have small magnitudes, with 94% of JPY and CHF opportunities existing at a difference of 1 basis point, which translates into a potential arbitrage profit of $100 USD per $1 million USD transacted.

Tests for seasonality in the amount and duration of triangular arbitrage opportunities have shown that incidence of arbitrage opportunities and mean duration is consistent from day to day. However, significant variations have been identified during different times of day. Transactions involving the JPY and CHF have demonstrated a smaller number of opportunities and long average duration around 01:00 and 10:00 UTC, contrasted with a greater number of opportunities and short average duration around 13:00 and 16:00 UTC. Such variations in incidence and duration of arbitrage opportunities can be explained by variations in market liquidity during the trading day. For example, the foreign exchange market is found to be most liquid for Asia around 00:00 and 10:00 UTC, for Europe around 07:00 and 17:00 UTC, and for America around 13:00 and 23:00 UTC. The overall foreign exchange market is most liquid around 08:00 and 16:00 UTC, and the least liquid around 22:00 and 01:00 UTC. The periods of highest liquidity correspond with the periods of greatest incidence of opportunities for triangular arbitrage. This correspondence is substantiated by the observation of narrower bid-ask spreads during periods of high liquidity, resulting in a greater potential for mispricings and therefore arbitrage opportunities. However, market forces are driven to correct for mispricings due to a high frequency of trades that will trade away fleeting arbitrage opportunities.

Researchers have shown a decrease in the incidence of triangular arbitrage opportunities from 2003 to 2005 for the Japanese yen and Swiss franc and have attributed the decrease to broader adoption of electronic trading platforms and trading algorithms during the same period. Such electronic systems have enabled traders to trade and react rapidly to price changes. The speed gained from these technologies improved trading efficiency and the correction of mispricings, allowing for less incidence of triangular arbitrage opportunities.

Profitability

Mere existence of triangular arbitrage opportunities does not necessarily imply that a trading strategy seeking to exploit currency mispricings is consistently profitable. Electronic trading systems allow the three constituent trades in a triangular arbitrage transaction to be submitted very rapidly. However, there exists a delay between the identification of such an opportunity, the initiation of trades, and the arrival of trades to the party quoting the mispricing. Even though such delays are only milliseconds in duration, they are deemed significant. For example, if a trader places each trade as a limit order to be filled only at the arbitrage price and a price moves due to market activity or new price is quoted by the third party, then the triangular transaction will not be completed. In such a case, the arbitrageur will face a cost to close out the position that is equal to the change in price that eliminated the arbitrage condition.

In the foreign exchange market there are many market participants competing for each arbitrage opportunity; for arbitrage to be profitable a trader would need to identify and execute each arbitrage opportunity faster than competitors. Competing arbitrageurs are expected to persist in striving to increase their execution speed of trades by engaging in what some researchers describe as an "electronic trading 'arms race'." The costs involved in keeping ahead in such a competition present difficulty in consistently beating other arbitrageurs over the long term. Other factors such as transaction costs, brokerage fees, network access fees, and sophisticated electronic trading platforms further challenge the feasibility of significant arbitrage profits over prolonged periods.

Exchange Rate Theories

Forecasting exchange rate is easier said than done. In the market, there are thousands of trading software known as "forex robots" (described in Session 4.3) are available which help in forecasting forex rates and promise to get rich quick!! However, until now nobody is known to have been amassed great riches by predicting forex rates and making a killing. Interestingly we know of the many traders have companies which have gone kaput on account forex trading going horribly wrong. Irrespective of this fact, all and sundry anything remotely to do with forex rates wants to learn the tools to predict forex rates. Significant research work is also being carried out to find out newer models to predict forex rates and make a killing!

A person interested on forecasting forex would get to hear simpler techniques based one age old basics like "Fibonacci series" and "time series analysis" to complex models based on neural network, artificial intelligence and genetic algorithms etc.

In fact, while browsing through the web, the author comes across an interesting write up. A researcher has claimed to develop a theory, which he is intending to sale/license, and generate revenue from the sale/license. The researcher also mentions that the theory would help users "24 hrs non-stop wealth building"!! The website content goes like this ... "The brand new theory towards analyzing and forecasting the forex market and it has come after 700 years of Fibo and 150 years of Elliot waves, the two most popular indicators". Anybody will be quite intrigued by the phrases like "700 years of Fibo and 150 years of Elliot waves" – how on the earth he got a time series data for 700 years forex quotations!!

As there is no end to the number of theories developed based on mathematical model, let us focus more on understating macroeconomic parameters like interest rate, inflation etc, those that have bearing on forex rate.

There are certain fundamental macroeconomic conditions which influence the exchange rates. One of the fundamental parity conditions is known as "Purchasing Power Parity" and the Law of One Price (LOOP). These aspects are discussed in detail.

Purchasing Power Parity

Purchasing power parity (PPP) is an economic theory that states that the exchange rate between two currencies equal the ratio of the currencies' respective purchasing power. Theories that invoke purchasing power parity assume that in some circumstances (for example, as a long-run tendency) it would cost exactly the same number of, for example, US dollars to buy euros and then to use the proceeds to buy a market basket of goods as it would cost to use those dollars directly in purchasing the market basket of goods. A fall in either currency's purchasing power would lead to a proportional decrease in that currency's valuation on the foreign exchange market.

The concept of purchasing power parity allows one to estimate what the exchange rate between two currencies would have to be in order for the exchange to be at par with the purchasing power of the two countries' currencies. Using that PPP rate for hypothetical currency conversions, a given amount of one currency thus has the same purchasing power whether used directly to purchase a market basket of goods or used to convert at the PPP rate to the other currency and then purchase the market basket using that currency. Observed deviations of the exchange rate from purchasing power parity are measured by deviations of the real exchange rate from its PPP value of 1.

PPP exchange rates help costing but exclude profits. So, it is reckoned as more efficient methodology than the use of market exchange rates. For example, suppose that two countries produce the same physical amounts of goods as each other in each of two different years. Since market exchange rates fluctuate substantially, when the GDP of one country measured in its own currency is converted to the other country's currency using market exchange rates, one country might be inferred to have higher real GDP than the other country in one year but lower in the other; both of these inferences would fail to reflect the reality of their relative levels of production. But if one country's GDP is converted into the other country's currency using PPP exchange rates instead of observed market exchange rates, the false inference will not occur. Essentially GDP PPP controls for the different costs of living and price levels, usually relative to the United States Dollar, thus enabling a more accurate depiction of a given nation's level of production.

Concept

The idea originated with the School of Salamanca in the 16th century, and was developed in its modern form by Gustav Cassel in 1918. The concept is based on the law of one price, where in the absence of transaction costs and official trade barriers, identical goods will have the same price in different markets when the prices are expressed in the same currency.

Another interpretation is that the difference in the rate of change in prices at home and abroad—the difference in the inflation rates—is equal to the percentage depreciation or appreciation of the exchange rate.

Deviations from parity imply differences in purchasing power of a "basket of goods" across countries, which means that for the purposes of many international comparisons, countries' GDPs or other national income statistics need to be "PPP-adjusted" and converted into common units. The best-known purchasing power adjustment is the Geary–Khamis dollar (the "international dollar"). The real exchange rate is then equal to the nominal exchange rate, adjusted for differences in price levels. If purchasing power parity held exactly, then the real exchange rate would always equal one. However, in practice the real exchange rates exhibit both short run and long run deviations from this value, for example due to reasons illuminated in the Balassa–Samuelson theorem.

There can be marked differences between purchasing power adjusted incomes and those converted via market exchange rates. For example, the World Bank's *World Development Indicators 2005* estimated that in 2003, one Geary-Khamis dollar was equivalent to about 1.8 Chinese yuan by purchasing power parity—considerably different from the nominal exchange rate. This discrepancy has large implications; for instance, when converted via the nominal exchange rates GDP per capita in India is about US$1,965 while on a PPP basis it is about US$7,197. At the other extreme, Denmark's nominal GDP per capita is around US$62,100, but its PPP figure is US$37,304.

Functions

The purchasing power parity exchange rate serves two main functions. PPP exchange rates can be useful for making comparisons between countries because they stay fairly constant from day to day or week to week and only change modestly, if at all, from year to year. Second, over a period of years, exchange rates do tend to move in the general direction of the PPP exchange rate and there is some value to knowing in which direction the exchange rate is more likely to shift over the long run.

Measurement

The PPP exchange-rate calculation is controversial because of the difficulties of finding comparable baskets of goods to compare purchasing power across countries.

Estimation of purchasing power parity is complicated by the fact that countries do not simply differ in a uniform price level; rather, the difference in food prices may be greater than the difference in housing prices, while also less than the difference in entertainment prices. People in different countries typically consume different baskets of goods. It is necessary to compare the cost of baskets of goods and services using a price index. This is a difficult task because purchasing patterns and even the goods available to purchase differ across countries.

Thus, it is necessary to make adjustments for differences in the quality of goods and services. Furthermore, the basket of goods representative of one economy will vary from that of another: Americans eat more bread; Chinese more rice. Hence a PPP calculated using the US consumption as a base will differ from that calculated using China as a base. Additional statistical difficulties arise with multilateral comparisons when (as is usually the case) more than two countries are to be compared.

Various ways of averaging bilateral PPPs can provide a more stable multilateral comparison, but at the cost of distorting bilateral ones. These are all general issues of indexing; as with other price indices there is no way to reduce complexity to a single number that is equally satisfying for all purposes. Nevertheless, PPPs are typically robust in the face of the many problems that arise in using market exchange rates to make comparisons.

For example, in 2005 the price of a gallon of gasoline in Saudi Arabia was USD 0.91, and in Norway the price was USD 6.27. The significant differences in price wouldn't contribute to accuracy in a PPP analysis, despite all of the variables that contribute to the significant differences in price. More comparisons have to be made and used as variables in the overall formulation of the PPP.

When PPP comparisons are to be made over some interval of time, proper account needs to be made of inflationary effects.

Law of One Price

Although it may seem as if PPPs and the law of one price are the same, there is a difference: the law of one price applies to individual commodities whereas PPP applies to the general price level. If the law of one price is true for all commodities then PPP is also therefore true; however, when discussing the validity of PPP, some argue that the law of one price does not need to be true exactly for PPP to be valid. If the law of one price is not true for a certain commodity, the price levels will not differ enough from the level predicted by PPP.

The purchasing power parity theory states that the exchange rate between one currency and another currency is in equlibirium when their domestic purchasing powers at that rate of exchange are equivalent.

Big Mac Index

Big Mac hamburgers, like this one from Japan, are similar worldwide.

Another example of one measure of the law of one price, which underlies purchasing power parity, is the Big Mac Index, popularized by *The Economist*, which compares the prices of a Big Mac burger in McDonald's restaurants in different countries. The Big Mac Index is presumably useful because although it is based on a single consumer product that may not be typical, it is a relatively standardized product that includes input costs from a wide range of sectors in the local economy, such as agricultural commodities (beef, bread, lettuce, cheese), labor (blue and white collar), advertising, rent and real estate costs, transportation, etc.

In theory, the law of one price would hold that if, to take an example, the Canadian dollar were to be significantly overvalued relative to the U.S. dollar according to the Big Mac Index, that gap should be unsustainable because Canadians would import their Big Macs from or travel to the U.S. to consume them, thus putting upward demand pressure on the U.S. dollar by virtue of Canadians buying the U.S. dollars needed to purchase the U.S.-made Big Macs and simultaneously placing downward supply pressure on the Canadian dollar by virtue of Canadians selling their currency in order to buy those same U.S. dollars.

The alternative to this exchange rate adjustment would be an adjustment in prices, with Canadian McDonald's stores compelled to lower prices to remain competitive. Either way, the valuation difference should be reduced assuming perfect competition and a perfectly tradable good. In practice, of course, the Big Mac is not a perfectly tradable good and there may also be capital flows that sustain relative demand for the Canadian dollar. The difference in price may have its origins in a variety of factors besides direct input costs such as government regulations and product differentiation.

However, in some emerging economies, Western fast food represents an expensive niche product priced well above the price of traditional staples—i.e. the Big Mac is not a mainstream 'cheap' meal as it is in the West, but a luxury import. This relates back to the idea of product differentiation: the fact that few substitutes for the Big Mac are available confers market power on McDonald's. For example, in India, the costs of local fast food like vada pav are comparative to what the Big Mac signifies in the U.S.A. Additionally, with countries like Argentina that have abundant beef resources, consumer prices in general may not be as cheap as implied by the price of a Big Mac.

The following table, based on data from *The Economist*'s January 2013 calculations, shows the under (−) and over (+) valuation of the local currency against the U.S. dollar in %, according to the Big Mac index. To take an example calculation, the local price of a Big Mac in Hong Kong when converted to U.S. dollars at the market exchange rate was $2.19, or 50% of the local price for a Big Mac in the U.S. of $4.37. Hence the Hong Kong dollar was deemed to be 50% undervalued relative to the U.S. dollar on a PPP basis.

Country or region	Price level (% relative to the US)
India	-59
South Africa	-54
Hong Kong	-50
Ukraine	-47
Egypt	-45
Russia	-45
Taiwan	-42
Mainland China	-41
Malaysia	-41
Sri Lanka	-37
Indonesia	-35
Mexico	-34
Philippines	-33
Poland	-33
Bangladesh	-32

Country or region	Price level (% relative to the US)
Saudi Arabia	-33
Thailand	-33
Pakistan	-32
Lithuania	-30
Latvia	-25
UAE	-25
South Korea	-22
Japan	-20
Singapore	-17
Estonia	-16
Czech Republic	-15
Argentina	-13
Hungary	-13
Peru	-11
Israel	-8
Portugal	-8
United Kingdom	-3
New Zealand	-1
Chile	0
United States	**0 (by definition)**
Costa Rica	1
Greece	3
Austria	5
Netherlands	7
Ireland	8
Spain	9
Turkey	10
Colombia	11
Australia	12
Euro area	12
France	12
Germany	13
Finland	17
Belgium	18
Denmark	19
Italy	20
Canada	24
Uruguay	25
Brazil	29

Country or region	Price level (% relative to the US)
Switzerland	63
Sweden	75
Norway	80
Venezuela	108

iPad Index

Like the Big Mac Index, the iPad index (elaborated by CommSec) compares an item's price in various locations. Unlike the Big Mac, however, each iPad is produced in the same place (except for the model sold in Brazil) and all iPads (within the same model) have identical performance characteristics. Price differences are therefore a function of transportation costs, taxes, and to a lesser extent, the prices that may be realized in individual markets. An iPad will cost about twice as much in Argentina as in the United States.

Country or region	Price (US Dollars)
Argentina	$1,094.11
Australia	$506.66
Austria	$674.96
Belgium	$618.34
Brazil	$791.40
Brunei	$525.52
Canada (Montréal)	$557.18
Canada (no tax)	$467.36
Chile	$602.13
Mainland China	$602.52
Czech Republic	$676.69
Denmark	$725.32
Finland	$695.25
France	$688.49
Germany	$618.34
Greece	$715.54
Hong Kong	$501.52
Hungary	$679.64
India	$512.61
Ireland	$630.73
Italy	$674.96
Japan	$501.56
Luxembourg	$641.50
Malaysia	$473.77

Country or region	Price (US Dollars)
Mexico	$591.62
Netherlands	$683.08
New Zealand	$610.45
Norway	$655.92
Philippines	$556.42
Pakistan	$550.00
Poland	$704.51
Portugal	$688.49
Russia	$596.08
Singapore	$525.98
Slovakia	$674.96
Slovenia	$674.96
South Africa	$559.38
South Korea	$576.20
Spain	$674.96
Sweden	$706.87
Switzerland	$617.58
Taiwan	$538.34
Thailand	$530.72
Turkey	$656.96
UAE	$544.32
United Kingdom	$638.81
US (California)	$546.91
United States (no tax)	$499.00
Vietnam	$554.08

KFC Index

Similar to the Big Mac Index, the KFC Index measures PPP amongst African countries, created by Sagaci Research (a market research firm focusing solely on Africa). Instead of comparing a Big Mac, this index compares a KFC Original 12/15 pc. bucket.

For example, the average price of KFC´s Original 12 pc. Bucket in America in January 2016 was $20.50; in Namibia it was only $13.40 at market exchange rates. Therefore, the index states the Namibian dollar was undervalued by 33% at that time.

OECD Comparative Price Levels

Each month, the Organisation for Economic Co-operation and Development measures the difference in price levels between its member countries by calculating the ratios of

PPPs for private final consumption expenditure to exchange rates. The OECD table below indicates the number of US dollars needed in each of the countries listed to buy the same representative basket of consumer goods and services that would cost 100 USD in the United States.

According to the table, an American living or travelling in Switzerland on an income denominated in US dollars would find that country to be the most expensive of the group, having to spend 62% more US dollars to maintain a standard of living comparable to the USA in terms of consumption.

Country	Price level (USA = 100)
Australia	123
Austria	99
Belgium	101
Canada	105
Chile	67
Czech Republic	59
Denmark	128
Estonia	71
Finland	113
France	100
Germany	94
Greece	78
Hungary	52
Iceland	111
Ireland	109
Israel	109
Italy	94
Japan	96
South Korea	84
Luxembourg	112
Mexico	66
Netherlands	102
New Zealand	118
Norway	134
Poland	51
Portugal	73
Slovak Republic	63
Slovenia	75
Spain	84
Sweden	109
Switzerland	162

Country	Price level (USA = 100)
Turkey	61
United Kingdom	121
United States	100

Measurement Issues

In addition to methodological issues presented by the selection of a basket of goods, PPP estimates can also vary based on the statistical capacity of participating countries. The International Comparison Program, which PPP estimates are based on, require the disaggregation of national accounts into production, expenditure or (in some cases) income, and not all participating countries routinely disaggregate their data into such categories.

Some aspects of PPP comparison are theoretically impossible or unclear. For example, there is no basis for comparison between the Ethiopian laborer who lives on teff with the Thai laborer who lives on rice, because teff is not commercially available in Thailand and rice is not in Ethiopia, so the price of rice in Ethiopia or teff in Thailand cannot be determined. As a general rule, the more similar the price structure between countries, the more valid the PPP comparison.

PPP levels will also vary based on the formula used to calculate price matrices. Different possible formulas include GEKS-Fisher, Geary-Khamis, IDB, and the superlative method. Each has advantages and disadvantages.

Linking regions presents another methodological difficulty. In the 2005 ICP round, regions were compared by using a list of some 1,000 identical items for which a price could be found for 18 countries, selected so that at least two countries would be in each region. While this was superior to earlier "bridging" methods, which do not fully take into account differing quality between goods, it may serve to overstate the PPP basis of poorer countries, because the price indexing on which PPP is based will assign to poorer countries the greater weight of goods consumed in greater shares in richer countries.

Need for Adjustments to GDP

The exchange rate reflects transaction values for traded goods *between* countries in contrast to non-traded goods, that is, goods produced for home-country use. Also, currencies are traded for purposes other than trade in goods and services, *e.g.*, to buy capital assets whose prices vary more than those of physical goods. Also, different interest rates, speculation, hedging or interventions by central banks can influence the foreign-exchange market.

The PPP method is used as an alternative to correct for possible statistical bias. The

Penn World Table is a widely cited source of PPP adjustments, and the associated Penn effect reflects such a systematic bias in using exchange rates to outputs among countries.

For example, if the value of the Mexican peso falls by half compared to the US dollar, the Mexican Gross Domestic Product measured in dollars will also halve. However, this exchange rate results from international trade and financial markets. It does not necessarily mean that Mexicans are poorer by a half; if incomes and prices measured in pesos stay the same, they will be no worse off assuming that imported goods are not essential to the quality of life of individuals. Measuring income in different countries using PPP exchange rates helps to avoid this problem.

PPP exchange rates are especially useful when official exchange rates are artificially manipulated by governments. Countries with strong government control of the economy sometimes enforce official exchange rates that make their own currency artificially strong. By contrast, the currency's black market exchange rate is artificially weak. In such cases, a PPP exchange rate is likely the most realistic basis for economic comparison. Similarly, when exchange rates deviate significantly from their long term equilibrium due to speculative attacks or carry trade, a PPP exchange rate offers a better alternative for comparison.

Extrapolating PPP Rates

Since global PPP estimates —such as those provided by the ICP— are not calculated annually, but for a single year, PPP exchange rates for years other than the benchmark year need to be extrapolated. One way of doing this is by using the country's GDP deflator. To calculate a country's PPP exchange rate in Geary–Khamis dollars for a particular year, the calculation proceeds in the following manner:

$$\text{PPPrate}_{X,i} = \frac{\text{PPPrate}_{X,b} \cdot \dfrac{\text{GDPdef}_{X,i}}{\text{GDPdef}_{X,b}}}{\text{PPPrate}_{U,b} \cdot \dfrac{\text{GDPdef}_{U,i}}{\text{GDPdef}_{U,b}}}$$

Where $\text{PPPrate}_{X,i}$ is the PPP exchange rate of country X for year i, $\text{PPPrate}_{X,b}$ is the PPP exchange rate of country X for the benchmark year, $\text{PPPrate}_{U,b}$ is the PPP exchange rate of the United States (US) for the benchmark year (equal to 1), $\text{GDPdef}_{X,i}$ is the GDP deflator of country X for year i, $\text{GDPdef}_{X,b}$ is the GDP deflator of country X for the benchmark year, $\text{GDPdef}_{U,i}$ is the GDP deflator of the US for year i, and $\text{GDPdef}_{U,b}$ is the GDP deflator of the US for the benchmark year.

Difficulties

There are a number of reasons that different measures do not perfectly reflect standards of living.

Range and Quality of Goods

The goods that the currency has the "power" to purchase are a basket of goods of different types:

1. Local, non-tradable goods and services (like electric power) that are produced and sold domestically.
2. Tradable goods such as non-perishable commodities that can be sold on the international market (like diamonds).

The more that a product falls into category 1, the further its price will be from the currency exchange rate, moving towards the PPP exchange rate. Conversely, category 2 products tend to trade close to the currency exchange rate.

More processed and expensive products are likely to be tradable, falling into the second category, and drifting from the PPP exchange rate to the currency exchange rate. Even if the PPP "value" of the Ethiopian currency is three times stronger than the currency exchange rate, it won't buy three times as much of internationally traded goods like steel, cars and microchips, but non-traded goods like housing, services ("haircuts"), and domestically produced crops. The relative price differential between tradables and non-tradables from high-income to low-income countries is a consequence of the Balassa–Samuelson effect and gives a big cost advantage to labour-intensive production of tradable goods in low income countries (like Ethiopia), as against high income countries (like Switzerland).

The corporate cost advantage is nothing more sophisticated than access to cheaper workers, but because the pay of those workers goes farther in low-income countries than high, the relative pay differentials (inter-country) can be sustained for longer than would be the case otherwise. (This is another way of saying that the wage rate is based on average local productivity and that this is below the per capita productivity that factories selling tradable goods to international markets can achieve.) An equivalent cost benefit comes from non-traded goods that can be sourced locally (nearer the PPP-exchange rate than the nominal exchange rate in which receipts are paid). These act as a cheaper factor of production than is available to factories in richer countries.

The Bhagwati–Kravis–Lipsey view provides a somewhat different explanation from the Balassa–Samuelson theory. This view states that price levels for nontradables are lower in poorer countries because of differences in endowment of labor and capital, not because of lower levels of productivity. Poor countries have more labor relative to capital, so marginal productivity of labor is greater in rich countries than in poor countries. Nontradables tend to be labor-intensive; therefore, because labor is less expensive in poor countries and is used mostly for nontradables, nontradables are cheaper in poor countries. Wages are high in rich countries, so nontradables are relatively more expensive.

PPP calculations tend to overemphasise the primary sectoral contribution, and underemphasise the industrial and service sectoral contributions to the economy of a nation.

Trade Barriers and Nontradables

The law of one price, the underlying mechanism behind PPP, is weakened by transport costs and governmental trade restrictions, which make it expensive to move goods between markets located in different countries. Transport costs sever the link between exchange rates and the prices of goods implied by the law of one price. As transport costs increase, the larger the range of exchange rate fluctuations. The same is true for official trade restrictions because the customs fees affect importers' profits in the same way as shipping fees. According to Krugman and Obstfeld, "Either type of trade impediment weakens the basis of PPP by allowing the purchasing power of a given currency to differ more widely from country to country." They cite the example that a dollar in London should purchase the same goods as a dollar in Chicago, which is certainly not the case.

Nontradables are primarily services and the output of the construction industry. Nontradables also lead to deviations in PPP because the prices of nontradables are not linked internationally. The prices are determined by domestic supply and demand, and shifts in those curves lead to changes in the market basket of some goods relative to the foreign price of the same basket. If the prices of nontradables rise, the purchasing power of any given currency will fall in that country.

Departures from Free Competition

Linkages between national price levels are also weakened when trade barriers and imperfectly competitive market structures occur together. Pricing to market occurs when a firm sells the same product for different prices in different markets. This is a reflection of inter-country differences in conditions on both the demand side (*e.g.*, virtually no demand for pork in Islamic states) and the supply side (*e.g.*, whether the existing market for a prospective entrant's product features few suppliers or instead is already near-saturated). According to Krugman and Obstfeld, this occurrence of product differentiation and segmented markets results in violations of the law of one price and absolute PPP. Over time, shifts in market structure and demand will occur, which may invalidate relative PPP.

Differences in Price Level Measurement

Measurement of price levels differ from country to country. Inflation data from different countries are based on different commodity baskets; therefore, exchange rate changes do not offset official measures of inflation differences. Because it makes predictions about price changes rather than price levels, relative PPP is still a useful concept. However, change in the relative prices of basket components can cause relative PPP to fail tests that are based on official price indexes.

Global Poverty Line

The global poverty line is a worldwide count of people who live below an international poverty line, referred to as the dollar-a-day line. This line represents an average of the national poverty lines of the world's poorest countries, expressed in international dollars. These national poverty lines are converted to international currency and the global line is converted back to local currency using the PPP exchange rates from the ICP. PPP exchange rates include data from the sales of high end none poverty related items which skews the value of food items and necessary goods which is 70 percent of poor peoples' consumption. Angus Deaton argues that PPP indexes need to be reweighted for use in poverty measurement; they need to be redefined to reflect local poverty measures, not global measures, weighing local food items and excluding luxury items that are not prevalent or are not of equal value in all localities.

PPP calculated by comparing price of one good across in different currencies is known as Absolute PPP. However the absolute law of one price never holds good when prices of one commodity is compared. (For example, price of one KG of Potato, Price of a similar brand car, price of a mobile phone etc.)

Another form of less stringent PPP stresses on comparing price index of basket of goods in both countries rather than comparing any one good/service.

$$\text{Spot Rate} = \frac{\text{Price Index}^{\text{INR}}}{\text{Price Index}^{\text{USD}}}$$

It indicates that if a country is experiencing higher inflation (higher price level) compared to another country, its currency will depreciate relative to other currency.

In other words, the spot rate between two countries can be determined by comparing the price index of a basket of similar goods and services. It is very important to understand at this point is that price index should comprise of "similar" goods & services" consumed by residents of both countries.

On a given date, suppose a basket of goods & services costs INR 5000 and a similar basket of goods & services cots USD300, the spot exchange rate on that date should be,

$$\text{Spot Rate} = \frac{\text{INR } 5000}{\text{USD } 300} = \text{INR } 16.67 / \text{USD}$$

If the actual spot exchange rate equals the rate calculated by PPP, then PPP holds true. However, it is empirically proved that PPP in absolute form based on single product or based on a price index does not hold good.

Law of One Price (LOOP)

PPP is based on the concept of "Law of One Price". The LOOP indicates that identical good/services should sell for the same price in two separate markets when there are no transportation costs and no differential tax rates exists in the two markets. If there is a price difference, then exchange rate would move in such a manner so that, in both markets the product will sell at same price.

The law of one price (LoP) is an economic concept which posits that "*a good must sell for the same price in all locations*". This law is derived from the assumption of the inevitable elimination of all arbitrage.

The law of one price constitutes the basis of the theory of purchasing power parity, an assumption that in some circumstances (for example, as a long-run tendency) it would cost exactly the same number of, for example, US dollars to buy euros and then to use the proceeds to buy a market basket of goods as it would cost to use those dollars directly in purchasing the market basket of goods.

History

The law of one price has been applied towards the analysis of many public events such as:

- In 2015, The International Monetary Fund holds that the law of one price holds for most tradeable products in Brazil but does not apply in the same way to its non-tradeable goods.
- A director of the Council on Foreign Relations held in 2013 that the then-current Apple iPad mini followed the law of one price, as far as its price nearly reached the same US dollar exchange rate in each applicable country.
- Indonesian governmental oil subsidies against oil smugglers; The smugglers selling stolen government-discounted oil back to its market rate.
- An apparent violation of the law involving international Royal Dutch/Shell stocks. After merging in 1907, holders of Royal Dutch Petroleum (traded in Amsterdam) and Shell Transport shares (traded in London) were entitled to 60% and 40% respectively of all future profits. Royal Dutch shares should therefore automatically have been priced at 50% more than Shell shares. However, they diverged from this by up to 15%. This discrepancy disappeared with their final merger in 2005.

Overview

The intuition behind the law of one price is based on the assumption that differences between prices are eliminated by market participants taking advantage of arbitrage opportunities.

Example in Regular Trade

Assume different prices for a single identical good in two locations, no transport costs and no economic barriers between both locations. The arbitrage mechanism can now be performed by both the supply and/or the demand site: All sellers have an incentive to sell their goods in the higher-priced location, driving up supply in that location and reducing supply in the lower-priced location.

If demand remains constant, the higher supply will force prices to decrease in the higher-priced location, while the lowered supply in the alternative location will drive up prices there.

Conversely, if all consumers move to the lower-priced location in order to buy the good at the lower price, demand will increase in the lower-priced location, and - assuming constant supply in both locations - prices will increase, whereas the decreased demand in the higher-priced location leads the prices to decrease there.

Both scenarios result in a single, equal price per homogeneous good in all locations. In efficient markets the convergence on one price is instant.

Example in Formal Financial Markets

Commodities can be traded on financial markets, where there will be a single offer price (asking price), and bid price. Although there is a small spread between these two values the law of one price applies (to each).

No trader will sell the commodity at a lower price than the market maker's bid-level or buy at a higher price than the market maker's offer-level. In either case moving away from the prevailing price would either leave no takers, or be charity.

In the derivatives market the law applies to financial instruments which appear different, but which resolve to the same set of cash flows.

> *"A security must have a single price, no matter how that security is created. For example, if an option can be created using two different sets of underlying securities, then the total price for each would be the same or else an arbitrage opportunity would exist."*

A similar argument can be used by considering arrow securities as alluded to by Arrow and Debreu (1944).

Non-application

- The law does not apply *intertemporally*, so prices for the same item can be different at different times in one market. The application of the law to financial markets is obscured by the fact that the market maker's prices are continually moving in liquid markets. However, at the *moment* each trade is executed, the law is in force (it would normally be against exchange rules to break it).

- The law also need not apply if buyers have less than perfect information about where to find the lowest price. In this case, sellers face a tradeoff between the frequency and the profitability of their sales. That is, firms may be indifferent between posting a high price (thus selling infrequently, because most consumers will search for a lower one) and a low price (at which they will sell more often, but earn less profit per sale).
- The Balassa-Samuelson effect argues that the law of one price is not applicable to all goods internationally, because some goods are not tradable. It argues that the consumption may be cheaper in some countries than others, because nontradables (especially land and labor) are cheaper in less developed countries. This can make a typical consumption basket cheaper in a less developed country, even if some goods in that basket have their prices equalized by international trade.

Relative Purchasing Power Parity

Relative purchasing power parity is an economic theory which predicts a relationship between the inflation rates of two countries over a specified period and the movement in the exchange rate between their two currencies over the same period. It is a dynamic version of the absolute PPP theory.

Explanation

Suppose that the currency of Country A is called the A$ (A-dollar) and the currency of country B is called the B$.

The theory states that if the price P in country A of a basket of commodities and services is P A-dollars, then the price Q of the same basket in country B will be C×P A-dollars, where C is a constant which does not vary over time, or, equivalently, C×P×S B-dollars, where S is the (variable) number of B-dollars required to buy one A-dollar, i.e. the exchange rate.

If (1) and (2) denote two different dates, then it follows that:

$$\frac{1}{C} = \frac{P(1) \times S(1)}{Q(1)} = \frac{P(2) \times S(2)}{Q(2)}$$

and hence

$$\frac{S(2)}{S(1)} = \frac{\left(\frac{Q(2)}{Q(1)}\right)}{\left(\frac{P(2)}{P(1)}\right)}$$

or, in words, the factor representing the movement in market exchange rates is equal to the ratio of the inflation factors (changes in price levels) of the two countries (as one would intuitively expect).

Absolute purchasing power parity occurs when C=1, and is a special case of the above.

According to this theory, the change in the exchange rate is determined by price level changes in both countries. For example, if prices in the United States rise by 3% and prices in the European Union rise by 1% the purchasing power of the EUR should appreciate by approximately 2% compared to the purchasing power of the USD (equivalently the USD will depreciate by about 2%).

Note that it is incorrect to do the calculation by subtracting these percentages – one must use the above formula, giving $\frac{1.01}{1.03}$ = 0.98058, i.e. a 1.942% depreciation of the USD. With larger price rises, the difference between the incorrect and the correct formula becomes larger.

Absolute Purchasing Power Parity

Commonly called *absolute* purchasing power parity, this theory assumes that equilibrium in the exchange rate between two currencies will force their purchasing powers to be equal. This theory is likely to hold well for commodities which are easily transportable between the two countries (such as gold, assuming this is freely transferable) but is likely to be false for other goods and services which cannot easily be transported, because the transportation costs will distort the parity.

Inflation and Measurement of Rate of Inflation

Inflation rate measures the rate of change of increase in prices of goods and services during a given time period. Normally the prices of goods and services are measured by construction of an index. The index can be Consumer price index (CPI) or Wholesale price index(WPI).

Composition of CPI: The basket of goods and services consumed by different classes of consumers in India varies. Hence based on economic groups, 4 different CPIs are calculated. These 4 indices are CPI for Industrial Workers [CPI(IW)] CPI for Urban Non-Manual Employees [CPI(UNME)], CPI for Agricultural Labourers [CPI(AL)], and CPI for Rural Labourers [CPI(RL)].

Composition of WPI: The WPI for all-India consists of 435 commodities. The 435 items details are given in Table 17.5. Basically it consists of 98 primary articles, 19 articles on fuel, power etc, and 318 items of manufactured products. The base year for calculation of WPI is 1993-94. These three major groups have 22.025%, 14.226% and 63.749% respectively.

Effective Exchange Rate

The effective exchange rate is an index that describes the strength of a currency relative to a basket of other currencies. Suppose a country has N trading partners and denote Trade_i and E_i as the trade and exchange rate with country i respectively. Then the effective exchange rate is calculated as:

$$E_{\text{effective}} = E_1 \frac{\text{Trade}_1}{\text{Trade}} + \ldots + E_N \frac{\text{Trade}_N}{\text{Trade}}$$

Although typically that basket is trade-weighted, the trade-weighted effective exchange rate index is not the only way to derive a meaningful effective exchange rate index. Ho (2012) proposed a new approach to compiling effective exchange rate indices. It defines the effective exchange rate as the ratio of the "normalized Exchange Value of Currency i against the US dollar" to the normalized exchange value of the "benchmark currency basket" against the US dollar. The US dollar is here used as numeraire for convenience, and since it cancels out, in principle any other currency can be used instead without affecting the results. The benchmark currency basket is a GDP-weighted basket of the major fully convertible currencies of the world.

Bilateral exchange rate involves a currency pair, while an effective exchange rate is a weighted average of a basket of foreign currencies, and it can be viewed as an overall measure of the country's external competitiveness. A nominal effective exchange rate (NEER) is weighted with the inverse of the asymptotic trade weights. A real effective exchange rate (REER) adjusts NEER by the appropriate foreign price level and deflates by the home country price level. There are four aspects for alternative measures of REER which are (a) using end-of-period or period averages of the nominal exchange rate. (b) choosing price indexes. (c) in obtaining the real effective exchange rates, deciding upon the number of trading partners in calculating the weights. (d) deciding upon the formula to use in aggregation. Considering all these aspects together led to the calculation of a great number of alternative series.

The Bank for International Settlements provides four sets of effective exchange rates, updated monthly. One pair uses a "narrow" set of 27 countries with data going back to 1964, both in nominal terms and as a "real" effective exchange rate adjusted using consumer price inflation. The "broad" set covers 61 economies, but with data only from 1994, again available both as a nominal series and adjusted for relative inflation. The trade weights are not updated monthly; as of March 2016, the base period was the average over 2011-13.

Effective exchange rates are useful for gauging whether a currency has appreciated overall relative to trading partners. For example, in 2015 the Chinese RMB depreciated about 8% against the US dollar. However, more of China's trade is with Asia and Europe than with the United States, and the dollar appreciated against those currencies.

The net effect was that once weighted by trade shares the value of the Chinese currency actually appreciated approximately 10% relative to its trading partners.

EER are still volatile over short periods of time and a poor guide for comparing standards of living across countries. For that purpose Purchasing Power Parity measures are more appropriate.

Effective Exchange Rate Index

The effective exchange rate index describes the strength of a currency relative to a basket of other currencies. Although typically the basket is trade weighted, there are others besides the trade-weighted effective exchange rate index.

Ho (2012) proposed a new approach to compiling effective exchange rate indices. Under this approach, the effective exchange rate can be calculated as a ratio of the normalized exchange value of currency against the US dollar to the normalized exchange value of the benchmark currency basket against the US dollar. Normalized exchange rate refers to the current exchange rate divided by the exchange rate against the US dollar in the base year, which effectively scales up the exchange rate of a "small value" currency like the Japanese yen, worth a small fraction of a dollar, and scales down the exchange rate of a "big value" currency like the British pound, worth much more than a dollar. Thus, all standardized or normalized currencies in the base year are worth US$1 in the base year. The US dollar is used for convenience, but, in principle, any other currency could be used instead without affecting the results. The benchmark currency basket is a GDP-weighted basket of the major fully convertible currencies of the world. Since GDP data are available with a lag, the GDP weights used in Ho are GDPs dated two years ago. The use of GDP weights has been found to be superior to direct trade weights since countries with bigger GDPs will tend to attract imports from other countries, both direct and indirect.

Value of the benchmark currency basket at time t = Σ (GDP weight of currency i(dated 2 years ago from year of time t)* normalized exchange rate of currency i against the US dollar at time t;

Effective exchange rate of currency j = Normalized exchange rate of currency j against the US dollar/Value of the benchmark currency basket against US dollar.

Ho's procedure allows effective exchange rate indices to be easily compiled for any country.

Exchange Rate Indices: NEER and REER

As country's currency can be compared with any other currency and a given country's currency can be expected to appreciate compared some currencies while expected to depreciate against some other currency. But can we generalize, whether a given country currency is expected to appreciate or depreciate? This can be done so by comparing the currency value of any country with the currency value of its major trading partners. Since countries trade with many other countries, to determine the relative purchasing power of a given currency, it needs to be evaluated against all other currency values so that the currency's true value can be identified. In other words, whether a currency is "over valued" or "under valued" compared to its major trading partners needs to be determined. This is done by calculating exchange rate indices.

These indices are calculated by trade weighing bilateral exchange rates between the currency and its trading partners. Two types of Exchange rate indices are calculated NEER (Nominal Effective Exchange Rate) and REER (Real Effective Exchange Rate).

Let us understand more on how these two indices are calculated. However more than the methodology, the interpretation of NEER and REER values is crucial to understand the direction of future exchange rate movement.

Exchange Rate Pass-through

Exchange rate pass through measure the percentage change in domestic prices of goods resulting from one percentage change in the exchange rate. If 1 percentage change in exchange rate results in 1 percentage change in domestic goods prices, then pass through is 100% or a complete pass through. Less than one-to-one change in domestic price compared to exchange rate is an incomplete or partial pass through.

For example, if the domestic currency depreciates against foreign currency, the imported goods become costlier. Hence consumers start replacing the imported goods with domestic goods, thus leading to an increase in prices of domestic goods. Depreciation of home currency also affects the cost of production of domestic goods, if the domestic good has some imported component, thus increasing the domestic goods price.

Change in exchange rate's impact on intermediate goods price is known as "first stage" pass through. The impact on domestic goods is known as "second stage" pass through.

A complete exchange rate pass through indicates that PPP holds i.e, that the prices of tradable goods when expressed in the same currency are same across countries.

It is pertinent to note here that change in exchange rate does not affect only the import goods and domestic goods prices, it also affects the export prices. Change in exchange rate affects 4 economic factors in a country i.e, import and export prices, consumer prices, investments and trade volumes. Of these four factors, exchange rate pass-through measures the effects of exchange rate changes on import and export prices.

Many empirical studies have focused on understating the degree of these pass through and came to the conclusion that complete pass through never occurs, though incomplete pass though occurs with varying degree – thus refuting the purchasing parity hypothesis. In other words, price level alone between countries has limited impact on future exchange rate. Hence companies trying forecast exchange rate should look beyond the price level parity conditions. Other parity condition i.e, interest rate parity and its impact on exchange rate is discussed in later sessions.

Exchange-rate pass-through (ERPT) is a measure of how responsive international prices are to changes in exchange rates.

Formally, exchange-rate pass-through is the elasticity of local-currency import prices with respect to the local-currency price of foreign currency, often measured as the percentage change, in the local currency, of import prices resulting from a one percent change in the exchange rate between the exporting and importing countries. A change in import prices affects retail and consumer prices. When exchange-rate pass-through is greater, there is more transmission of inflation between countries. Exchange-rate pass-through is also related to the law of one price and purchasing power parity.

Example

Suppose that the US imports widgets from the UK. The widgets cost $10 and £1 costs $1. Then the British Pound appreciates against the dollar and now £1 costs $1.50. Also suppose that the widgets now cost $12.50.

There has been a 50% change in the exchange rate and a 25% change in price. The exchange rate pass-through is,

$$\frac{25\%}{50\%} = .5.$$

For every 1% increase in the exchange rate, there has been a.5% increase in the price of the widgets.

Measurement

The “standard pass-through regression” is,

$$\Delta \ln p_t = \alpha + \sum_{i=0}^{N} \gamma_i \Delta \ln e_{t-i} + \delta \Delta \ln c_t + \psi \Delta \ln d_t + \epsilon_t,$$

where p is import price, e is the exchange rate, c is marginal costs, d is demand, and Δ denotes a first difference. The exchange-rate pass-through after N periods is,

$$\sum_{i=0}^{N} \gamma_i .$$

Campa and Goldberg (2005) estimated the long-run exchange-rate pass-through to import prices for the following countries, averaging across the countries from which imports came:

Country	Long-Run Exchange-Rate Pass-Through
Australia	0.69
Canada	0.68
Switzerland	0.94
Czech Republic	0.61
Germany	0.79
Denmark	0.68
Spain	0.56
Finland	0.82
France	1.21
United Kingdom	0.47
Hungary	0.85
Ireland	1.37
Iceland	0.76
Italy	0.62
Japan	1.26
Netherlands	0.77
Norway	0.79
New Zealand	0.62
Poland	0.99
Portugal	0.88
Sweden	0.59
USA	0.41

Measurement of exchange-rate pass-through is typically performed using aggregate price indexes. Some studies have examined how firms in different industries or with different production costs differ in their responses to exchange rates. Studies of firm-level differences explain why exchange-rate pass-through is not equal to one and how globalization caused a decrease in exchange-rate pass-through.

Elasticity (Economics)

In economics, elasticity is the measurement of how responsive an economic variable is to a change in another. It gives answers to questions such as:

- "If I lower the price of a product, how much more will sell?"

- "If I raise the price of one good, how will that affect sales of this other good?"
- "If the market price of a product goes down, how much will that affect the amount that firms will be willing to supply to the market?"

An *elastic* variable (with elasticity value greater than 1) is one which responds more than proportionally to changes in other variables. In contrast, an *inelastic* variable (with elasticity value less than 1) is one which changes less than proportionally in response to changes in other variables. A variable can have different values of its elasticity at different starting points: for example, the quantity of a good supplied by producers might be elastic at low prices but inelastic at higher prices, so that a rise from an initially low price might bring on a more-than-proportionate increase in quantity supplied while a rise from an initially high price might bring on a less-than-proportionate rise in quantity supplied.

Elasticity can be quantified as the ratio of the percentage change in one variable to the percentage change in another variable, when the latter variable has a causal influence on the former. A more precise definition is given in terms of differential calculus. It is a tool for measuring the responsiveness of one variable to changes in another, causative variable. Elasticity has the advantage of being a unitless ratio, independent of the type of quantities being varied. Frequently used elasticities include price elasticity of demand, price elasticity of supply, income elasticity of demand, elasticity of substitution between factors of production and elasticity of intertemporal substitution.

Elasticity is one of the most important concepts in neoclassical economic theory. It is useful in understanding the incidence of indirect taxation, marginal concepts as they relate to the theory of the firm, and distribution of wealth and different types of goods as they relate to the theory of consumer choice. Elasticity is also crucially important in any discussion of welfare distribution, in particular consumer surplus, producer surplus, or government surplus.

In empirical work an elasticity is the estimated coefficient in a linear regression equation where both the dependent variable and the independent variable are in natural logs. Elasticity is a popular tool among empiricists because it is independent of units and thus simplifies data analysis.

A major study of the price elasticity of supply and the price elasticity of demand for US products was undertaken by Hendrik S. Houthakker and Lester D. Taylor.

Specific Elasticities

Elasticities of Supply

Price elasticity of supply

The price elasticity of supply measures how the amount of a good that a supplier wishes to supply changes in response to a change in price. In a manner analogous to the price elasticity of demand, it captures the extent of horizontal movement along the supply curve relative to the extent of vertical movement. If the price elasticity of supply is zero the supply of a good supplied is "totally inelastic" and the quantity supplied is fixed.

Elasticities of scale

Elasticity of scale or *output elasticity* measures the percentage change in output induced by a collective percent change in the usages of all inputs. A production function or process is said to exhibit constant returns to scale if a percentage change in inputs results in an equal percentage in outputs (an elasticity equal to 1). It exhibits increasing returns to scale if a percentage change in inputs results in greater percentage change in output (an elasticity greater than 1). The definition of decreasing returns to scale is analogous.

Elasticities of Demand

Price elasticity of demand

Price elasticity of demand is a measure used to show the responsiveness, or elasticity, of the quantity demanded of a good or service to a change in its price. More precisely, it gives the percentage change in quantity demanded in response to a one percent change in price (ceteris paribus, i.e. holding constant all the other determinants of demand, such as income).

Cross-price elasticity of demand

Cross-price elasticity of demand is a measure of the responsiveness of the demand for one product to changes in the price of a different product. It is the ratio of percentage change in the former to the percentage change in the latter. If it is positive, the goods are called substitutes because a rise in the price of the other good causes consumers to substitute away from buying as much of the other good as before and into buying more of this good. If it is negative, the goods are called complements.

Applications

The concept of elasticity has an extraordinarily wide range of applications in economics. In particular, an understanding of elasticity is fundamental in understanding the response of supply and demand in a market.

Some common uses of elasticity include:

- Effect of changing price on firm revenue.
- Analysis of incidence of the tax burden and other government policies.

- Income elasticity of demand, used as an indicator of industry health, future consumption patterns and as a guide to firms' investment decisions.
- Effect of international trade and terms of trade effects.
- Analysis of consumption and saving behavior.
- Analysis of advertising on consumer demand for particular goods.

Variants

In some cases the discrete (non-infinitesimal) arc elasticity is used instead. In other cases, such as modified duration in bond trading, a percentage change in output is divided by a unit (not percentage) change in input, yielding a semi-elasticity instead.

References

- Moffett, Michael H.; Stonehill, Arthur I.; Eiteman, David K. (2009). Fundamentals of Multinational Finance, 3rd Edition. Boston, MA: Addison-Wesley. ISBN 978-0-321-54164-2
- Chatterjee, Devalina (2010). Three essays in forward rate unbiasedness hypothesis (Thesis). Utah State University. pp. 1–102. Retrieved 13, July 2020
- O'Sullivan, Arthur; Steven M. Sheffrin (2003). Economics: Principles in action. Upper Saddle River, New Jersey 07458: Pearson Prentice Hall. p. 458. ISBN 0-13-063085-3
- Feenstra, Robert C.; Taylor, Alan M. (2008). International Macroeconomics. New York, NY: Worth Publishers. ISBN 978-1-4292-0691-4
- Zivot, Eric (2000). "Cointegration and forward and spot exchange rate regressions". Journal of International Money and Finance. 19 (6): 785–812. doi:10.1016/S0261-5606(00)00031-0. Retrieved 20, May 2020
- Narasimhan, Anand; Dogra, Aparna (3 September 2012). "The case study: Goli Vada Pav". Financial Times. Retrieved 01, March 2020
- Dunn, Robert M., Jr.; Mutti, John H. (2004). International Economics, 6th Edition. New York, NY: Routledge. ISBN 978-0-415-31154-0
- Madura, Jeff (2007). International Financial Management: Abridged 8th Edition. Mason, OH: Thomson South-Western. ISBN 0-324-36563-2
- Ho, Tsung-Wu (2003). "A re-examination of the unbiasedness forward rate hypothesis using dynamic SUR model". The Quarterly Review of Economics and Finance. 43 (3): 542–559. doi:10.1016/S1062-9769(02)00171-0. Retrieved 21, May 2020
- Cook, J.A. (2014). "The Effect of Firm-Level Productivity on Exchange Rate Pass-Through". Economics Letters. 122 (1): 27–30. doi:10.1016/j.econlet.2013.10.028

- FBF Master Agreement for Financial Transactions, Supplement to the Derivatives Annex, Edition 2004 (PDF), 2004, retrieved 27, August 2020
- Moosa, Imad A. (2003). International Financial Operations: Arbitrage, Hedging, Speculation, Financing and Investment. New York, NY: Palgrave Macmillan. ISBN 0-333-99859-6

6

International Trade Barriers

International trade barriers are government-induced restrictions on international trade, which decrease overall economic deficiency. They can be broadly classified into tariff and non-tariff barriers. The custom levies or taxes on imported goods are called tariff barriers. The barriers outside the purview of tariff barriers like import licenses, export licenses, import quotas, subsidies, etc. are known as Non-tariff. This chapter discusses the subject of trade barriers and their effects on International trade.

Trade barriers are government-induced restrictions on international trade. Man-made trade barriers come in several forms, including:

- Tariffs,
- Non-tariff barriers to trade,
- Import licenses,
- Export licenses,
- Import quotas,
- Subsidies,
- Voluntary Export Restraints,
- Local content requirements,
- Embargo,
- Currency devaluation,
- Trade restriction.

Most trade barriers work on the same principle–the imposition of some sort of cost on trade that raises the price of the traded products. If two or more nations repeatedly use trade barriers against each other, then a trade war results.

Economists generally agree that trade barriers are detrimental and decrease overall economic efficiency. This can be explained by the theory of comparative advantage. In theory, free trade involves the removal of all such barriers, except perhaps those considered necessary for health or national security. In practice, however, even those countries promoting free trade heavily subsidize certain industries, such as agriculture and steel. Trade barriers are often criticized for the effect they have on the developing world. Because rich-country players set trade policies, goods, such as agricultural products that developing countries are best at producing, face high barriers. Trade barriers, such as taxes on food imports or subsidies for farmers in developed economies, lead to overproduction and dumping on world markets, thus lowering prices and hurting poor-country farmers. Tariffs also tend to be anti-poor, with low rates for raw commodities and high rates for labor-intensive processed goods. The Commitment to Development Index measures the effect that rich country trade policies actually have on the developing world. Another negative aspect of trade barriers is that it would cause a limited choice of products and, therefore, would force customers to pay higher prices and accept inferior quality.

In general, for a given level of protection, quota-like restrictions carry a greater potential for reducing welfare than do tariffs. Tariffs, quotas, and non-tariff barriers lead too few of the economy's resources being used to produce tradable goods. An export subsidy can also be used to give an advantage to a domestic producer over a foreign producer. Export subsidies tend to have a particularly strong negative effect because in addition to distorting resource allocation, they reduce the economy's terms of trade. In contrast to tariffs, export subsidies lead to an over allocation of the economy's resources to the production of tradable goods.

Ethical Barriers

Despite international trading laws and declarations, countries continue to face challenges around ethical trading and business practices. International trade is the exchange of goods and services across national borders. In most countries, it represents a significant part of gross domestic product (GDP). The rise of industrialization, globalization, and technological innovation has increased the importance of international trade, as well as its economic, social, and political effects on the countries involved. Internationally recognized ethical practices such as the UN Global Compact have been instituted to facilitate mutual cooperation and benefit between governments, businesses, and public institutions. Nevertheless, countries continue to face challenges around ethical trading and business practices, especially regarding economic inequalities and human rights violations.

Arguments against International Trade

Capital markets involve the raising and investing money in various enterprises. Although some argue that the increasing integration of these financial markets between countries leads to more consistent and seamless trading practices, others point out that capital flows tend to favor the capital owners more than any other group. Likewise, owners and workers in specific sectors in capital-exporting countries bear much of the burden of adjusting to increased movement of capital. The economic strains and eventual hardships that result from these conditions lead to political divisions about whether or not to encourage or increase integration of international trade markets.

Moreover, critics argue that income disparities between the rich and poor are exacerbated, and industrialized nations grow in power at the expense of under-capitalized countries.

Anti-Globalization Movements

The anti-globalization movement is a worldwide activist movement that is critical of the globalization of capitalism. Anti-globalization activists are particularly critical of the undemocratic nature of capitalist globalization and the promotion of neoliberalism by international institutions such as the International Monetary Fund (IMF) and the World Bank. Other common targets of anti- corporate and anti-globalization movements include the Organisation for Economic Co-operation and Development (OECD), the WTO, and free trade treaties like the North American Free Trade Agreement (NAFTA), Free Trade Area of the Americas (FTAA), the Multilateral Agreement on Investment (MAI), and the General Agreement on Trade in Services (GATS). Meetings of such bodies are often met with strong protests, as demonstrators attempt to bring attention to the often devastating effects of global capital on local conditions.

On November 30, 1999, close to fifty thousand people gathered to protest the WTO meetings in Seattle, Washington. Labor, economic, and environmental activists succeeded in disrupting and closing the meetings due to their disapproval of corporate globalization. This event came to symbolize the increased debate and growing conflict around the ethical questions on international trade, globalization and capitalization.

Cultural Barriers

It is typically more difficult to do business in a foreign country than in one's home country due to cultural barriers.

Culture and Global Business

It is typically more difficult to do business in a foreign country than in one's home country, especially in the early stages when a firm is considering either physical investment in or product expansion to another country. Expansion planning requires an in-depth knowledge of existing market channels and suppliers, of consumer preferences and current purchase behavior, and of domestic and foreign rules and regulations. Language and cultural barriers present considerable challenges, as well as institutional differences among countries.

With the process of globalization and increasing global trade, it is unavoidable that different cultures will meet, conflict, and blend together. People from different cultures find it hard to communicate not only due to language barriers but also because of cultural differences.

In a survey of Texas agricultural exporting firms, Hollon found that from a firm management perspective, the initial entry into export markets was significantly more difficult than either the handling of ongoing export activities or the consideration of expansion to new export product lines or markets. From a list of 38 items in three categories (knowledge gaps, marketing aspects, and financial aspects) over three time horizons (start-up, ongoing, and expansion), the three problems rated most difficult were all start-up phase marketing items:

- Poor knowledge of emerging markets or lack of information on potentially profitable markets.
- Foreign market entry problems and overseas product promotion and distribution.
- Complexity of the export transaction, including documentation and "red tape."

Two of these items, market entry and transaction complexity, remained problematic in ongoing operations and in new product market expansion. Import restrictions and export competition became more problematic in later phases, while financial problems were pervasive at all phases of the export operation.

Tools for Understanding Cultural Deviations in Business

Recognizing that different geographic regions and/or nationalities represent vastly different business operating characteristics, often due to differences in cultural predisposition, is a critical building block for successful global business leaders. As a result, various researchers in global business have generated business models to illustrate key cultural considerations between different countries. The most recognized and utilized in the field is Geert Hofstede's Cultural Dimensions Theory, which encompasses six cultural deviations highly relevant to business managers.

The six dimensions underline differences in perspective in each category. Two countries (or more) are selected for comparison, at which point can identify differences in business practices based on cultural barriers. For example, Country A demonstrates lower power distance compared to Country B. This means that a resident of Country A operating in Country B must understand that lines of authority are more rigid in Country B and act accordingly. To briefly explain each dimension:

- PDI rating represents a stronger acceptance of authority in a given culture.
- IDV (individualism) rating indicates the degree to which individuals are focused upon as opposed to the broader group.
- UAI represents the degree to which risk-taking is commonplace (a higher rating meaning a lower propensity for risk).

- MAS represent the scale between competitiveness, materialism and aggressiveness (high rating) compared to focusing on relationships and quality of life.
- LTO indicates the tendency to plan for longer-term agenda items as opposed to pursuing short-term goals.
- IVR is simply the frugal (or spendthrift) habits of the average individual in a culture (purchasing beyond necessity).

Technological Barriers

Standards-related trade measures, known in WTO parlance as technical barriers to trade play a critical role in shaping global trade. U.S. companies, farmers, ranchers, and manufacturers increasingly encounter non- tariff trade barriers in the form of product standards, testing requirements, and other technical requirements as they seek to sell products and services around the world. As tariff barriers to industrial and agricultural trade have fallen, standards-related measures of this kind have emerged as a key concern. Governments, market participants, and other entities can use standards-related measures as an effective and efficient means of achieving legitimate commercial and policy objectives. But when standards-related measures are outdated, overly burdensome, discriminatory, or otherwise inappropriate, these measures can reduce competition, stifle innovation, and create unnecessary technical barriers to trade. These kinds of measures can pose a particular problem for small- and medium-sized enterprises (SMEs), which often do not have the resources to address these problems on their own. Significant foreign trade barriers in the form of product standards, technical regulations and testing, certification, and other procedures are involved in determining whether or not products conform to standards and technical regulations.

These standards-related trade measures, known in World Trade Organization (WTO) parlance as "technical barriers to trade," play a critical role in shaping the flow of global trade. Standards-related measures serve an important function in facilitating global trade, including by enabling greater access to international markets by SMEs. Standards-related measures also enable governments to pursue legitimate objectives, such as protecting human health and the environment and preventing deceptive practices. But standards-related measures that are non-transparent, discriminatory, or otherwise unwarranted can act as significant barriers to U.S. trade. These kinds of measures can pose a particular problem for SMEs, which often do not have the resources to address these problems on their own.

The Argument for Barriers

Some argue that imports from countries with low wages have put downward pressure on the wages of Americans and therefore we should have trade barriers. It is asserted that trade has created jobs for foreign workers at the expense of American workers. It is more accurate to say that trade both creates and destroys jobs in the economy in line with market forces.

Economy-wide trade creates jobs in industries that have comparative advantage and destroys jobs in industries that have a comparative disadvantage. In the process, the economy's composition of employment changes; but, according to economic theory, there is no net loss of jobs due to trade. Over the course of the last economic expansion, from 1992 to 2000, U.S. imports increased nearly 240%. Over that same period, total employment grew by 22 million jobs, and the unemployment rate fell from 7.5% to 4.0% (the lowest unemployment rate in more than 30 years.). Foreign outsourcing by American firms, which has been the object of much recent attention, is a form of importing and also creates and destroys jobs, leaving the overall level of employment unchanged. There is no denying that with international trade there will be short-run hardship for some, but economists maintain the whole economy's living standard is raised by such exchange. They view these adverse effects as qualitatively the same as those induced by purely domestic disruptions, such as shifting consumer demand or technological change. In that context, economists argue that easing adjustment of those harmed is economically more fruitful than protection given the net economic benefit of trade to the total economy. Many people believe that an import from countries with low wages has put downward pressure on the wages of Americans.

There is no doubt that international trade can have strong effects, good and bad, on the wages of American workers. The plight of the worker adversely affected by imports comes quickly to mind. But it is also true that workers in export industries benefit from trade. Moreover, all workers are consumers and benefit from the expanded market choices and lower prices that trade brings. Yet, concurrent with the large expansion of trade over the past 25 years, real wages (i.e., inflation adjusted wages) of American workers grew more slowly than in the earlier post-war period, and the inequality of wages between the skilled and less skilled worker rose sharply. Was trade the force behind this deteriorating wage performance? Some industries, or at least components of some industries, are vital to national security and possibly may need to be insulated from the vicissitudes of international market forces. This determination needs to be made on a case-by-case basis since the claim is made by some who do not meet national security criteria. Such criteria may also vary from case to case. It is also true that national security could be compromised by the export of certain dual-use products that, while commercial in nature, could also be used to produce products that might confer a military advantage to U.S. adversaries. Controlling such exports is clearly justified from a national security standpoint; but, it does come at the cost of lost export sales and an economic loss to the nation. Minimizing the economic welfare loss from such export controls hinges on a well- focused identification and regular re-evaluation of the subset of goods with significant national security potential that should be subject to control.

The Argument against Barriers

Economists generally agree that trade barriers are detrimental and decrease overall economic efficiency. Trade barriers are often criticized for the effect they have on the developing world. Because rich-country players call most of the shots and set trade policies, goods, such as crops that developing countries are best at producing, still face high barriers. Trade barriers, such as taxes on food imports or subsidies for farmers in developed economies, lead to overproduction and dumping on world markets, thus lowering prices and hurting poor-country farmers. Tariffs also tend to be anti-poor, with low rates for raw commodities and high rates for labor-intensive processed goods.

If international trade is economically enriching, imposing barriers to such exchanges will prevent the nation from fully realizing the economic gains from trade and must reduce welfare. Protection of import-competing industries with tariffs, quotas, and non-tariff barriers can lead to an over-allocation of the nation's scarce resources in the protected sectors and an under-allocation of resources in the unprotected tradable goods industries. In the terms of the analogy of trade as a more efficient productive process used above, reducing the flow of imports will also reduce the flow of exports. Less output requires less input. Clearly, the exporting sector must lose as the protected import-competing activities gain. But, more importantly, from this perspective the overall economy that consumed the imported goods must also lose, because the more efficient production process–international trade–cannot be used to the optimal degree, and, thereby, will have generally increased the price and reduced the array of goods available to the consumer. Therefore, the ultimate economic cost of the trade barrier is not a transfer of well-being between sectors, but a permanent net loss to the whole economy arising from the barriers distortion toward the less efficient the use of the economy's scarce resources.

Tariffs

A tariff is a duty or tax imposed by the government of a country upon the traded commodity as it crosses the national boundaries. Tariff can be levied both upon exports and imports. The tariff or duties imposed upon the goods originating in the home country and scheduled for abroad are called as the export duties. Countries, interested in maximising their exports generally avoid the use of export duties. Tariffs have, therefore, become synonymous with import duties.

The import duties or import tariffs are levied upon the goods originating from abroad and scheduled for the home country. Sometimes a country may also resort to what is called as a transit duty. It is imposed upon the goods originating in the foreign country and scheduled for a third country crossing the borders of the home country.

The imposition of import tariff results in the relative changes in prices of products and factors. That brings about a significant change in the structure of international trade. High tariffs certainly have the effect of restricting the volume of international trade. A negative tariff or subsidy is often supposed to expand foreign trade over and above its volume in the absence of subsidy.

Types of Tariffs

Tariffs are of several types and these can be classified into different groups or sub-groups as below:

Classification on the Basis of Criterion for Imposition

On the basis of the criterion for imposition of tariffs. These can be of such types as:

- Specific tariff,
- Ad Valorem tariff,
- Compound tariff,
- Sliding scale tariff.

Specific Tariff

Specific tariff is the fixed amount of money per physical unit or according to the weight or measurement of the commodity imported or exported. Such duties can be levied on goods like wheat, rice, fertilizers, cement, sugar, cloth etc. Specific duties are quite easy to administer, as they do not involve the evaluation of the goods.

The determination of the value of the traded goods may be difficult as there are several variants of price such as demand price, supply price, market price, contract price, invoice price, f.o.b, (free on board) price, c.i.f (cost, insurance, freight) price etc. The resort to specific duties enables the government to keep out of complexities of prices. However, the specific duties cannot be levied on high valued goods such as diamonds, jewelry, watches, T.V. sets, motor cars, works of arts like paintings etc.

Ad Valorem Tariff

When the duty is levied as a fixed percentage of the value of the traded commodity, it is called as valorem tariff. Such duties are levied on the products the value of which is disproportionately higher compared to their physical characteristics such as weight or measurement.

These duties are more equitable as the costly goods, generally consumed by the rich, bear greater burden of duty, while the cheaper goods bought by the poor, bear lesser burden of tariff. For instance, if the import of watches is subject to 70 percent ad valorem tariff, a watch valued at Rs. 1000 will be subject to a duty of Rs. 700 and a watch valued at Rs. 1200 will be subject to a tariff amounting to Rs. 840. The ad valorem duties have an additional advantage that the international comparison of tariffs, in their case, can be easily made.

Compound Tariff

The compound tariff is a combination of specific and ad valorem tariff. The structure of compound tariff includes specific duty on each unit of the commodity plus a percentage of ad valorem duty. The compound tariffs not only impart a greater elasticity to revenues but also assure a more effective protection to the home industries.

Sliding Scale Tariff

The import duties which vary with the prices of the commodities are termed as sliding scale duties. These may either be on specific or ad valorem basis. In practice, these are generally on a specific basis.

Classification on the Basis of Purpose for which Tariff is Imposed

On the basis of purpose of levying the tariff. These can be of two types:

- Revenue Tariff.
- Protective Tariff.

Revenue Tariff

The tariff, which is imposed primarily for generating more revenues for the government is called as the revenue tariff. In advanced countries, the introduction and diversification of direct taxes has reduced the importance of tariff as a source of government revenues. But in the less developed countries, there is still much reliance of the governments on this source of revenue.

Generally pure revenue tariff is not possible. The imposition of tariff, even for the purpose of securing revenues, does have protective effect when it leads to switch of demand by the domestic consumers from the imported to home- produced goods.

Protective Tariff

The tariff may be imposed by the government to protect the home industries from the cut-throat competition from the foreign produced goods. The higher the tariff, greater may be the protective effect of tariff. A perfect protective tariff is likely to prohibit completely the import from abroad.

In practice, the perfect protective tariff may not exist. If the domestic demand for import remains strong, there can be the possibility of smuggling imported goods. In addition, such a tariff will not yield any revenue to the government. A high rate of protective tariff can make the domestic producers more lethargic and inefficient and unable to face foreign competition even in the long run.

Classification on the Basis of Discrimination

If the tariff is influenced the consideration of discrimination. There can be two types of tariffs:

- Non-discriminatory.
- Discriminatory.

Non-Discriminatory Tariff

If the uniform tariff rates are applicable to all the commodities irrespective of the country of origin, these are known as non-discriminatory tariffs. It is possible that low rates of tariffs on certain commodities exist because of commercial agreements with some countries but the tariff-imposing home country extends the same low tariff rates to the commodities of all the countries.

Such a system of nondiscriminatory tariff is called as single column tariff. This system of tariff is easy and simple to administer. There is, however, one deficiency that it is not elastic enough to adjust according to the changing needs of the industries of the home country. From the viewpoint of revenues too, it may not be satisfactory for the tariff-imposing country.

Discriminatory Tariff

In case of discriminatory tariff, the varying tariff rates exist for different commodities. The products originating from favoured countries are subject to a lower tariff rate than those of other countries. The discriminatory tariffs can be double or multiple column tariffs.

In case of the double column tariff, two different rates of duty exist for all or some commodities. Both the rates are either announced by the government right from the beginning and the two rates come into existence after the country enters into favoured-nation commercial agreement with some foreign countries. The favoured rates of tariff may either be on a unilateral basis or on a reciprocal basis. The double column tariff can be further classified as:

- General and conventional tariff.
- Maximum and minimum tariff.
- Multiple Column Tariff.

General and Conventional Tariff

The general tariff schedule is determined by the state legislature. It also makes provision for the adjustment in tariff rates as and when required to fulfill the obligations of international commercial agreements. The conventional tariff schedule is evolved through the commercial agreements of the home country with other countries. It does not permit changes in tariff rates according to the changes in domestic conditions or requirements.

The changes can be possible only after negotiations and agreements are reached between the concerned countries or after the expiry of the existing agreement. It is clear that there is some rigidity in the conventional tariff schedule. In contrast, the general tariff schedule is more flexible.

Maximum and Minimum Tariff

Under this system, a country has maximum and minimum tariff rates for every commodity. These tariff rates are fixed by the legislature and the government is authorised to apply specific rates of tariff to the goods imported from the different countries. The minimum tariff rates are applied to the products originating from the countries treated as 'The Most Favoured Nations'. The maximum tariff rates are applied for the purpose of improving the bargaining position of the home country vis-a-vis the foreign countries.

Multiple Column Tariff

The multiple column tariff consists of three different rates of tariff – a general rate, an international rate and a preferential rate. The general and international tariff rates can be considered equivalent to the maximum and minimum tariff rates discussed above. The preferential tariff is generally applied by a subject country to the products originating from the colonial countries.

The preferential tariff rate is kept lower than the general rate of tariff. For instance, the goods imported by India from Britain before independence were subjected to a lower tariff or duty free on account of Imperial Preferences. On the other hand, the goods imported from other countries such as Japan, Germany and others were subject to higher rates of tariff.

Classification on the Basis of Product

Whether a product is imported or exported can be the basis of tariff. On this basis, the tariffs can be of the types of:

- Import duties.
- Exports duties.

Import Duties

If the home country imposes tariff upon the products of the foreign countries as they enter its territory, the tariff is known as import tariff or import duty.

Export Duties

If the products of the home country become subject to tax as they leave its territory to be sold in the foreign market, the tax or duty is called as export tariff or export duty. The import tariffs have remained the matter of deep interest both for analytical and policy reasons. These are far more wide-spread, and almost every country takes resort to them. In contrast, the export duties are applied to a very limited extent. Some countries like the USA have prohibited export duties by law. Even in those countries, where these are in vogue, the basic purpose is to secure larger revenues.

Classification on the Basis of Retaliation

On this basis, the tariffs can be of the types of:

- Retaliatory tariffs.
- Countervailing tariffs.

Retaliatory Tariffs

If a foreign country has imposed tariffs upon the exports from the home country and the latter imposes tariffs against the products of the former, the tariffs resorted to by the home country will be regarded as the retaliatory tariffs. The home country, while adopting this measure does not either has the object of raising revenues or protecting home industries but of acting in retaliation.

Countervailing Tariffs

If the foreign country has been exporting large quantities of its products in the market of the home country on the strength of export subsidies, the home country can neutralise the 'unfair advantage' enjoyed by foreign products through imposing duties upon them as they enter the territory of the home country. The latter has full justification for resorting to these countervailing duties in order that the unfair advantage given by exports subsidies to the foreign products is offset and the competition takes place on equal footing between the foreign and home produced goods.

International trade increases the number of goods that domestic consumers can choose from, decreases the cost of those goods through increased competition, and allows domestic industries to ship their products abroad. While all of these effects seem beneficial, free trade isn't widely accepted as completely beneficial to all parties.

Who Collects a Tariff?

In simplest terms, a tariff is a tax. It adds to the cost borne by consumers of imported goods and is one of several trade policies that a country can enact. Tariffs are paid to the customs authority of the country imposing the tariff. Tariffs on imports coming into the United States, for example, are collected by Customs and Border Protection, acting on behalf of the Commerce Department. In the U.K., it's HM Revenue & Customs (HMRC) that collects the money.

It is important to recognize that the taxes owed on imports are paid by domestic consumers, and not imposed directly on the foreign country's exports. The effect is nonetheless to make foreign products relatively more expensive for consumers - but if manufacturers rely on imported components or other inputs in their production process, they will also pass the increased cost on to consumers. Often, goods from abroad are cheaper because they offer cheaper capital or labor costs, if those goods become more expensive, then consumers will choose the relatively costlier domestic product. Overall, consumers tend to lose out with tariffs, where the taxes are collected domestically.

Why are Tariffs and Trade Barriers Used?

Tariffs are often created to protect infant industries and developing economies but are also used by more advanced economies with developed industries. Here are five of the top reasons tariffs are used:

Protecting Domestic Employment

The levying of tariffs is often highly politicized. The possibility of increased competition from imported goods can threaten domestic industries. These domestic companies may fire workers or shift production abroad to cut costs, which means higher unemployment and a less happy electorate. The unemployment argument often shifts to domestic industries complaining about cheap foreign labor, and how poor working conditions and lack of regulation allow foreign companies to produce goods more cheaply. In economics, however, countries will continue to produce goods until they no longer have a comparative advantage.

Protecting Consumers

A government may levy a tariff on products that it feels could endanger its population. For example, South Korea may place a tariff on imported beef from the United States if it thinks that the goods could be tainted with a disease.

Infant Industries

The use of tariffs to protect infant industries can be seen by the Import Substitution Industrialization (ISI) strategy employed by many developing nations. The government of a developing economy will levy tariffs on imported goods in industries in which it wants to foster growth. This increases the prices of imported goods and creates a domestic market for domestically produced goods while protecting those industries from being forced out by more competitive pricing. It decreases unemployment and allows developing countries to shift from agricultural products to finished goods.

Criticisms of this sort of protectionist strategy revolve around the cost of subsidizing the development of infant industries. If an industry develops without competition, it could wind up producing lower quality goods, and the subsidies required to keep the state-backed industry afloat could sap economic growth.

National Security

Barriers are also employed by developed countries to protect certain industries that are deemed strategically important, such as those supporting national security. Defense industries are often viewed as vital to state interests, and often enjoy significant levels of protection. For example, while both Western Europe and the United States are industrialized, both are very protective of defense-oriented companies.

Retaliation

Countries may also set tariffs as a retaliation technique if they think that a trading partner has not played by the rules. For example, if France believes that the United States has allowed its wine producers to call its domestically produced sparkling wines "Champagne" (a name specific to the Champagne region of France) for too long, it may levy a tariff on imported meat from the United States. If the U.S. agrees to crack down on the improper labeling, France is likely to stop its retaliation. Retaliation can also be employed if a trading partner goes against the government's foreign policy objectives.

Common Types of Tariffs

There are several types of tariffs and barriers that a government can employ:

- Specific tariffs.
- Ad valorem tariffs.
- Licenses.
- Import quotas.
- Voluntary export restraints.
- Local content requirements.

Specific Tariffs

A fixed fee levied on one unit of an imported good is referred to as a specific tariff. This tariff can vary according to the type of good imported. For example, a country could levy a $15 tariff on each pair of shoes imported, but levy a $300 tariff on each computer imported.

Ad Valorem Tariffs

The phrase "ad valorem" is Latin for "according to value," and this type of tariff is levied on a good based on a percentage of that good's value. An example of an ad valorem tariff would be a 15% tariff levied by Japan on U.S. automobiles. The 15% is a price increase on the value of the automobile, so a $10,000 vehicle now costs $11,500 to Japanese consumers. This price increase protects domestic producers from being undercut but also keeps prices artificially high for Japanese car shoppers.

How Do Tariffs Affect Prices?

Tariffs increase the prices of imported goods. Because of this, domestic producers are not forced to reduce their prices from increased competition, and domestic consumers are left paying higher prices as a result. Tariffs also reduce efficiencies by allowing companies that would not exist in a more competitive market to remain open.

The figure below illustrates the effects of world trade without the presence of a tariff. In the graph, DS means domestic supply and DD means domestic demand. The price of goods at home is found at price P, while the world price is found at P*. At a lower price, domestic consumers will consume Qw worth of goods, but because the home country can only produce up to Qd, it must import Qw-Qd worth of goods.

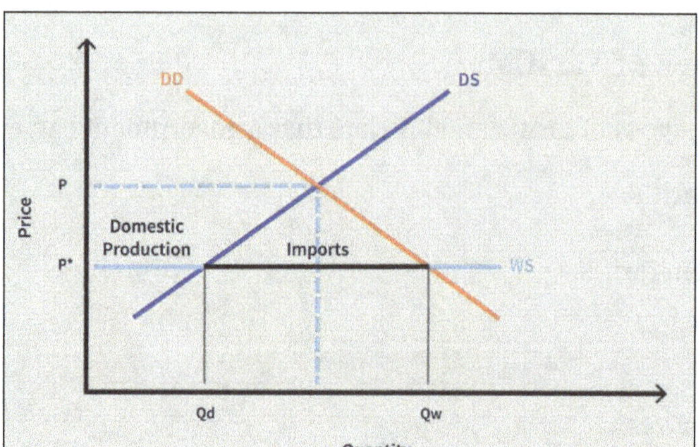

When a tariff or other price-increasing policy is put in place, the effect is to increase prices and limit the volume of imports. In the figure below, price increases from the non-tariff P* to P'. Because the price has increased, more domestic companies are willing to produce the good, so Qd moves right. This also shifts Qw left. The overall effect is a reduction in imports, increased domestic production, and higher consumer prices.

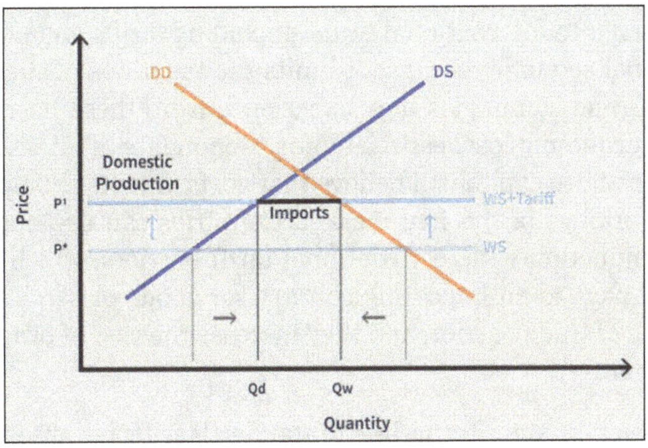

Tariffs and Modern Trade

The role tariffs play in international trade has declined in modern times. One of the primary reasons for the decline is the introduction of international organizations designed to improve free trade, such as the World Trade Organization (WTO). Such organizations make it more difficult for a country to levy tariffs and taxes on imported goods, and can reduce the likelihood of retaliatory taxes. Because of this, countries have shifted to non-tariff barriers, such as quotas and export restraints. Organizations like the WTO attempt to reduce production and consumption distortions created by tariffs. These distortions are the result of domestic producers making goods due to inflated prices, and consumers purchasing fewer goods because prices have increased.

Since the 1930s, many developed countries have reduced tariffs and trade barriers, which has improved global integration and brought about globalization. Multilateral agreements between governments increase the likelihood of tariff reduction, while enforcement of binding agreements reduces uncertainty.

Non-Tariff Barrier to Trade

A nontariff barrier is a way to restrict trade using trade barriers in a form other than a tariff. Nontariff barriers include quotas, embargoes, sanctions, and levies. As part of their political or economic strategy, some countries frequently use nontariff barriers to restrict the amount of trade they conduct with other countries.

How Non-tariff Barriers Work

Countries commonly use nontariff barriers in international trade. Decisions about when to impose nontariff barriers are influenced by the political alliances of a country and the overall availability of goods and services.

In general, any barrier to international trade–including tariffs and non-tariff barriers–influences the global economy because it limits the functions of the free market. The lost revenue that some companies may experience from these barriers to trade may be considered an economic loss, especially for proponents of laissez-faire capitalism. Advocates of laissez-faire capitalism believe that governments should abstain from interfering in the workings of the free market. Countries can use nontariff barriers in place of, or in conjunction with, conventional tariff barriers, which are taxes that an exporting country pays to an importing country for goods or services. Tariffs are the most common type of trade barrier, and they increase the cost of products and services in an importing country.

Often times countries pursue alternatives to standard tariffs because they release countries from paying added tax on imported goods. Alternatives to standard tariffs can have a meaningful impact on the level of trade (while creating a different monetary impact than standard tariffs).

Types of Non-tariff Barriers

- Licenses: Countries may use licenses to limit imported goods to specific businesses. If a business is granted a trade license, it is permitted to import goods that would otherwise be restricted for trade in the country.
- Quotas: Countries often issue quotas for importing and exporting both goods and services. With quotas, countries agree on specified limits for products and services allowed for importation to a country. In most cases, there are no restrictions on importing these goods and services until a country reaches its quota, which it can set for a specific timeframe. Additionally, quotas are often used in international trade licensing agreements.
- Embargoes: Embargoes are when a country–or several countries–officially ban the trade of specified goods and services with another country. Governments may take this measure to support their specific political or economic goals.
- Sanctions: Countries impose sanctions on other countries to limit their trade activity. Sanctions can include increased administrative actions–or additional customs and trade procedures–that slow or limit a country's ability to trade.
- Voluntary Export Restraints: Exporting countries sometimes use voluntary export restraints. Voluntary export restraints set limits on the number of goods and service a country can export to specified countries. These restraints are typically based on availability and political alliances.

Example of Non-tariff Barriers

In December 2017, the United Nations adopted a round of nontariff barriers against North Korea and the Kim Jong Un regime. The nontariff barriers included sanctions that cut exports of gasoline, diesel, and other refined oil products to the nation. They also prohibited the export of industrial equipment, machinery, transport vehicles, and industrial metals to North Korea. The intention of these nontariff barriers was to put economic pressure on the nation to stop its nuclear arms and military exercises.

Import Licence

The import licence may include tariff and non-tariff barriers. A tariff is an import and export tax between countries. A non-tariff barrier is an obstacle and comes in a form of a quota, Government regulations or licensing which means that the import licence is a non-tariff barrier.

A national government provides an official import license to authorize the importation of certain goods into a country. The document is used to specify the amount of goods that need to be transported where carriers make sure they do not exceed the already determined quota.

Which Goods are Controlled by Import Licence?

A specific Government may put certain restrictions on what type of goods and services are imported. The import licence defines the number which is why it needs to be issued. In addition, some of the goods controlled by the licence are the following:

- Agricultural products,
- Plants,
- Medicine,
- Food,
- Chemicals,
- Military weapons,
- Wood products,
- Technology.

Why Importing is Crucial

There are many reasons why importing may be crucial. The right definition for all would be to make human living easier. It is good for the economy, for other industries and mainly, it is beneficial for the society. As an explanation, importing is advantageous because it has become a necessity, and it offers the following:

- Accessibility: There are goods or services that are not produced in specific countries and importing makes them available for the society. With importing, people can advantage from door to door delivery and have their goods shipped right at their door.
- Preference: Some prestigious textile products like cashmere, silk or specific cotton are available in a few countries only. They need to be imported in other countries for availability and preferences of businesses or buyers. Other products like Italian furniture, cashmere or French perfume are more authentic to a foreign country.
- Price: There are products which are found cheaper in other countries. Electronics, technology and clothing are one of them and buyers are constantly purchasing online in the previous years. On the other hand, there are toys and clothing which can be manufactured for a cheaper price in other countries, so importing is the best option for businesses.

Why Import Licences are Needed?

An import licence is needed because some of the goods may be restricted, a subject to a specific quota, or a subject to monitoring. For example, if you want to transport dangerous goods or hazardous chemicals, you will need an import licence.

As previously mentioned, goods that can be banned are military or other offensive weapons, self-defense sprays etc. Examples of goods that can be subject to monitoring are firearms.

Export Licence

An export license is a document issued by the appropriate licensing agency after which an exporter is allowed to transport his product in a foreign market. The license is only issued after a careful review of the facts surrounding the given export transaction. Export license depends on the nature of goods to be transported as well as the destination port. So, being an exporter it is necessary to determine whether the product or good to be exported requires an export license or not. While making the determination one must consider the following necessary points:

- What are you exporting?
- Where are you exporting?
- Who will receive your item?
- What will your items will be used?

Canalisation

Canalisation is an important feature of Export License under which certain goods can be imported only by designated agencies. For an example, an item like gold, in bulk, can be imported only by specified banks like SBI and some foreign banks or designated agencies.

Application for an Export License

To determine whether a license is needed to export a particular commercial product or service, an exporter must first classify the item by identifying what is called ITC (HS) Classifications. Export license are only issued for the goods mentioned in the Schedule 2 of ITC (HS) Classifications of Export and Import items. A proper application can be submitted to the Director General of Foreign Trade (DGFT). The Export Licensing Committee under the Chairmanship of Export Commissioner considers such applications on merits for issue of export licenses.

Exports Free Unless Regulated

The Director General of Foreign Trade (DGFT) from time to time specifies through a public notice according to which any goods, not included in the ITC (HS) Classifications of Export and Import items may be exported without a license. Such terms and conditions may include Minimum Export Price (MEP), registration with specified authorities, quantitative ceilings and compliance with other laws, rules, regulations.

Import Quotas

The import quota means physical limitation of the quantities of different products to be imported from foreign countries within a specified period of time, usually one year. The import quota may be fixed either in terms of quantity or the value of the product.

For instance, the government may specify that 60,000 colour T.V. sets may be imported from Japan. Alternatively, it may specify that T.V. sets of the value of Rs. 50 crores can be imported from that country during a given year. For the purpose of restricting imports, it may adopt one of the alternative ways such as:

- Issue of import licence to the highest bidder in the open market.
- Issue of import licence by calling for the tenders form prospective importers, the highest tenderer getting the licence.
- Issue of import licence on first-come first-serve basis.
- Issue of import licences of specific categories of importers such as established importers, star trading houses, actual users etc.

- Issue of import licences to some government agency such as the State Trading Corporation.

Objectives of Import Quotas

The system of prescribing import quota is resorted to by the government of a country for realising some of the following objectives:

- To afford protection to domestic industries through restricting foreign competition by limiting the imports from abroad.
- To make adjustment in the adverse balance of payments. The restriction of imports through quotas can reduce the balance of payments deficit faced by the country.
- To conserve the scarce foreign exchange resources of the country and to direct their use for high-priority import items.
- To ensure the stabilisation of the internal price level by properly regulating the imports of goods from abroad.
- To discourage conspicuous consumption by the wealthy sections through placing quota restrictions on the import of luxury goods.
- To improve the international bargaining position of the country through allocating larger import quotas for the products of such countries as allow a liberal inflow of the products of the home country.
- To retaliate against the restrictive trade policies adopted by some of the foreign countries.
- To check the speculative imports in anticipation of changes in exchange rates, tariff rates and internal money and credit policies, the government may take resort to import quota.

Types of Import Quotas

Tariff or Custom Quota

In the case of tariff or custom quota, a certain specified quantity of a commodity is allowed to be imported by the government of the importing country either duty free or at a low rate of import duty. The imports in excess of this specified quantity are subject to a relatively higher rate of tariff. A tariff quota is either an autonomous quota or agreed quota. The autonomous tariff quota is fixed by decree or law. On the opposite, the agreed tariff quota is one, which is the result of some agreement between the quota-imposing country and one or more foreign countries.

This variant of import quota has some merits. Firstly, this system has the advantage of flexibility and it synthesises the tariff and import quota. Secondly, as the imports above-a specific limit are subject to a higher rate of tariff, this system, on the one hand, restricts imports and conserves scarce foreign exchange resources and, on the other hand, yields revenues to the government.

Thirdly, this system does not completely prohibit imports. Some quantity of the importable goods is allowed to enter the home market either without duty or at very low rate of duty. Fourthly, the prices of domestic products under this system remain related to the prices of the foreign products. The home prices of a given product are not supposed to exceed the foreign prices by more than the amount of custom duty leviable upon it.

Although this system has some merits, yet its drawbacks cannot be overlooked. The main drawbacks of this system are- Firstly, since the imports upto a specified limit are allowed duty free or at low rates of tariffs, the entire gain from low rates is enjoyed by the exporting country.

Secondly, the rush of imports at low rates of tariff is likely to have disturbing effect upon the domestic price structure.

Thirdly, this system discriminates against the relatively poor consuming sections, as they cannot import goods at higher tariff rates. On the contrary, the wealthy consuming sections can continue to secure the supply of foreign products even at higher tariff rates.

Unilateral Quota

Under the system of unilateral quota, a country places an absolute limit upon the quantity of a commodity to be imported during a specified period. This limit is fixed without any prior negotiation or agreement with the foreign countries. The unilateral quota can be broadly of two types – (a) global quota and (b) allocated quota. In the case of global quota, the entire quantity to be imported may be obtained from any one or more countries during the specified period. Under the allocated quota system, the total quantity of import quota is allocated or distributed among the different exporting countries on the basis of certain criteria.

The global quota system allows the importing country to import even entire quota from anyone country. This greatly improves the bargaining position of the importing country. The exporting countries compete among themselves to capture the market of the importing country. They offer their products at lower prices and assure more favourable terms of trade compared with the rival countries.

However, the global quota system suffers from certain defects. Firstly, the global quota system generally favours the nearby exporting countries than the distant countries.

Secondly, as the quota is announced by the government, the importers rush to make imports. This results in the flooding of home market and unnecessary stock-piling of goods. Such a situation may cause rapid fall in prices.

Thirdly, in the subsequent stages when the quota does not permit further imports, shortages and consequent rise in-prices occur. Fourthly, in the global quota system, the small and less organised countries are at a disadvantage compared with the large and advanced industrialised countries. Fifthly, the global quota system does not provide sufficient protection to the home industries from foreign competition.

Bilateral Quota

In case of the bilateral quota system, the import quota is fixed after negotiations between the importing and exporting countries. Haberler has called the bilateral quotas as agreed quotas. The system has the following merits:

- As the quotas are fixed after negotiations among the countries, there is discrimination against one or the other country.
- There is no possibility of excessive fluctuations in imports and prices.
- The exporting countries are not likely to resort to monopolistic practices.
- It is not arbitrary. Therefore, it may not provoke opposition and retaliation by the foreign countries.

This system, at the same time, has the following drawbacks:

- This system promotes the formation of international cartels.
- It opens the floodgate of corruption on an extensive scale.
- The exporting countries, after securing the desired quota, may raise the prices of their products to the detriment of importing countries.
- This system greatly intensifies competition.
- It is an open invitation to monopolies in the exporting countries.

Mixing Quota

Under this system, which is also known as indirect quota, the domestic producers in the quota-fixing country are required to make use of domestic raw materials along with the imported raw material in a specified proportion. This system of import quota has the following merits:

- It affords protection to the producers of raw materials.

- It saves the valuable and scarce foreign exchange resources of the country.
- It induces the domestic processing of semi-finished goods and manufacturing of finished goods.

The system of mixing quota is, however, is subjected to some objections on the following grounds:

- If the domestic materials, which are required to be used in a fixed proportion along with imported materials, are of poor quality, there is a danger of deterioration in the quality of production in the quota-enforcing country.
- It causes deviation from the principle of comparative cost advantage and thus results in inefficiency and higher cost structure.

Licensing of Imports

The government of a country may prescribe any one of the systems of import quota. The most crucial aspect of any system of fixation of quota is its administration. For this purpose, the government may follow the mechanism of issuing licences to different categories of importers on the basis of specific terms, conditions and norms. The system of issuing licences for the regulation of imports has the following main merits:

- The licensing authority can have an effective control over the volume of imports.
- The system tends to discourage the speculation in foreign exchange.
- It does not permit wide fluctuations in prices.
- It assures continuous supply of scarce products from abroad and prevents domestic shortages in a more efficient manner.
- This system has a great deal of flexibility and is easily adaptable to changing situations.
- It ensures the economical use of foreign exchange resources of the country.

The system of licensing of imports, at the same time, suffers from certain defects indicated below:

- This system generally favours the established, and prevents the entry of new importers. Thus the system of licensing of imports tends to encourage the growth of monopolies in the import trade.
- This system promotes bureaucratic corruption, favouritism and nepotism.

- Another defect of the system is that it tends to create 'premium market' for licences. Some of the unscrupulous importers transfer their licenses to the others and pocket substantial amounts of premia. This practice increases greatly the prices of imported goods and can intensify the inflationary condition within the quota enforcing country.
- The licensing tends to make the system more rigid.
- It causes concentration of economic power in the hands of small and privileged groups of established importers.

The import quotas can have various effects such as price effect, protective or production effect, consumption effect, revenue effect, redistributive effect, terms of trade effect and balance of payments effect. Some of them can be studied under the partial equilibrium analysis while some others under general equilibrium system. However, these effects have been almost exclusively analysed under the partial equilibrium conditions.

The effects of import quotas can be discussed with the help of Figure below. In this figure, S_0 is the foreign supply curve under free trade and it is perfectly elastic. S_1 is the domestic supply curve which slopes positively. D is the demand curve for the given commodity and it slopes negatively. The quantity demanded and supplied of the given commodity is measured along the horizontal scale and price is measured along vertical scale. In the conditions of free trade, the quantity supplied is OQ and the quantity demanded is OQ_1. The excess of demand over supply is met through the import from abroad.

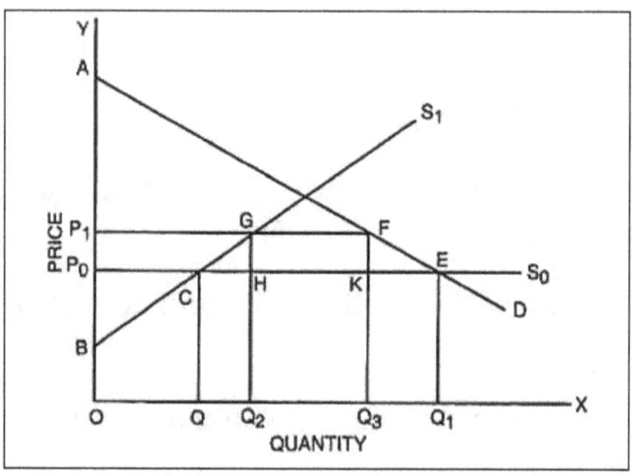

Price Effect

Import quota is the direct physical limitation of the quantity of the given commodity imported from the foreign country. The enforcement of import quota restricts its availability in the home market and creates shortage and consequent rise in its price. Originally, the price of the commodity was Po and the quantity imported amounted to QQ_1. The government of the home country fixes the import quota to the extent of Q_2Q_3.

The initial total supply in the home market, made up of OQ as the domestic output and QQ_1 as the import, amounted to $OQ + QQ_1 = OQ_1$. After the enforcement of import quota, the total supply is OQ_3 out of which domestic production is OQ_2 and import quota is Q_2Q_3 ($OQ_3 = OQ_2 + Q_2Q_3$). It signifies a shortage of the commodity compared with the original situation. As a consequence, given the supply OQ_3 and demand curve D, the price rises from P_0 to P_1. This rise in the price of the commodity is the price effect of import quota.

Protective or Production Effect

An import quota has a protective effect. As it reduces the imports, the domestic producers are induced to increase the production of import substitutes. The increased domestic production due to import quota is called as the protective or production effect. According to Figure, originally the domestic production was OQ. After the import quota is fixed at Q_2Q_3, the domestic production expands from OQ to OQ_2. Thus there is an increase in domestic production by QQ_2. This is the protective or production effect.

Consumption Effect

After the import quota is prescribed, there is a rise in the domestic price of the given commodity. As a consequence, the consumption of the commodity gets reduced. This is known as the consumption effect. In Figure, the consumption under free trade situation is OQ_1. After the fixation of import quota up to Q_2Q_3, the total consumption at the higher price P1 is reduced to OQ_3. Thus there is a reduction in consumption by $OQ_1 - OQ_3 = Q_1Q_3$, subsequent to the fixation of import quota. This is the consumption effect.

Revenue Effect

Unlike tariff, the revenue effect of import quota is complex and difficult to determine. If the government follows the policy of auctioning the import licenses, the revenue accruing to the government will amount to $P_0P_1 \times Q_2Q_3$=GHKF. Such a revenue effect is equivalent to the revenue effect in the event of equivalent tariff. But in fact the governments do not auction the import licenses in recent times.

In such an event, the revenue effect is either captured by the domestic importers or foreign exporters, or shared between the domestic importers and foreign exporters in some proportion. It is, therefore, not easy to quantify exactly what the revenue effect of import quota will be and to which group or groups will it accrue and in which proportion.

Redistributive Effect

The fixation of import quota leads to a rise in the price of the given commodity. It may result in a loss in consumer's surplus for the importing country. At the same time, higher price and increased production ensures a gain in producer's surplus. Thus import quota causes redistributive effect in the quota enforcing country. According to Figure after the fixation of import quota, the price rises from P_0 to P_1 and the loss in consumer's surplus amounts to P_0EFP_1.

The gain is producer's surplus amounts to P_0CGP_1. If importers are organised, an amount equal to the revenue effect GHKF will accrue to them. Consequently, the net loss to the community will be $P_0EFP_1 - (P_0CGP_1 + GHKF) = \Delta GCH + \Delta FKE$. If the revenue effect neither accrues to the government nor to the importers, the redistribution effect will involve a large net loss in welfare. In this case, the net loss in welfare will amount to $P_0EFP_1 - P_0CGP_1 = GCEF$.

Balance of Payments Effect

One of the objectives of enforcing import quota is to reduce the balance of payments deficit by restricting imports. That portion of national income going into imports can be utilised for investment in the import- substitution or export industries. The expansion in exports, coupled with restriction of imports is likely to bring about improvement in the balance of payments position of the country.

According to Figure the quantity imported under free trade conditions at the price P_0 is QQ_1 and the total value of imports is $QCEQ_1$. In case, the government prescribes the imports quota as Q_2Q_3, the physical quantity imported has been slashed.

Since price of imported commodity rises to P_1, the value of imports is Q_2GFQ_3. If the government auctions the import licenses, its revenue receipt is GFKH. Alternatively, if the importers are organised, the gain due to higher price in the form of additional profit can be obtained by them. In either of the case, there can be saving of foreign exchange of the size of GFKH and actual payment to foreign country is Q_2HKQ_3 which is less than the payment $QCEQ_1$ for imports under the free trade. Thus import quota brings about a reduction in the balance of payments deficit.

The imposition of import quota can influence the terms of trade of a country in a favourable or unfavourable way depending upon the elasticity of the offer curve or monopolistic and monopoly power of the importing and exporting countries respectively. If the offer curve of importing country is elastic or it has a monopsony power, the terms of trade will become favourable to it.

On the contrary, if the offer curve of exporting country is elastic or it has some monopolistic control on the given commodity, the terms of trade are likely to become favourable for it and unfavourable for the importing country.

It is possible that the terms of trade effect of import quota may be uncertain and indeterminate. In the words of Kindelberger, "As in the case of bilateral monopoly—with a monopoly buyer and a monopoly seller, the outcome is theoretically indeterminate."

The terms of trade effect of import quota can be explained through Figure below. Cloth is the exportable commodity and steel is the importable commodity of the quota-imposing home country A. OA is the offer curve of country A and OB is the offer curve of foreign country B.

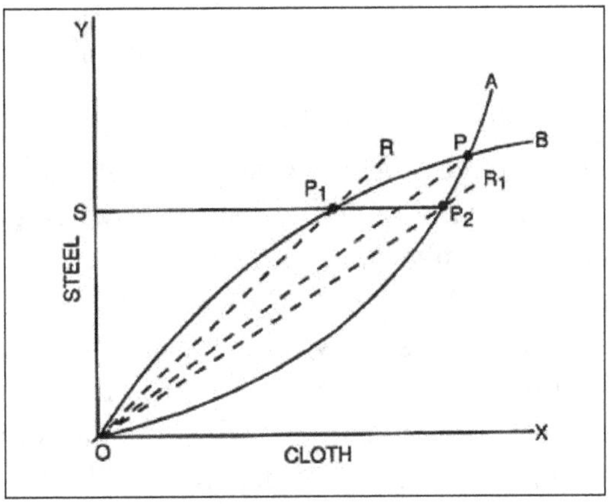

Originally P is the point of exchange and the terms of trade are measured by the slope of the line OP. If the county A imposes an import quota OS upon the importable commodity steel, the exchange can take place either at P_1 or P_2. If P_1 is the point of exchange, the terms of trade are measured by the slope of the line OR. Since OR is more steep than OP, the terms of trade become favourable to the home country A.

On the opposite, if exchange takes place at P_2, the terms of trade are measured by the line OR_1 which is less steep than OP. In this case, the terms of trade become unfavourable to the quota-imposing country A. It shows that the terms of trade may be uncertain or indeterminate consequent upon the enforcement of a specified quota upon imports.

Voluntary Export Restraints

A VER is a measure by which the government or an industry in the importing country arranges with the government or the competing industry in the exporting country for a restriction on the volume of the latter's exports of one or more products. By this definition, the term VER is a generic reference for all bilaterally agreed measures to restrain exports. Strictly speaking, however, a VER is an action unilaterally taken and administered by the exporting country and is "voluntary" in the sense that the country has a formal right to eliminate or modify it. Usually a VER arises because of pressure from an importing country; it can then be thought of as "voluntary" only in the sense that the exporting country may prefer it to alternative trade barriers that the importing country might use. Further, in a noncompetitive, especially oligopolistic, industry exporting firms might find it to their advantage to negotiate a VER, which is then truly "voluntary."

A VER that consists of a government-to-government agreement is normally referred to as an orderly marketing arrangement and often specifies export management rules, consultation rights, and the monitoring of trade flows. In some countries, notably the United States, orderly marketing arrangements are legally distinct from a VER as strictly defined. Agreements which involve industry participation are often referred to as voluntary restraint arrangements. The distinction between these forms of VER is largely legal and terminological and has little bearing on the economic impact of VERs.

A typical VER limits the supply of exports, by commodity type, by country, and by volume. GATT Articles, which are concerned with governmental actions affecting trade, prohibit export restraints under normal circumstances; when permitted, they must be nondiscriminatory and applied only through duties, taxes, and charges. However, the involvement of governments in VERs is not always clear. Also, VERs do not always have firm market-sharing provisions; they may, for example, be in the form of an export forecast and thus become cautionary in nature. For these reasons, VERs fall into a "grey area" in that there can be doubt as to their illegality under GATT. Further, parties to a VER are unlikely to request a finding under the GATT's dispute settlement procedures—they have never done so—while third parties can often appear to benefit from a VER and may therefore be reluctant to initiate dispute procedures.

Why are VERs introduced?

Broadly speaking, restrictive trade measures are taken usually for two purposes: to protect or improve the balance of payments situation, and to provide relief for industries adversely affected by foreign competition, in principle allowing them time to undertake the adjustments necessary to regain external competitiveness. VERs are employed for this latter purpose and, compared to other forms of protectionism, offer several advantages from the viewpoint of the protecting country.

Under GATT rules, safeguard provisions exist for the temporary, emergency protection of domestic industries injured by import competition. Such safeguard actions, however, involve negotiating compensation with the countries affected by the measures. These negotiations can be difficult and may not succeed. In that case, the protecting country risks retaliation by the exporting country. In either case—compensation or retaliation—the exports of the country taking the safeguard action may suffer. VERs, on the other hand, have built-in compensation, in the form of rents (i.e., higher earnings arising out of the scarcity of a product). This makes acceptance by the exporting source more likely and retaliation less probable.

The importing country, in negotiating a VER, tends to avoid the frequently lengthy, public, and often multilateral, debate that invariably precedes other forms of protectionism, such as increasing tariffs or imposing quotas. In such a debate, the cost of the protective measure is likely to become more clearly recognized, making the action politically expensive and risky. A VER then has the advantage that, as an action taken by a foreign source, a domestic legislative struggle may be avoided; it often can be negotiated quickly without its costs becoming obvious. Further, in the context of exports which are, or are suspected of being, subsidized, the domestic authorities can bypass the often expensive and time-consuming process of a countervailing-duty investigation by coming to a VER agreement with the exporter. Finally, it can be argued that a VER, by addressing the source of the problem, that is the one or few low-cost suppliers disrupting the domestic industry, obviates the need for wider action that could harm third countries, as would be the case with a nondiscriminatory import quota of equivalent import-reducing effect (see below). For any of these reasons domestic policymakers often prefer a VER to alternative measures; it offers relatively quick, politically inexpensive assistance to an industry threatened by import competition.

A VER can also be attractive to the exporting country. As indicated above, it offers rents which, at least in the short-run, are windfall gains to the extent that demand in the rest of the world is elastic so that terms of trade losses are minimal or zero. This can be important relative to alternative trade barriers that the importing country might take; tariff revenues, for example, accrue to the government that levies them. Also, VERs can serve to assure the exporter of market access to the importing country, terminate the uncertainty inherent in a countervailing-duty investigation, and provide the exporting government with an element of control over its domestic industry. These factors suggest that when faced with the probability of protection by the importing country, particularly if it is an important market for other products, the exporter might agree readily to a VER.

Prevalence of VERs

Quantitative export restraints first seem to have appeared in 1935 when Japan was induced to limit its textiles exports to the United States. However, only in the past decade or so have they come into widespread use. The accompanying table lists almost 100 major, known VERs. The actual number may well be greater as there are reported to be various undisclosed industry-to-industry and government-to-industry arrangements. Of the known number of VERs, 55 restrict exports to the European Community or its individual member states, and 32 restrain exports to the United States. In general, VERs have been introduced to protect industries in OECD markets where certain developing countries, East European countries, or Japan have become serious competitors. Indeed, the exports of these countries are restrained by about 80 VERs.

The above numbers do not include the Multi-Fibre Arrangement (MFA), which together with its predecessor, the Long-Term Arrangement on Cotton Textiles, has been the model for VERs. The MFA is a negotiated, multilateral departure from GATT based on the principle that industrial countries, which are the main importers of textiles, require special protection against "market disruption" by lower-cost, normally developing-country, exports. Under its aegis a multiplicity of bilateral export restraint agreements have been concluded, covering approximately 50 percent of trade in textiles and clothing. In addition, as the table notes, there are 11 known VERs in this sector outside the scope of the MFA. As a result a considerable portion of world trade in textiles and clothing is managed, and thus not subject to the normal forces of international trade.

Apart from textiles and clothing, steel is the product category most heavily affected by VERs. Since the first restraint in this sector was negotiated in 1968 between the United States and several European and Japanese exporters, about a quarter of the total trade in steel has come under VERs, affecting exports from nearly all the major third country suppliers to the United States and the European Community, as well as exports from the European Community to the United States. Exports of agricultural products are also restrained by VERs, principally from the more efficient producers, such as Australia and Argentina, to the European Community. In automobiles and transport equipment, as well as in electronic products and machine tools, Japanese exporters limit their sales to both the European Community and the United States, while in footwear a number of OECD markets are protected by VERs with Korean exporters.

According to one calculation, in 1984 some 10 percent of total world trade, and 12 percent of non-fuel trade, was covered by VERs. This study also estimated that in the same year approximately 38 percent of Japanese exports to the European Community and 32 percent of Japanese exports to the United States were covered by VERs. Other commentators estimate that in 1983 about 11 percent of world trade in developing countries' manufactured goods was restrained by VERs. Further, the percentages appear to have risen rapidly in the early 1980s. By one estimate the share of exports of the newly industrialized countries of Asia and Japan affected by VERs rose from some 15 percent in 1980 to about 32 percent in 1983.

The Economics of VERs

In general, the effect of VERs is to reduce the level of imports and thus increase the price of the product in question in the importing country. This will happen as the normally low-cost, but now restricted, foreign suppliers raise their export prices to capture the rents created by the VER. The higher price will normally encourage an increase in domestic output of the product.

However, even if the VER is set at the free trade level of imports, in an oligopolistic industry prices can rise because a VER fundamentally changes the nature of competition in the affected industry. Given that the exporting industry (or country) administers the VER, producers in the protecting country become "price leaders" relative to those in the exporting country: any increase in the price by domestic producers must result in an appropriate rise in the price of the imported substitute if the VER is to be observed. In these circumstances the profits of both the domestic and foreign firms increase. Consumers will, of course, lose. Producers in the exporting country can be expected to agree willingly to a proposed VER, particularly since it can increase their share of the importing country's market, if the demand for the domestic product is more responsive to changes in the price of the home product than to changes in the price of the imported substitute. The VER then protects domestic producers, by raising their profits, but does not protect domestic production.

These results become less tenable the larger the number of firms in the industry. First, it becomes more difficult to persuade all domestic firms to be part of the price-leadership role; some may prefer to increase market share by price competition. Second, if not all foreign firms are covered by a VER, they, too, may seek a larger market share. Thus the larger the number of firms in the industry, the more likely that the VER will need to be set at an import-reducing level if the domestic price is to rise and encourage higher local production levels. However, the oligopolistic example does point to the important conclusion that, regardless of the number of firms in the industry, a VER provides an incentive for collusion between firms, to change the nature of competition. This creates vested interests in both the importing and exporting country. A VER may encourage, therefore, what anti-monopoly legislation is meant to forestall.

Price rises due to VERs can be substantial. In a recent study of the impact of the VER on Japan's automobile exports to the United it was estimated that the average price of a car sold in the United States in 1984 was about $1,650, or 17 percent, higher than it would have been in the absence of the VER. Of this estimated increase about $1,030 reflected improvements in quality. Exporters under a volume constraint have an incentive to upgrade the quality of their product on the restricted market in order to maximize profit per unit sold. Unrestricted foreign suppliers and domestic producers are likely to follow suit if their products are relatively close substitutes for the improved, export-restrained, product. In the above study the pure price effect was some $620 per car in 1984; this cost US consumers a total of $6.6 billion.

VERs can distort trade and production in a number of ways. First, in the importing country the market share of exporters not subject to VERs can increase. The price of the product subject to the VER in the importing country is likely to exceed the world price; the latter may in fact fall, particularly if the importing country's market is large and the VER well enforced. In these circumstances, non-restrained suppliers may divert exports to the protected market, thus distorting the pattern of trade. At the time of the 1977 orderly marketing arrangement for color television sets between Japan and the United States, Japan accounted for some 90 percent of US imports of such sets. Two years later Japan's share had fallen to about 50 percent, while that of the Republic of Korea and Taiwan; Province of China had grown significantly. Subsequently the OMA was extended to Korea and Taiwan.

Second, there may be an incentive for new firms in both the importing and other countries to enter the affected industry, making investments that might not have been efficient at the free trade level of imports. Third, the existing VER-affected firms in the exporting country may seek to circumvent their constraints by exporting via third countries. Finally, foreign suppliers may take to exporting, or increasing exports of, close substitutes for the VER-protected products to the importing market.

If VERs spread so as to cover imports of a product from all sources, the VER-system then resembles an import quota. The process, however, is quite different. A quota is normally applied on a global basis; it is nondiscriminatory, usually being allocated either on a "first-come, first-served" basis or by quota-shares in accord with the previous pattern of import shares. VERs is bilaterally negotiated, normally with one or a few suppliers. They are discriminatory, therefore, with export volumes depending on negotiating strength. They can bias the pattern of trade for the VER-covered product to the importing country against the more efficient exporters and may create investment signals for producers in third countries that could turn out to be wrong. As such, VERs can lead to larger efficiency losses than a globally applied quota of equivalent import-reducing volume.

VERs can—and have—spread from country to country and from product to product. In this respect their demonstration effect can be important. Moreover, as previously noted, a VER tends to lower the world price of the product, increasing demand in third countries, which might be satisfied by imports of the product. This effect could be reinforced to the extent that the VER-covered exporters are able to use their rents from the protected market to win market share in non-protected countries. These factors may help to persuade third countries, especially those that manufacture the product in question, also to negotiate VERs. Eventually, as in textiles and clothing, and steel, a VER network could effectively result in a globally managed market-sharing arrangement.

VERs tends to create rents, which can be substantial, for foreign producers. The OECD has estimated that the annual transfer from OECD countries to exporters of textiles and clothing in the newly industrialized countries of Asia is at least $2 billion under MFA bilateral export restraint arrangements. In the above-noted study of the VER on Japan's auto exports to the United States, it was calculated that Japanese exporters, on pure price effects alone, "earned" rents of $1 billion in 1984; the total transfer to foreign suppliers was $1.67 billion, indicating that third-country exporters not restrained by the VER may have benefited from it. M. Kostecki, using a VER tariff-equivalent method, has estimated that the rent transfers resulting from VERs worldwide in 1984 could have been as much as $27 billion.

Trade policymakers are not unaware of the effects discussed above, in particular of the efficiency losses in the allocation of resources. This is one reason why VERs are generally negotiated to have a relatively short lifespan. Nevertheless, VERs can be a tempting form of protection. Once they are in place, vested interests may work against their removal.

Do VERs Work?

The answer to this question depends on whether a VER serves its purpose of safeguarding employment and promoting adjustment in the protected sector, and, if so, at what price. These aims might not be consistent with each other. Modernization to regain competitiveness often entails switching to a more capital-intensive mode of production.

Similarly, if a VER implies a political constraint to retain employment, adjustment by the industry might be delayed. This might happen in any event as the VER, akin to other forms of protectionism, reduces competitive pressures and makes it easier to continue production with outdated and inefficient technology. The industry then retains low-quality staff, displacing potentially higher-skilled employees who could make a greater contribution to raising real incomes.

More generally, by raising domestic profits VERs can make resources available for adjustment. This appears to have happened in the US automobile industry and in certain parts of the textile and steel industries in both the European. Community and the United States. However, in these sectors the VER protection has also afforded the exporters an opportunity to upgrade the quality of their products. The domestic industries thus face increased competition in precisely those areas where they might otherwise have had a comparative advantage.

A recent GATT report shows that VERs have not prevented a loss of employment in the textiles, clothing, and steel industries in the protecting countries. In the period 1973-84, employment in the steel sectors of the European Community and the United States declined by 42 percent and 54 percent, respectively; in textiles and clothing the declines were 46 percent and 43 percent, respectively, in the European Community, and 22 percent and 18 percent, respectively, in the United States. Modernization, gains in productivity, and changes in macroeconomic conditions dominated the employment situation in these sectors, as they did in the US automobile industry where employment fell by some 250,000 jobs in the early 1980s. It is possible, however, that employment in these sectors would have fallen further in the absence of protective measures. Thus, by one estimate between 40,000–75,000 jobs were saved in the US automobile industry during 1981-84 as a result of the VER on Japan's car exports to the United States. Similarly it has been calculated that a 50 percent relaxation in the VERs protecting the Swedish clothing industry would reduce clothing employment in Sweden by about 6 percent.

Job maintenance by VERs can be very costly. Estimates for 1984 indicate that the annual cost, as a result of higher prices, to US consumers under VERs on textiles and clothing amounted to $50,000 and $39,000, respectively, per position saved, as compared with annual average textile and clothing wages of $13,400 and $10,500, respectively. The OECD has calculated that each job protected under the orderly marketing arrangement on Japan's color television exports to the United States cost about $60,000 per year.

Regulating VERs

The prevalence of VERs and their inherent drawbacks, especially their tendency to spread and fragment the trading system into a series of market-sharing arrangements dominated by the major trading nations, has led some commentators to suggest that they should be regulated and their use be subjected to strict conditions and multilateral surveillance. This would encourage greater adherence to internationally agreed trade rules. These observers also note that GATT already sanctions certain departures from the principle of nondiscrimination as, for example, in its provisions for customs unions and free trade areas. Others suggest that the principle of nondiscrimination is too vital to be further weakened by giving VERs official approval. Nondiscrimination in economic terms means that a given level of protection for domestic producers can be achieved at minimum cost to domestic consumers and the rest of the world. It also protects the interests of smaller trading nations and helps to ensure the access of new entrants to the international market place. Its role in GATT rules lends transparency and predictability to international trade relations and to domestic decision making. In this view, VERs would be controlled by a firmer commitment by trading nations to nondiscrimination in the formulation and practice of their trade policies.

This issue is on the agenda of the recently launched Uruguay Round of multilateral trade negotiations, especially in the context of GATT's safeguard provisions. The decisions of the negotiators could have an important effect on the future of the international trading system and by implication on the growth and employment prospects of its member countries.

Local Content Requirements

The aim of local content requirements is to create rent-based investment and import substitution incentives. Local content requirements are provisions (usually under a specific law or regulation) that commit foreign investors and companies to a minimum threshold of goods and services that must be purchased or procured locally. From a trade perspective, local content requirements essentially act as import quotas on specific goods and services, where governments seek to create market demand via legislative action. They ensure that within strategic sectors – particularly those such as oil and gas with large economic rents, or vehicles where the industry structure involves numerous suppliers – domestic goods and services are drawn into the industry, providing an opportunity for local content to substitute domestic value-addition for imported inputs. Thus – in contrast to the traditional protected export platform proposed by many development advocates in the 1960s and 1970s – local content requirements seek to attract foreign direct investment (FDI) by firms. Moreover, through local content requirements, government can achieve these goals often without sharing in the risk of commercial undertakings.

Local content requirements are often paired with investment incentives, as part of a "carrot and stick" approach to attracting FDI. While the use of local content measures has attracted outsized attention inside and outside the WTO, governments (both developed and developing) employ a range of measure to attract investment, using a "carrot and stick" approach.

- On the "stick" side, governments use performance requirements, which can be generally understood as stipulations – whether related to local content, export performance, technology transfer, R&D, employment and domestic equity/ ownership – imposed on investors, requiring them to meet certain specified goals with respect to their operations in the host country. The specific policy goals – strengthening infant industries, increasing revenue, improving the balance of trade and lowering unemployment – are not always accounted for in the decisions of private economic agents. The use of some measures is restricted at various levels – the WTO Agreement on Trade-Related Investment Measures (TRIMs) prohibits the use of measures related to local content, trade balancing, export controls and certain foreign-exchange restrictions, and certain bilateral treaties limit the use of other performance requirements. These measures however are nonetheless widely used by governments to align investment with industrial planning.
- On the "carrot" side, governments use a range of investment incentives to offset costs incurred by firms that choose to establish in the host market. These incentives range from direct transfers – e.g. grants (for R&D projects or new capital investment) and dedicated public-private investment funds – to indirect transfers, such as low- or no-cost government services in marketing and distribution. The sum of government resources used for investment incentives is significant: available information indicates that, in 2003, 21 developed countries spent nearly US$250 billion on subsidies; the total for the world was more than US$300 billion in that year, with state and local incentives in the United States (US$50 billion) nearly equally the total subsidies in developing countries.

This carrot-and-stick approach has been used successfully by several countries as an integrated package of industrial planning policies. Chile, for example, successfully used cash subsidies and local content requirements – prior to their phase-out under Chile's WTO obligations – to develop a more diversified exporting base, with small and medium-sized enterprises in particular seeing a rapid increase in growth and export volumes. Malaysia employed a combination of "pioneer status" tax incentives with employment requirements from the 1960s through the 1990s to achieve dramatic increases in manufacturing employment – from 318,000 in 1970 to 2.1 million persons in 2000; corresponding to a doubling of its share of total employment to 23%, and contributed to a reduction of unemployment to below 4%.

Local content requirements can be both explicit and implicit. In their most direct and explicit form, local content requirements can be explicit (i.e. numerical or qualitative) targets contained in national legislation or industry-specific regulations that specify a minimum share of locally-sourced goods and/or services (or conversely a maximum ceiling for imported inputs). Other, less direct, forms include the creation of 'weighting' or 'scorecard' systems where local content is one of usually several criteria (including export performance and whether or not the sector in question has been designated as strategic by the Government). This mixed system generally arises in the case of subsidy Programmes – such as the Nigerian Export Expansion Grant to encourage non-oil manufacturing – where the score determines the level of subsidy to be received, or for targeted goals within government procurement to ensure that government purchases are in line with employment policies and targets. Local content requirements may not necessarily need to be de jure (i.e. written in legislation, regulations or directives); for public procurement where selection processes can be heavily influenced by political considerations, a statement by relevant government officials that local content will be given heavy weighting in tender assessment could suffice to serve as a clear signal to potential bidders that a de facto local content standard will be applied.

Local content can take many different forms, affecting any number of sectors. Local content requirements can be fashioned for virtually any good or service that can be used as an input into most goods and services. This can include inter alia:

- Minimum thresholds on the amount of locallysourced materials for the production of goods – usually expressed as a percentage of volume, tonnage, length (e.g. for cables), or number – particularly for large/heavy industrial inputs.
- Minimum thresholds on the amount of locallysourced expenditure or man-hours for the use of services, ranging from engineering and transport to financial services and insurance.
- Explicit or implicit requirements that companies/entities take local content development into account in their project and strategic planning, or when undertaking feasibility studies.
- Requirements for companies, operators or investors to locally establish facilities, factories, production units or other operations for the purposes of carrying out any production, manufacturing or service provision currently being imported.

Although restricting trade is not always the primary aim of local content requirements, they can have significant impacts on trade. In a scenario where both (a) local content targets are high (i.e. greater than 20-30%) and (b) enforcement and compliance mechanisms are effective at both the sector and product level, a Government's use of local con tent requirements can dramatically effect the investment and sourcing patterns of firms in the host country market, and by extension on trade. For example, the use of targeted local content policies by the Thai Government in its automobile sector led to a 77% decrease in the value of imported parts and components in each domestically assembled vehicle; similar measures imposed by the South African government in its vehicles sector from 1965 to 1985 resulted in a nearly one-quarter decrease import penetration ratios.

The Positive Rationale for Local Content Requirements

The economic impetus can arise from several sources, primarily to strengthen a weakened or infant industrial base. The primary rationale for the use of local content requirements is either the development (i.e. the infant industry argument) or the strengthening of the domestic industrial base, particularly where a developing country has been historically engaged in enclave and/or low value-added activities, or where weak linkages exist between large industries and the rest of the manufacturing and service sectors. In many resource-rich developing countries, the capital flows and demand associated with the exploitation of fossil fuels has often led to overvalued exchange rates, a high propensity to consume (with associated balance-of-payments difficulties), a neglect of basic investment measures to bring down business costs, and a neglect in certain cases of entire sectors (e.g. agriculture, light manufacturing) that could serve as inputs into higher value-added activities. Local content requirements thus become a means of shifting the economic base away from both consumption and rent-based industries (e.g. mineral extraction), and towards the creation of an indigenous production platform focused on domestic value-added.

The industrial strengthening case is particularly strong in some developing countries in Sub-Saharan Africa. Immediately following independence, a number of Sub-Saharan African governments embarked on an ambitious programed of import substitution, public spending and development planning – for example, Nigeria channeled 14% of public investment towards industrial development from 1962-1968 – coupled with legislative measures to restrict strategic economic sectors for nationals, or place strict quotas on expatriate hiring. For some countries, the import substitution approach to industrial development, during its initial stages, saw arguable successes. In Nigeria for example the number of industrial firms grew at over 12% annually from 1964 to 1972; the annual average growth rate of wage bills and total gross domestic output increased by 17.9% and 16.4% respectively over the same time period. More ambitious initiatives however ran into significant obstacles, as the reality set in that many measures – which strongly affected key sectors such as banking, construction, tourism, and energy – were crafted with little consideration of capacity, industry competence or competitiveness, and that economic rents created by the investment restrictions quickly became a valuable trading commodity between established foreign companies, powerful politicians and private sector middlemen, whereby the latter two groups earned large commission fees with little real capacity building in the process. The combination of economic fluctuations due to commodity price swings (especially the price of oil) and the rapid expansion of the state's role in the economy created a powerful disincentive against long-term foreign investment, particularly for small and medium-size enterprises (SMEs) who could not afford access to political elites. Thus local content requirements are seen as a way to channel investment away from the often import-heavy, low value-added industrialization that often resulted from the post-independence period.

The industry-strengthening argument is mirrored in trade-related concerns over the balance of payments. A major motivation of developing countries in implementing local content requirements is the safeguarding of the balance of payments (BOP), given the often very high foreign currency drainage associated with the importation of goods and services for strategic industries. This concern is particularly true in the case of technologically-intensive resource extraction (e.g. offshore oil and gas) – in Nigeria's case, authorities in charge of implementing new local content legislation estimated in 2011 that orders from oil companies with foreign equipment manufacturers totaled US$15 billion per year. The balance-of-payment arguments is not always cited as a primary rationale behind new local content guidelines for the simple reason that the energy discoveries that prompt local content legislative efforts are often accompanied by dramatic increases in export values that either match or outpace the concomitant growth in exports. The concerns however tend to arise when energy prices suddenly fall; leading to a situation where the costs (and hence import bills) of production are maintained but export revenues are dramatically decreased.

A secondary use of local content requirements is to address a market or policy failures. Local content requirements can help in correcting an economic outcome whereby multinationals fail to respond to employment and sourcing opportunities available on the domestic market. This failure can arise due to, for example, governments being aware of, but multinationals or domestic firms not accounting for, the positive "externalities-from-entry", spillovers and learning effects that could be generating by local content. In simpler terms, local content requirement can help in closing the gap between social and private returns to certain FDI activities. Local content can also compensate for certain business practices undertaken by foreign or domestic firms that hinder the growth of local capacity – for example, if large firms become reluctant to cede their technological or market advantages by licensing or sub-contracting, or engage in restrictive practices such as price-fixing, collusion or manipulation of transfer prices that prevent wage and price signals from reaching domestic investors and firms.

Countries also use local content to "leap-frog" existing barriers to technological transfer. The use of performance requirements (particularly those on local content) are just one of many means to discipline and speed up the process whereby developing countries (or advanced economies seeking to quickly develop a new strategic sector) are able to learn, adopt and adapt technologies and production processes innovated elsewhere. The use of performance requirements is particularly prevalent not only (as noted above) in sectors with high rents and strong network effects, but also in highly sophisticated industries where these entry barriers are extremely high and potentially prohibitive for most developing countries. The barriers can be particularly high in the case of new technologies such as deep-water oil/gas extraction, or green technology.

The fundamental "leap frog" rationale, especially in the developing country context, is concisely captured by Veloso:

"The logic for performance standards seems straightforward. Governments in industrializing nations were aware that local firms needed to learn how to master the technologies of the developed world to be able to catch up and compete. Nevertheless market power and coordination problems may result in under-investment by both local firms and foreign investors in the types of skills and technologies that are critical for industrialization. The government response was to step in and intervene, setting targets and defining milestones that could steer the economy in the right direction. Some of their main targets were export promotion and backward linkage formation, exactly those that are recognized as having more importance for development, and also those that are more prone to be subject to increasing returns and externalities that generate under-investment."

Countries can also use local content to re-distribute rents arising from economic activities. One of the specific attractions of local content requirements to industrial policymakers is their ability to be carefully tailored, both in terms of which industries are targeted and in terms of what level local content targets are set. Local content requirements allow governments to re-direct the rents arising from economic undertakings (particularly in high-rent activities such as natural resource extractions) away from foreign investors and towards specific groups, firms or regions in the host country. This can either serve a beneficial purpose – e.g. to ensure that the profits and employment from natural resource extraction are felt directly in the communities where the extraction is done – or a negative purpose, e.g. where the distribution of rents, or the local content process itself, is used as a means to compensating certain individuals or firms for political reasons, or to fuel corruption. The re-distribution can also be aimed globally, such as when developing countries seek in the host country to offset subsidies and measures that foreign firms enjoy in their home countries – for example, subsidies on education, materials, or the tax treatment of profits.

Local content requirements may be preferable to other forms of protection. The specificity of local content requirements has led some observers to suggest that – from an overall welfare perspective, particularly in the developing-country setting – content policies might be preferable to other trade-distorting measures such as tariffs and subsidies. Tariffs, for example, create a cost penalty on imported inputs that does not exist in the case of local content requirements. While governments gain from higher tariff revenues, they lose the ability to ensure that the increase in demand is limited to the strategic good in question. Moreover, governments' abilities to increase tariffs may be limited either by their WTO commitments, or by FTA commitments with the country of origin of the imported inputs, or by participation in a regional trade agreement (RTA) common external tariff arrangement that sets certain tariff rates (usually low) for industrial inputs.

Current use and Best Practices

A Global Picture

Local content requirements have been widely used at the global level. While there is a paucity of recent global surveys, a mid-1980s UNIDO study of the use of local content requirements found that in just a single sector (automobiles), 27 (mostly developing) countries out of 50 employed local content guidelines to boost domestic value-added. In 1989, a study conducted by the United States Trade Representative (USTR) found that 23 of 31 developing countries (and one-third of developed countries) surveyed applied some form of local content requirements. A follow-up study in 2002, based on WTO notifications, found that large developing countries used local content guidelines in a range of industries (particularly automobiles). In some industries, such as the automotive sector, the use of performance requirements is particularly prevalent, with virtually every developed country using (at one point or another) local content requirements, export performance requirements or local equity requirements to build indigenous industrial capacity. Further studies however have found that in part as a response to WTO commitments – the overall global trend is a move away from strict local content targets, with both developing and developed countries tending to rely more on requirements linked to incentives.

The rationale for local content requirements is especially strong for the energy sector. Apart from the United Kingdom, very few new energy producers including Norway, long considered as the gold standard of local content – had, upon discovery of their oil and gas deposits, the requisite industrial capacity to serve as an internationally competitive platform for exploration, extraction, distribution and export. Given that the oil industry is nearly a century old, the dominance of established operators and the sophistication of energy technology – particularly for offshore de- posits – implies that emerging energy producers will, at the outset, nearly always depend on foreign firms. While energy sector investments (if properly managed) can ensures a steady revenue stream and constant (and in the case of developing countries, rising) demand levels, its exploitation requires sophisticated and cutting-edge technology, a ready-made demand for a wide network of suppliers in virtually all areas of manufacturing and services, and ongoing employment for trained staff, both at home and in other energy-producing countries around the world. The "fixed" and finite nature of energy deposits however gives host countries – even developing countries with weak institutions – a distinct bargaining power with respect to foreign firms seeking access to natural resources, vis-à-vis investment sectors (e.g. automobiles) where firms are able to consider a number of potential sites for investment.

The impetus is particularly strong for Sub-Saharan countries that have historically depended on a narrow range of fossil fuels. In the oil industry alone, services to producing firms have historically accounted for nearly 90% of total costs. Weak industrial capacity in many sub-Saharan economies, particularly in post-conflict environments such as

Angola, however implies that the overwhelming majority of expenditures on goods and services by energy companies go to foreign suppliers. In the Nigerian case for example, the market for oilfield services totals some $8 billion per year, with an expectation of a near-doubling in size due to supply increases from future projects. Despite the significant market for energy services however the shares (including materials procurement) that accrue to indigenous producers in Nigeria are estimated at between 3% and 11%. In 2000, industry experts estimated that up to 90% of capital input went overseas via equipment purchases, consulting/services fees and expatriate wages. Many developing countries continue to struggle to develop effective local content policies. In their pursuit of locally-focused industrial development, particularly based on the exploitation of natural re-sources, many developing countries have faced steep obstacles in their efforts to develop indigenous skills and production:

- Many countries (e.g. Angola, Libya, and Yemen) are emerging from protracted internal conflicts that have destroyed most national infrastructure, led to a global dispersion of skilled nationals, and reduced business confidence of overseas investors who are unwilling to make the often enormous investments required to make the remaining infrastructure viable.
- A number of countries' local content efforts continued to be stymied by governance issues at state-run oil companies, who tend to issue scattered or outdated regulations that are unevenly enforced, fail to coordinate with other government agencies and/or implement local content policies in a non- transparent or highly politicised manner.
- Geographical or logistical hurdles (e.g. in Papua New Guinea and Nigeria's offshore fields) implies that productive activities are inherently high-cost and require globally-competitive level of sophistication even for basic parts or services, leading to very low initial levels of local sourcing in countries with a weak industrial base.

Country Cases

Brazil is an often-cited success story, given its transformation of a protected state-run energy sector into a globally competitive industry. From the mid-20th century until the 1990s, Brazil's oil and gas industry developed in a highly protected market – where the state-owned Petrobras was the sole developer of all Brazilian oil and gas until the 1990s with licensing agreements with international firms allowed Brazilian suppliers to develop state of the art technologies in an environment isolated from overseas competition. Government policy in the energy sector explicitly sought to promote self-sufficiency in most petroleum products (a goal not yet reached at present) as well as develop national technical know-how in all aspects of petroleum production. Petrobras, as the appointed "national champion" for the energy sector, was given sole responsibility for developing a new national supply industry. The company also established a number of subsidiaries in other industrial areas, such as petrochemicals, fertilizers, sulphur and commercial distribution.

Brazil has successful used, at different times, a mix of protection and deregulation to create strong local content capacity. Under the pre-liberalization import substitution policy, Brazil was able to develop a protected – albeit technologically unsophisticated industrial base, both within the energy sec- tor and in the wider economy, despite facing political turbulence in the form of a military dictatorship. The Brazilian import-substitution approach however ran into difficulties during Latin America's "lost decade" of the 1980, with severe inflation and slow growth. The import substitution policy was then reversed in a series of policy reforms, including the restructuring of state-owned enterprises and the relaxation of barriers to trade. A key element was a complete re-organization and partial privatization of Petrobras in 1997, with a focus on improving performance, decentralization and cost-cutting, whereby the company headcount was reduced from 60,000 to slightly fewer than 40,000 employees. Government policy still acknowledged national ownership of mineral assets, but created a market whereby Petrobras was forced to compete with foreign suppliers. A key policy change in 1997 was the switch from a complete Petrobras monopoly on the supply of goods and services, to a policy where contractors are required to purchase local goods and services only when they are competitive on cost and quality with foreign suppliers. These measures have transformed Petrobras into a global energy player, and a key driver of local content at home.

Brazil has used a multi-prong approach towards increasing local content. The Brazilian government has adopted a policy of (Everything which can be done in Brazil should be done in Brazil). The Brazilian approach mixes over-arching government policies and programs – such as the National Program for the Mobilization and Development of Oil and Gas Industry, established by the Ministry of Mines and Energy and coordinated by Petrobras – with company- and contract level specifications for local content. For example, Petrobras sets explicit targets for local content in individual projects15 as well as pursuing macro objectives; the company has publicly stated its aims to create some new 100,000 jobs by 2010 through ratcheting up local content requirements and implementation, and its 2006-2010 Petrobras strategic investment plan calls for 65% of equipment and services to be sourced from domestic suppliers. This gradual increase in local content has been achieved through successive bidding rounds, with each round increasing the desired level of local content. The success of the local content build-up in Brazil's energy sector has led to the similar approaches in other strategic sectors, such as mining.

Malaysia, like Brazil, has developed a strong national petroleum company that drives local content development. Malaysia's state oil company Petronas has historically focused on an international expansion strategy to compensate for the relatively small domestic petroleum market. The company has been able to successfully pursue joint ventures with large petroleum multinationals and has pursued an aggressive human resources strategy, offering numerous training programs and establishing its own university to train management and technical staff. Petronas requires firms under production-sharing contracts to secure equipment, facilities, goods, materials and services locally unless a waiver is granted by Petronas. Similarly, contractors are required to fill positions with suitable Malaysian personnel, with exceptions only granted via a waiver from Petronas.

Malaysia's local content requirements however have been developed in the context of an institutionally strong, market- and export-oriented economy. Malaysia has over time used windfalls from the energy sector to invest in massive public-sector projects and heavy industries such as cement, petro-chemicals and steel – and like some other developing countries, these "white elephant" investments led to massive over-borrowing and fiscal-debt crises. The primary reason why in Malaysia's case these periods of fiscal profligacy did not lead to chronic fiscal crises lies in the overall export orientation of the economy:

"Since the early 1970s the country has led an export-oriented industrial policy welcoming foreign investment while developing infrastructure and local skills through heavy investment in infrastructure, education and health. In addition the country has had a stable policy environment, a competitive exchange rate and a reasonably prudent macroeconomic policy. Thus, except for relatively short spells of excesses, the Malaysian government has not let the petroleum sector drive up costs and wages in the economy. As a result, rapid non- oil industrialization has taken place in parallel with the expansion of the petroleum sector, an unusual achievement indeed. Perhaps the most important success factor is the checks and balances embedded in the Malaysian institutional setting. Malaysia has demonstrated an ability to adjust and rethink policy measures when they have turned out not to have the de- sired effects, or when unfavorable unintended side effects have arisen."

Thus the Malaysian Government's desire to enforce strict local content requirements on petroleum sector investors had to be balanced against the risk of negatively affecting the overall attractiveness of Malaysia as an export base, and thus compromise its ability to compete on an equal footing with other regional export bases such as Singapore and China.

In the case of Norway, the government took an early policy decision to actively develop a domestic industry, rather than solely rely on local content requirements. Upon discovery of Norway's offshore energy deposits, very little initial energy-related capacity existed in the primarily fisheries-based economy. The country did however boast internationally recognized shipyards, a strong overall maritime industry, and resilient democratic institutions. At an early stage the Norwegian government undertook numerous initiatives – many under its strong national petroleum company Statoil – to re-orient its local industrial base to serve the needs of the new energy industry. Statoil and associated Ministry of Petroleum played a key role in developing local technologies: the private companies developed products, but Statoil defined product requirements, ensured overall project control, and provided technical skills and advice on the newly developed products. The government sponsored a Supplier Development Programme to address the commercial needs of the industry with local firms. The Norwegian government invested significant sums in research and development, as well as building strong links between private firms and local academic centres to create industry "clusters", which in turn have grown into service suppliers for overseas petroleum markets.

While Norway has never implemented specific local content targets, strong incentives were put into place to encourage local industrial development. In Norway, domestic firms were given preference when they were considered competitive in terms of price, competitiveness and quality until 1996, when in response to EU legislation – equal conditions/access was granted to all operators regardless of origin. In developing its domestic supply sector however, the Norwegian government set in motion a series of deliberate policies and mandates that essentially forced the international oil companies to develop the Norwegian industry as a condition, and by-product, of their own operations. Commitments by foreign firms to transfer technology to their Norwegian counterparts were enshrined in legally binding agreements. Petroleum multinationals were placed in the role of technical assistants to both Statoil and smaller Norwegian firms, and joint teams were used to fast track the Norwegian companies into fully-fledged operators. Companies were required to conduct at least 50% of the research for technology needed to develop prospects in Norway at local institutions. Some of Norway's protective measures were gradually relaxed over time as the industry reached international standards of competitiveness.

The United Kingdom government has historically taken a very hands-on approach to developing local content. In developing its North Sea oil fields, the UK government implemented a series of local content measures, including discretionary licensing (as opposed to auctions), audits of purchases made by oil companies and provision of financial assistance to domestic suppliers. The successful implementation of these measures increased the UK local content in the North Sea oil sector from 30% in 1973 to 82% by 1986, with nearly 100% local content in post- development operations. Much like their Norwegian counterparts, local content policies have been successful in turning UK firms into competitive suppliers of petroleum services at the international level.

The UK's local content measures have however been taken in a much more favourable context than that of most new energy producing nations. The UK – at the time of the North Sea oil discoveries – already had a well-established industrial base and highly trained and educated workforce, with a high level of technical competence in manufacturing, shipbuilding and engineering. The UK also provided significant support to its domestic supplies industry, creating a dedicated agency (the Offshore Supplies Office) to develop the industry's competitiveness, develop R&D initiatives and advise on joint ventures with established operators. The UK government also instituted strict auditing procedures to ensure full and fair opportunities for domestic suppliers. Most importantly, government policy ensured that the focus of local content requirements was on creating high value addition, rather than mere local incorporation, low levels of transformation or local ownership. Firm-level sanctions for a lack of local content development were largely of the "soft" kind – i.e. difficulty in future bidding rounds – rather than legal mandates, prosecutions or fines. The UK government also recognized that in a highly specialized field such as offshore oil and gas, foreign (mostly US) involvement was inevitable at least in the initial stages of industry development, by providing strong support to a number of multinational subsidiaries in the North Sea fields.

Other emerging producer countries such as Trinidad and Tobago, Nigeria and Ghana are beginning to explore and/or implement local content regimes. Other developing-country energy producers are beginning to implement their own local content regimes, including:

- In Trinidad and Tobago, local content policies have been driven by the realization that the traditional approach – whereby preference was given to local suppliers if their services were of equal quality to the international competitor – was not yielding sufficient capacity building for domestic firms. At present, the government plans to institute several local content measures, including the establishment of an electronic clearinghouse between multi- nationals and local suppliers, and partnerships with several local academic institutions to create curricula specifically targeted at creating local technical and management staff. The local content approach has heavily benefited from participation by private sector operators and has benefited from a wider focus on using oil and gas local content for other areas of the economy, given the recognition of the finite nature of Trinidad's energy resources.
- Nigeria's 2010 Content Act creates and number of incentives throughout the bidding and contracting process to increase local content levels in its domestic oil and gas sector. The 2010 Act requires that "all regulatory authorities, operators, contractors, subcontractors, alliance partners and other entities involved in any project, operation, activity or transaction in the Nigerian oil and gas industry" to incorporate Nigerian content as a key element in project development and management. At the outset, the Act ensures that "first" and "exclusive" consideration to be given to Nigerian providers in certain instances, for example, where the indigenous providers have the requisite capacity. The key local content element of the Act is an annexed Schedule that provides for minimum percentage specifications of Nigerian content for any project to be executed in the Nigerian oil and gas industry.
- In Ghana, the government has set a 90% local content target and has mandated operators to create an Annual Local Content Plan and Annual Recruitment and Training Programme, and shall "as far as practicable" prefer local inputs to imported goods. The Ghanaian government has instituted the same 10% preference threshold as the Nigerian regime, and mandates a local content target of 10% in the first year, increasing by 10% each following year.

Embargo

An embargo is a government restriction placed on the import or export of goods, services, currency, and other values to any other country or state. It can be imposed both in war and peacetime, covering all aspects of trade and economic activity. Embargoes can be placed on specific categories of goods, scientific and technical information, transport and other services, etc.

In modern international relations, an embargo acts as an instrument of economic, scientific, technical, and financial pressure, aimed at forcing changes in the target state's internal and foreign policies.

Imposing an Embargo

The variety of historical and modern cases of establishing an embargo makes it possible to classify the use of such a policy in foreign trade activities on various grounds. Embargoes are most often directed at a country or a group of countries. For example, the embargo can be imposed against a criminal or terrorist organization.

The United Nations provides the possibility of imposing an embargo as a collective repressive measure against a specific country or countries whose actions pose a threat to international security. The restrictions may serve as a basis for suspending or terminating the performance of all or some specific obligations of specific countries, their organizations, and citizens.

Types of Embargoes

There are several forms of embargoes imposed on a state or country, including:

- A political embargo.
- An embargo of an economic nature or a trade embargo.
- An embargo to ensure the national security of the state.
- An embargo to prevent and respond to disputed questions about the territorial borders of countries.
- An embargo imposed to protect the health of the citizens of a state.
- An embargo of an environmental nature that are imposed to express a state's disagreement with another state's environmental policy or attitude toward animals.

Some trade embargoes allow the exchange of certain goods, such as food and medicine, to meet humanitarian needs. Also, most multinational embargoes contain provisions that allow certain types of exports or imports under a limited set of restrictions.

Consequences of an Embargo

Embargoes are not violent methods of influence, but they can still harm people and the economies of the countries involved. An embargo can block the importation of important goods and services to the civilian population of the state that is subject to the restriction. In a state that imposes an embargo, businesses may lose the ability to trade or invest in the state that is subject to the embargo.

Currency Devaluation

Competitive devaluation is a theoretical scenario in which one nation matches an abrupt devaluation in another country's currency, often in a tit-for-tat manner. In other words, one nation is matched by a currency devaluation of another, which in turn devalues their currency in response. The goal of devaluation in this case is to make a country's exports more attractive on the world market.

It is presumed that the devaluation initially tends to reduce the foreign prices of the country's exports in proportion to the devaluation. At these reduced prices, foreign demand for the country's exports will be increased, thus tending to bid up the foreign prices of these exports part-way back toward their pre-devaluation levels. How much the foreign currency proceeds of the country's exports will change then depends upon the elasticity of foreign demand for the country's exports and the elasticity of domestic supply of export goods. Similarly, on the import side, the initial effect of the devaluation is to raise the domestic price of imports, presumably leading to some reduction in the country's demand for imports, which in turn may tend to reduce the world price of the imported goods. The size of these reactions on imports depends upon the elasticity of domestic demand for imports and the elasticity of foreign supply of imports.

The Elasticities Approach

The conventional analysis is an extension, to imports and to exports as a whole, of the familiar Marshallian supply and demand analysis of the price and production of a single commodity. While supply and demand curves are very useful tools for analyzing the factors that determine price and output for a single good, their value is much more questionable when applied to imports and exports as a whole. Similarly, the extension of the Marshallian partial equilibrium analysis to the determination of total employment and output has been found to be of limited use. The most important reservation against the use of the Marshallian supply and demand curves in the analysis of the effects of devaluation arises from the complexity of the relationships which govern supply and demand conditions in international trade. The elasticities for which the conventional formulas are valid must be defined as total elasticities and not as partial elasticities.

Partial elasticities measure the effect of a change of price on the quantity supplied or demanded when all other things remain equal. Total elasticities relevant to a devaluation measure the corresponding relationship when the other things have changed that are likely to change as a result of the devaluation. Accordingly, a total elasticity does not measure the direct effects of price changes on quantity, but the covariation of price and quantity as the whole economic system seeks a new equilibrium. A total elasticity is the ratio of a percentage change in quantity to a percentage change in price. But the percentage change in quantity is the result not only of the price change to which it is related, but also of many other price and income changes which are themselves direct and indirect effects of devaluation. The percentage change in price is not generally equal to the percentage devaluation, but itself depends on the same complicated set of relationships. Therefore the total elasticities appropriate for the analysis of the effects of devaluation depend on the behavior of the whole economic system, and the statement that the effect of devaluation depends on the elasticities boils down to the statement that it depends on how the economic system behaves.

The Income-Absorption Approach

In examining the relationships of real expenditure to real income and of both of these to price levels, the analysis of the effects of devaluation should, of course, be applied to both the devaluing country and the rest of the world. It is generally recognized that a country's net foreign trade balance is equal to the difference between the total goods and services produced in that country and the total goods and services taken off the market domestically. For brevity, the taking of goods and services off the market will be referred to here as absorption. Absorption then equals the sum of consumption plus investment as usually defined (including in investment any change in the holding of inventories). If a devaluation is to affect the foreign balance, it can do so in only two ways: (1) It can lead to a change in the production of goods and services in the country; this change will have associated with it an induced change in the absorption of goods and services so that the foreign balance will be altered by the difference between the change in income and the income-induced change in absorption. (2) The devaluation may change the amount of real absorption associated with any given level of real income.

Any factors affecting the foreign balance of a country other than those connected with trade in goods and services will be ignored. Also, it will be assumed that there are no restrictions on trade and payments, although that assumption is not necessary for the validity of the subsequent analysis. Furthermore, only the simplest forms of the various relationships involved will be considered. For example, only one price level will be considered, and the change in that level will be denoted by p. Similarly, y will denote the change in the aggregate net production of goods and services, i.e., in national income.2 Finally, the relationships in the devaluing country will be examined; to complete the picture, a similar analysis, with some of the terms reversed, would have to be applied to the rest of the world.

A starting point is the identity that the foreign balance, B, is equal to the difference between the total production of goods and services, Y, and the total absorption of goods and services, A:

$$B = Y - A.$$

Changes in these quantities may be denoted by the corresponding small letters, so that is our fundamental identity. It indicates that the change in the foreign balance equals the difference between the change in output and the change in absorption of goods and services. It shows that the first question to be investigated is how the devaluation will affect the two terms, y and a. The above relationships hold, of course, both in real and in money terms. The present discussion will deal only with real quantities, not with money values.

$$b = y - a$$

Account may first be taken of the fact that the absorption of goods and services depends, at least in part, on real income, which itself is equal to the output of goods and services. Absorption may also depend on the price level, or other factors related to the devaluation, so that:

$$a = cy - d$$

where c is the propensity to absorb, equal to the propensity to consume plus an analogous effect of income on investment, which may be called the propensity to invest. The term d may be called the direct effect of the devaluation on absorption. It expresses whatever tendency there may be for the devaluation to induce a change in the amount of real absorption at any given level of real income.

$a = cy - d$ therefore states that the change in the absorption of goods and services in real terms as a result of devaluation is made up of two parts. The first, *cy*, is the change in real consumption plus real investment that is induced by the change in real income that results from the devaluation. The other part, *d*, is the change in absorption which results other than through the income effect.

A combination of the functional relationship $a = cy - d$ with the fundamental identity $b = y - a$ yields:

$$b = (1 - c)y + d.$$

This formulation is useful in that it directs the investigation to three basic questions: How does the devaluation affect income? How does a change in the level of income affect absorption, i.e., how large is c? How does the devaluation directly affect absorption at any given level of income, i.e., how large is d? In order to analyze these questions in precise terms, the entire economic structure of the devaluing country and of the rest of the world would have to be considered. Such an analysis would be far more complicated than is desirable for the presentation of the main ideas of this paper. Consequently, what follows is a summary of these main ideas, rather than a precise formulation of the relationships.

Effect of Devaluation on Income

Idle Resources Effect

The principal effect of a devaluation on income is associated with the increased exports of the devaluing country and the induced stimulation of domestic demand through the familiar multiplier relationship, provided there are unemployed resources. In addition to the multiplier itself, the limiting factors on the process of inducing enlarged output are (1) the degree to which an increased output of goods and services is forthcoming without an extensive price rise in the devaluing country, and (2) the degree to which the rest of the world can absorb the increase in exports that is associated with the decline in the foreign prices of exports made possible by the devaluation—after allowance for the counteracting upward movement of the domestic prices of export goods, which occurs as the demand for these goods expands.

It must be emphasized that the net effect of the recovery of income and production on the foreign balance is not the total amount of additional production induced, but merely the difference between that amount and the induced increase in absorption. This difference between the real production or income and the real expenditure on goods and services may be termed real hoarding. The foreign balance is, by the fundamental identity, equal to the aggregate real hoarding of the economy as a whole. The income-induced change in the balance, b, is accordingly equal to the income-induced change in real hoarding, i.e., the change in income, y, multiplied by the propensity to hoard, 1–c. The existence of the business cycle makes it plausible that c may be greater than unity, that an increase in income may stimulate an even greater increment in the absorption of goods and services into consumption and investment. Many of the current theories of the business cycle do depend on the assumption that c is greater than unity. If c is equal to or greater than unity, the foreign balance will not be improved as a result of the increased output. Under such circumstances, the devaluation might be effective in stimulating recovery but not in improving the foreign balance except possibly through direct effects.

At any rate, under conditions of unemployment, devaluation may be expected to exert a favorable effect on production and employment. This fact became evident in the devaluations of the thirties, and was recognized even before the promulgation of the Keynesian theory, though not in so systematic or analytic a framework.5 The competitive depreciations of the thirties were largely associated with a recognition of the income effects of a devaluation, a recognition that was perhaps dim and intuitive on the part of many of those responsible for the devaluations, but nevertheless clear enough to motivate those devaluations. Of course, to the extent that the additional exports of the devaluing country displace those of its competitors, the levels of production and income in the competitor countries will be adversely affected.

From the point of view of a devaluing country that has unemployed resources, the effect on income, as well as the favorable effect on the balance of payments if c is less than unity, must constitute the most attractive potentiality of a devaluation. If the country is at full employment, this potentiality does not exist and the effects of devaluation must depend on the more tenuous and less attractive direct effects on absorption.

Terms of Trade Effect

Another income effect frequently considered as influencing the foreign balance is that of the terms of trade. It is usually presumed, frequently with justification that devaluation will result in a decline of export prices in foreign currency greater than the decline of import prices in foreign currency. This presumption is based on the fact that a country's exports are usually more specialized than its imports, so that the price of exports will be much more subject to the influence of devaluation than will the price of imports. There may be some compensation, though probably only to a minor degree, if imports greatly exceed exports prior to the devaluation. Thus, if before the devaluation the country concerned was importing twice as much as it was exporting, and if as a result of the devaluation the fall in foreign prices of exports is 2 per cent and of imports 1 per cent, the deficit in foreign currency would be unchanged if the physical values of imports and exports were unchanged. It may, however, be assumed that the normal result of a devaluation will be such a deterioration of the terms of trade of the devaluing country as to make the balance of payments deteriorate by the amount t. That is, t is the measure of the reduction of the country's real income associated with the deterioration of the terms of trade.

A fallacious argument, frequently encountered, is that a deterioration of the terms of trade on account of devaluation will improve the foreign balance since it reduces the real income of the country and hence the demand for imports. It is true that the reduced income associated with a deterioration of the terms of trade will reduce the demand for imports as well as for domestic goods. Thus the decline in income, *t*, resulting from the changed terms of trade will induce a reduction of absorption by the amount *ct*, which will permit an equivalent improvement in the foreign balance partly through the direct reduction of imports included in *ct* and partly through the eventual transfer to the production of exports or of import substitutes of the resources formerly used to produce the domestic components of *ct*. The effects of the deterioration of the terms of trade accordingly will be, after resources are transferred, an improvement of the amount, *ct*. But the entire deterioration, *t*, of the national income as a result of the changed terms of trade is initially a reduction in the foreign balance. That is, the change of the terms of trade initially imposes a reduction, *t*, in the foreign balance and then has the effect of stimulating an improvement, *ct*, so that the change in the balance associated with the initial terms of trade effect on income, *t*, is *t-ct* or *(1-c) t*. This might have been seen directly from equation (3). If t is negative, as assumed, and if c is less than unity, then deterioration in the terms of trade also implies a deterioration in the foreign balance.

Only if *c* is greater than unity will the adverse terms of trade effect improve the foreign balance.

The aggregate income effects may then be expressed as (*1-c*) multiplied by the change of income. That change of income will have two components. One, presumably positive, is the idle resources effect, i.e., the increased production stimulated by the devaluation. The other, presumably negative, is the effect on income of the change in the terms of trade. The resulting change in income, *y*, will induce a change in absorption, *cy*, so that it will, according to $b = y - a$, result in a change of the foreign balance equal to *y-cy* or (*1-c*)*y*.

Direct Effect on Absorption

If there is initially full employment, or if c is almost unity or greater than unity, the principal favorable influence of a devaluation on the foreign balance is through the direct effect on absorption. This direct effect is largely associated with a tendency for a high or rising price level to discourage consumption or investment out of a given level of real income. It is important to recognize that this effect is not connected with any tendency for higher prices to force a reduction of consumption or investment out of a given money income. That would be an effect through real income, since if prices go up relative to money income, real income goes down. Except for the terms of trade effect on income, the real income of the devaluing country should not be expected to decline; at full employment, money income and money prices can be expected to move together. The direct effect on absorption is any influence toward lower real expenditure as money income and money prices rise together as a result of the devaluation.

In order most clearly to illustrate the nature of the forces behind d, the direct effect on absorption, certain assumptions which imply that all other effects are absent can be made. Accordingly, assume that the devaluing country is at full employment so that real income produced cannot be increased as a result of devaluation. Furthermore, assume that the foreign supply of imports and the foreign demand for exports are perfectly elastic, so that the foreign currency prices of imports and exports, and hence the terms of trade, will be unchanged. Thus there will be no income effects, either through increased production or through a change in the terms of trade.

The higher import and export prices in domestic currency resulting from devaluation will initially induce an attempt by individuals and enterprises in the devaluing country to shift their demand from imports to the home market and to export more. The resulting increased demand for the country's production would tend to raise domestic prices and money incomes to the point where the increased demands are choked off by the combined operation of the direct absorption effect and the narrowing price differential between the foreign and the domestic markets. If there were no direct absorption effect, domestic prices would continue to rise until there was no longer any tendency to substitute domestic goods for imports, or to try to export more, and there would be no change of the foreign balance as a result of the devaluation.

The relationship involved may be illustrated by a crude example. Suppose, under the assumed conditions of full employment and perfectly elastic foreign supply and demand, that there is a 10 per cent devaluation and an elasticity of direct absorption of 0.1. This would mean that a 1 per cent increase in the general price level would induce a 0.1 per cent reduction of absorption at a given level of real income. It may also be assumed that the substitutability of domestic goods for imports in consumption, and of resources as between the production of domestic goods and exports, is such as to link the domestic price level to the prices of foreign goods by a factor of 0.5, so that the 10 per cent increase of import and export prices in domestic currency leads to a 5 per cent rise of the general domestic price level. Then the devaluation would lead to a reduction of absorption by one-half of one per cent of total absorption. If imports furnish about 20 per cent of total absorption, the improvement of the foreign balance would amount to 2½ per cent of imports. In terms of the conventional analysis, the inelasticity of domestic supply of exports and of import substitutes reduces the effect of the devaluation in spite of the perfect elasticities of foreign supply and demand. At full employment, the elasticity of domestic supply for import substitutes and exports taken together must be just another way of expressing the direct absorption effect.

It is frequently taken for granted that, even when the devaluing country is at full employment, a devaluation will lead to increased exports and reduced imports. If it does so, then clearly domestic absorption will have been reduced. The question to be explored is why, with a given real income, when money incomes and prices rise in the same proportion there should be a reduction of real consumption or investment.

The direct absorption effect can be divided into a cash balance effect, an income redistribution effect, a money illusion effect, and possibly into other, miscellaneous direct absorption effects.

Cash Balance Effect

The cash balance effect is perhaps the best known of the direct absorption effects. If the money supply is inflexible, and if money holders desire to maintain cash holdings of a certain real value, they must, as prices rise, accumulate more cash. This will require a reduction in their real expenditures relative to their real incomes. It might be possible for any individual to increase his cash holdings by selling other assets, but this is clearly impossible for the country as a whole as long as the banking system or government does not create more money, except to the extent that goods or services may be sold abroad and the domestic money supply thereby increased. Capital movements are ruled out here; if they were allowed they might change or eliminate the cash balance effect.

One result of the attempt to maintain real cash balances by increasing their money amounts while prices rise may be to drive down the prices of assets, i.e., to increase the rate of interest. This in turn might have some effect on real consumption or investment relative to real income: thus the cash balance effect may operate directly on the income-expenditure relationship through the foregoing of expenditure in order to build up cash, or indirectly through the rate of interest as the result of an attempt to shift from other assets into cash—an attempt that can be discouraged only by a rise in the rate of interest. Clearly, one of the most important components of the direct absorption effect would be the cash balance effect. A hypothetical example applied to the United Kingdom may illustrate the possible magnitude of that effect. Suppose that in the United Kingdom the total money supply is £5 billion, and that devaluation raises domestic prices by 5 per cent and thus cuts the real value of cash balances by about 5 per cent or £250 million. Suppose that cash balances were previously in adjustment with the level of real incomes, and that for each £10 that they are out of adjustment there is a cut of expenditure of £1 to rebuild them. There would then be a cash balance effect (ignoring any repercussions through the rate of interest and assuming no change in real income) of about £25 million per year on absorption, and therefore on the foreign balance.

It is possible that the reduction of absorption on account of the cash balance effect, or of the other direct absorption effects, might be directed toward certain domestic goods and services, from whose production it is not easy to transfer resources to the production of exports or import substitutes; therefore, some unemployment might result. The results of this unemployment might then be traced throughout the economy. If c is less than one, the net result of this adverse effect on income produced would be a deterioration of the foreign balance which would tend to counteract the improvement from the direct absorption effects.

Redistribution of Income

The redistribution of income effect is also well recognized. There may be a long lag of wages behind prices, and profits might therefore gain at the expense of wages as a result of the devaluation. Rising prices will transfer income from fixed money income groups to the rest of the economy. Taxes, at least in advanced countries, can be expected to take a larger share of a given real income when the price level is higher. To the extent that income is shifted from those with a high marginal propensity to absorb to those with a low propensity, the foreign balance will be improved by the devaluation. It must be remembered, however, that absorption includes both consumption and investment, so that it is by no means certain that a shift to profits will lead to reduced absorption. Although the proportion of any increment of income consumed by the profit recipient may be smaller than the proportion consumed by the wage earner, the higher profits may stimulate investment demand. The government can, in advanced countries, usually be expected to have a low marginal propensity to absorb, so that the tax shift might be a significant factor influencing the relationship of absorption to income, and so affecting the foreign balance.

Money Illusion

The money illusion may contribute a favorable effect to devaluation if it actually leads people to pay more attention to money prices than to money incomes. If at higher prices people choose to buy and consume less even though their money income has increased in proportion, over and above what can be attributed to the cash balance effect, the result on the balance of payments will be favorable. But rising money incomes and rising prices may actually operate in the opposite manner; for example, annual savings may be calculated in money terms and may fail to rise in proportion to money incomes and prices.

Miscellaneous Direct Absorption Effects

There may be other direct absorption effects, some working toward a favorable, others toward an unfavorable, change in the foreign balance. Expectations of price rises may be inspired, leading to increased absorption with adverse effects on the foreign balance, at least in the short run. If investment goods come largely from abroad, investment may be much less attractive after the devaluation than before because of the rise in the domestic price of investment goods, provided no close substitutes are produced domestically. More generally, the goods imported may be such that when the domestic prices rise, the domestic purchasers cut their expenditures on those goods but save or hoard the difference, rather than shift the expenditures to other goods. The importance of such a tendency in any actual case is open to doubt, but it is a theoretical possibility.

Impermanence and Non-proportionality of Effects

Many of the direct absorption effects may be transitory. Thus the money supply may respond to the increased demand for cash balances, so that the cash balance effect may gradually disappear or be counterbalanced by additional absorption financed by credit creation. Similarly, some of the income-distribution effects are associated with lags, but the lagged income may eventually catch up, e.g., wages may eventually rise to restore the pre-devaluation wage-profit relationship. Other effects depend on dynamic movements, on rising prices rather than on high prices. As the rise in prices comes to a halt, these effects will tend to disappear.

Furthermore, some of the effects may be non-proportional. A small devaluation may take advantage of the money illusion, or of wage inertia; a large devaluation may shatter the money illusion, or impart a dynamic momentum to the wage inertia, or impart a dynamic momentum to the wage inertia, or lead to modifications of tax rates, etc.

In general, then, many of the effects of a devaluation on the balance of payments through the direct absorption effects may be expected to be transitory and non-proportional. It does not necessarily follow that, in the absence of unemployment, a devaluation cannot have a strong influence on the balance of payments; that depends on the strength of the various effects. In many cases, in which the question of devaluation is likely to become a live issue under conditions of full employment, the favorable direct absorption effects are likely to be weak. It would seem to be much more effective to operate on absorption directly through monetary and credit policy—limitation of government expenditures, of private investment and, possibly, of private consumption—provided these can be brought to bear on the foreign balance without adversely affecting income and employment. They must, of course, "adversely" affect absorption, since, at full employment, it is possible to improve the foreign balance only through reducing absorption.

The main conclusion of this paper. The main conclusion is that the most fruitful approach to the general problem of obtaining a satisfactory foreign balance, and in particular of appraising the effects on the foreign balance of devaluation, is via the analysis of the income-absorption relationship. It is theoretically possible to obtain the same answers in terms of supply and demand elasticities, but one is more likely to be misled. It seems more in accord with the realities of the situation to recognize that, if the foreign balance is to be improved, the community as a whole must reduce its absorption of goods and services relative to its income. The inquiry can then best follow the line of asking who is to cut his absorption relative to his income, or what is to be the shift of income from those who, on the margin, absorb more to those who absorb less. Supply and demand conditions, in the sense of partial elasticities, may be useful tools in this analysis. But the total elasticities, for which the conventional formulas alone are valid, are not only poor tools; they may mislead, or at least obscure the analysis.

Devaluation Compared with Other Methods

If an improvement of the foreign balance is required, it may possibly be achieved either through a devaluation or through some other method of reducing absorption relative to production. The general alternative to devaluation is sometimes referred to as deflation, but that term has a narrower connotation than it is desirable to give to the alternatives to devaluation. These alternatives, which may for brevity be referred to as disabsorption, may be characterized as the discouragement of absorption relative to income by means other than devaluation. Disabsorption may be attained through monetary policy, as for example, by discouraging investment and consumption through tightening credit. It may be achieved by direct controls, such as investment licensing or rationing of consumers goods. It may be applied over the whole economy, as in the form of a sales tax or income tax, or in selected spheres, as in the form of investment licensing or import controls. The means to disabsorption are many and varied, but they may all be characterized as domestic measures calculated to change the relationship of absorption to income, and hence to affect the foreign balance.

An analysis of the relative advantages, from the point of view of a single country, of devaluation and trade restrictions has been presented elsewhere.8 That analysis is appropriate only to conditions of full employment. It can be extended to any other domestic measure for achieving a given balance of trade at full employment. Measures tending to reduce imports are of benefit to the country concerned as long as the relative domestic welfare value of import goods relative to export goods does not exceed the marginal terms of trade, i.e., the rate at which export goods can be exchanged for import goods at the margin on foreign markets, account being taken of any tendency for the prices of exports to fall relative to imports as more exports are offered and imports demanded.

When consideration is given to measures to improve the foreign balance under conditions of widespread unemployment, the above criterion must be so modified as to be abandoned for all practical purposes. That criterion is based on the proposition that, if the marginal rate of exchange of export goods for import goods in the foreign market is less favorable than their domestic welfare values, it would pay to cut back on imports and thus gain a greater welfare value in the export goods saved for the domestic economy. But if the resources used to make those export goods would, under those conditions, become unemployed, then there would be no gain from the restriction but rather a considerable loss. It is generally recognized that under conditions of widespread unemployment a domestic expansion policy is appropriate. Any adverse effects on the foreign balance can, except in extreme cases of inelasticity of foreign demand and supply, be appropriately handled by devaluation rather than by disabsorption under such circumstances. Disabsorption becomes an attractive policy only as full employment is approached.

If disabsorption of a general nature, say through a broad deflationary policy, should lead from full employment to the idleness of certain resources which cannot be expected to be transferred to the production of exports or import substitutes, it is to that extent undesirable. It is well recognized that when deflation leads to unemployment it is an undesirable measure for improving the foreign balance. Other means, such as import restriction or devaluation, would be preferable. In actual practice, therefore, the choice between devaluation and disabsorption will be affected not only by the considerations of the terms of trade on which the above criterion is based, but more immediately by considerations of other effects of any particular measure on the domestic economy. Considerations of the desirability of the resulting changes in the distribution of income as among individuals are ignored here, although in practice these considerations may be important and sometimes governing. One of the most important effects of any measure to improve the foreign balance is the influence it has on production as well as on absorption.

In the analysis both of devaluation and of disabsorption, the issues turn largely on the price rigidities and general inflexibilities of the economy. A satisfactory analysis of the problems depends on the identification and the appraisal of these inflexibilities. This is strictly analogous to the familiar question of whether, for stimulating employment, a reduction of wages can be as effective as an increase in aggregate monetary demand. That question hinges on whether the supply of labor is related to real wages or to money wages; that is, whether the effect of a given change in real wages that comes from a reduction of the general price level differs from that which comes from an increase in money wages.

Similarly, in evaluating various measures likely to affect the balance of payments, an identification of the rigidities and inflexibilities is vital to the conclusions. Thus, in the foregoing theory no attempt was made to distinguish between those components of a reduction in total absorption, a, which actually provide additional exports or import substitutes and those which do not. This constituted an implicit assumption that the resources freed by a reduction in absorption anywhere in the economy could be applied anywhere else, and in particular to the production of exports or import substitutes. It is, accordingly, necessary in any actual case to deal with a far more complicated set of components of the quantities, such as income and absorption. It must first be ascertained whether the contemplated measure will actually bring about the desired disabsorption and whether there may not merely be a shift of absorption to other objects, e.g., to clothing if food is rationed. It is further necessary to consider whether the resources to be set free by any contemplated disabsorption will in fact find their way into the production of exports or import substitutes. Thus what is required is a highly detailed analysis of the locus of impact of the contemplated measure and the nature of the adjustments in absorption and in production that will consequently be made.

Even where some form of disabsorption—for example, restriction of investments through licensing—can be achieved in such a manner that the investment goods can then be exported, the choice between that measure and devaluation must depend on whether the economy can spare the investment goods better than the different set of goods that would be foregone as the result of a devaluation or a restriction on imports. At this level of generality, it is possible to distinguish between two important lines of inquiry that must be followed in evaluating the relative merits of various possible measures to improve the balance of payments. The first concerns the effects on income, the second the relative welfare value of the absorption that must be foregone. These two considerations must be appraised jointly. Thus, for example, an import restriction may not reduce income at all but merely change the level of absorption in the country concerned. A devaluation at full employment that achieved an equal improvement in the foreign balance might have a tendency to reduce the real income by the terms of trade effect. Imports may, however, have a domestic welfare value sufficiently above that of exports so that the reduction in real income associated with a more desirable composition of absorption is preferable to the higher real income but less desirable composition of absorption associated with import restrictions. This paradox contains an implicit criticism of the measure of real income used here; it implies that a lower real income can have a higher welfare value. The paradox could be eliminated by an improved method of measuring real income, but the fundamental principle remains. In evaluating alternative measures for improving the balance of payments, the final criterion must be the welfare value of the goods and services absorbed at the given balance of payments to be achieved. This will depend not only on the level of employment and production but also on the composition of that production, and on the level and composition of trade.

References

- International-trade-barriers, boundless-business: courses.lumenlearning.com, Retrieved 11, May 2020
- Tariffs-meaning-and-types-international-trade-economics-30413: economicsdiscussion.net, Retrieved 24, June 2020
- Nontariff-barrier: investopedia.com, Retrieved 14, July 2020
- Import-quotas-meaning-objectives-and-types-international-economics-30454: economicsdiscussion.net, Retrieved 17, August 2020
- Economics, embargo, knowledge: corporatefinanceinstitute.com, Retrieved 17, June 2020

Permissions

All chapters in this book are published with permission under the Creative Commons Attribution Share Alike License or equivalent. Every chapter published in this book has been scrutinized by our experts. Their significance has been extensively debated. The topics covered herein carry significant information for a comprehensive understanding. They may even be implemented as practical applications or may be referred to as a beginning point for further studies.

We would like to thank the editorial team for lending their expertise to make the book truly unique. They have played a crucial role in the development of this book. Without their invaluable contributions this book wouldn't have been possible. They have made vital efforts to compile up to date information on the varied aspects of this subject to make this book a valuable addition to the collection of many professionals and students.

This book was conceptualized with the vision of imparting up-to-date and integrated information in this field. To ensure the same, a matchless editorial board was set up. Every individual on the board went through rigorous rounds of assessment to prove their worth. After which they invested a large part of their time researching and compiling the most relevant data for our readers.

The editorial board has been involved in producing this book since its inception. They have spent rigorous hours researching and exploring the diverse topics which have resulted in the successful publishing of this book. They have passed on their knowledge of decades through this book. To expedite this challenging task, the publisher supported the team at every step. A small team of assistant editors was also appointed to further simplify the editing procedure and attain best results for the readers.

Apart from the editorial board, the designing team has also invested a significant amount of their time in understanding the subject and creating the most relevant covers. They scrutinized every image to scout for the most suitable representation of the subject and create an appropriate cover for the book.

The publishing team has been an ardent support to the editorial, designing and production team. Their endless efforts to recruit the best for this project, has resulted in the accomplishment of this book. They are a veteran in the field of academics and their pool of knowledge is as vast as their experience in printing. Their expertise and guidance has proved useful at every step. Their uncompromising quality standards have made this book an exceptional effort. Their encouragement from time to time has been an inspiration for everyone.

The publisher and the editorial board hope that this book will prove to be a valuable piece of knowledge for students, practitioners and scholars across the globe.

Index

www.ingramcontent.com/pod-product-compliance
Lightning Source LLC
LaVergne TN
LVHW080617210926
848485LV00003B/172